GREAT COMPANIONS

GREAT COMPANIONS

GREAT COMPANIONS

READINGS ON THE MEANING
AND CONDUCT OF LIFE FROM
ANCIENT AND MODERN SOURCES

Compiled by
ROBERT FRENCH LEAVENS

Collaborator
MARY AGNES LEAVENS

1946
THE BEACON PRESS
BOSTON, MASS.

First Printing, April, 1927
Twelfth Printing, June, 1946

Our growing thought makes growing revelation.

GEORGE ELIOT

PREFACE

As John Ruskin said, to the reader there is continually open the society of the wisest of earth. This small volume may give the reader, "the heir of all the ages," the enlightenment and inspiration of such association.

It includes passages from the sacred books of the great religions; selections from Greeks and Romans; expressions of the long struggle for human liberty and solidarity; thoughts of seers and prophets, poets and philosophers, of courageous men and women—of those who have served their fellow-men intimately, and with distinction; and writings of recent times which throw upon the way of man the light of the widely increased knowledge of history and science. Religious thought through the ages, from the time when men began to outgrow primitive conceptions of the cosmos and to discriminate between right and wrong in the art of living, reveals essential unity in the midst of diversity; and it is this universal character which has determined the choice of these passages.

A body of scriptures is usually an unconscious development, a literary cathedral to which succeeding generations make additions. But when the larger Bible, The Scriptures of Mankind, is written, it will be a deliberate production, drawing its material from records of the deeds and thoughts of humanity, the canon never closed.

Great Companions may help to meet the long recognized need for a collection of readings of this nature, convenient in form, for use in church services; and to the individual, the school, and the family, it should be a source of strength and guidance, of renewed faith in the order of the universe and the things of the spirit.

This anthology is the work of many minds. My sister, Mary Agnes Leavens, by her assistance in selecting and preparing material, has made possible its publication at the present time and in its present scope. To my wife, I wish to express my affectionate gratitude for her loyal devotion throughout its preparation. Members of three churches which I have served and colleagues in the ministry who have expressed the desire for such a book have given me valuable suggestions. I am indebted to Dr.

Samuel A. Eliot for his unfailing encouragement; to W. Forbes Robertson of The Beacon
Press, Inc., for his hearty coöperation; to Pro-
fessors William R. Arnold and James H. Ropes
of Harvard University for examining the Biblical passages with special attention to accuracy
of dates; and to Professor George Foot Moore,
also of Harvard University, for reviewing the
oriental selections with reference to authenticity
of dates and translations.

In editing, we have exercised constant care
to quote from authorized texts, to cite authentic
historical data, and in abridging or arranging
to alter neither meanings nor words.

R. F. L.

An asterisk following the title indicates that
the selection is an abridgment or an arrangement.

Certain early English and American selections appear in their original form to suggest
their times.

Except where otherwise stated, the Biblical
passages are from the English Revised Version.

Samuel A. Eliot, for his unfailing encouragement; to W. Forbes Robinson of The Beacon
Press, Inc., for his hearty cooperation; to Pro-
fessors William R. Arnold and James H. Ropes
of Harvard University for examining the Biblical passages with sympathetic attention to accuracy
of detail and to Professor George Foot Moore,
also of Harvard University, for reviewing the
choice of selections with reference to authenticity
of source and translations.

In editing, we have exercised constant care
to quote from authorized texts, to cite authentic
historical data, and in abridging or arranging
to alter neither meanings nor words.

R. E. L.

An asterisk following the title indicates that
the selection is an abridgment or an arrangement.

Certain early English and American selections appear in their original forms to a great
extent ... their lines.

Except where otherwise stated, the Biblical
passages are from the English Revised Version.

CONTENTS

BOOK I

MAN IN THE UNIVERSE

BOOK II

THE CONDUCT OF LIFE

BOOK III

THE COMMONWEALTH

BOOK I

MAN IN THE UNIVERSE

The World Without

NATURE *

WILLIAM WORDSWORTH
English poet, 1770–1850

                    I have learned
To look on nature not as in the hour
Of thoughtless youth but hearing oftentimes
The still, sad music of humanity,
Nor harsh nor grating, though of ample power
To chasten and subdue.   And I have felt
A presence that disturbs me with the joy
Of elevated thoughts; a sense sublime
Of something far more deeply interfused,
Whose dwelling is the light of setting suns,
And the round ocean and the living air,
And the blue sky, and in the mind of man:
A motion and a spirit that impels
All thinking things, all objects of all thought,
And rolls through all things.   Therefore am I
     still
A lover of the meadows and the woods
And mountains; and of all that we behold
From this green earth; of all the mighty world

Of eye, and ear,—both what they half create,
And what perceive; well pleased to recognize
In nature and the language of the sense
The anchor of my purest thoughts, the nurse,
The guide, the guardian of my heart, and soul
Of all my moral being.

           Nature never did betray
The heart that loved her; 'tis her privilege
Through all the years of this our life to lead
From joy to joy; for she can so inform
The mind that is within us, so impress
With quietness and beauty, and so feed
With lofty thoughts, that neither evil tongues,
Rash judgments, nor the sneers of selfish men,
Nor greetings where no kindness is, nor all
The dreary intercourse of daily life
Shall e'er prevail against us, or disturb
Our cheerful faith that all which we behold
Is full of blessings.

                From *Tintern Abbey*

THE SPACIOUS FIRMAMENT

JOSEPH ADDISON
English essayist, 1672–1719

The spacious firmament on high,
  With all the blue ethereal sky,

The spangled heavens, a shining frame,
Their great Original proclaim:
The unwearied sun, from day to day,
Does his Creator's power display,
And publishes to every land
The work of an almighty hand.

Soon as the evening shades prevail,
The moon takes up the wondrous tale,
And nightly to the listening earth
Repeats the story of her birth;
Whilst all the stars that round her burn,
And all the planets in their turn,
Confirm the tidings as they roll
And spread the truth from pole to pole.

What though, in solemn silence, all
Move round the dark terrestrial ball?
What though nor real voice nor sound
Amid their radiant orbs be found?
In reason's ear they all rejoice
And utter forth a glorious voice,
For ever singing, as they shine,
"The hand that made us is divine."

From The Spectator, 464

THE STARRY HEAVENS AND THE MORAL LAW

IMMANUEL KANT

German: founder of critical philosophy; 1724–1804

Two things fill the mind with ever new and increasing admiration and awe, the oftener and the more steadily we reflect on them: the starry heavens above and the moral law within. I have not to search for them and conjecture them as though they were veiled in darkness or were in the transcendent region beyond my horizon; I see them before me and connect them directly with the consciousness of my existence. The former begins from the place I occupy in the external world of sense, and enlarges my connection therein to an unbounded extent with worlds upon worlds and systems of systems, and moreover into limitless times of their periodic motion, its beginning and continuance. The second begins from my invisible self, my personality, and exhibits me in a world which has true infinity, but which is traceable only by the understanding, and with which I discern that I am not in a merely contingent, but in a universal and necessary, connection, as I am also thereby with all those visible worlds. The former view of a countless multitude of worlds annihilates, as it were, my importance as an animal creature, which after it has been for some time provided with vital power, one knows not how, must again give back the matter of which it was formed to the planet it inhabits (a mere speck in the universe). The second, on the contrary, infinitely elevates my worth as an intelligence by my personality, in which the moral law reveals to me a life independent of animality and even of the whole sensible world, at least so far as may be inferred from the destination assigned to my existence by this law, a destination not restricted to conditions and limits of this life, but reaching into the infinite.

The Critique of Practical Reason
Trans. Thomas Kingsmill Abbott

THE MUSIC OF THE SPHERES *
ALFRED NOYES
English poet, 1880—

We, who are borne on one dark grain of dust
Around one indistinguishable spark
Of star-mist, lost in one lost feather of light,
Can by the strength of our own thought ascend
Through universe after universe; trace their
  growth

Through boundless time, their glory, their
    decay;
And, on the invisible road of law, more firm
Than granite, range through all their length and
    breadth,
Their height and depth, past, present and to
    come.

Oh, holy night, deep night of stars, whose peace
Descends upon the troubled mind like dew,
Healing it with the sense of that pure reign
Of constant law, enduring through all change;
Shall I not, one day, after faithful years,
Find that thy heavens are built on music too
And hear once more above thy throbbing worlds
This voice of all compassion, "Comfort ye"—
Yes—"comfort ye, my people," saith your God?

Watchers of the Sky

(In this passage, William Herschel, musician and
astronomer, is represented as lost in meditation
while waiting to conduct his orchestra.)

AT HOME AMONG THE STARS *
EDWARD YOUNG
English clergyman and author, 1683–1765

This prospect vast, what is it?—weighed
    aright,

'Tis nature's system of divinity,
And every student of the night inspires.
'Tis elder scripture, writ by God's own hand:
Scripture authentic! uncorrupt by man.
The soul of man was made to walk the skies.
Nor, as a stranger, does she wander there;
But, wonderful herself, through wonder strays;
Contemplating their grandeur, finds her own;
Dives deep in their economy divine,
Sits high in judgment on their various laws,
And, like a master, judges not amiss.
Hence greatly pleased, and justly proud, the
    soul
Grows conscious of her birth celestial; breathes
More life, more vigor, in her native air;
And feels herself at home among the stars.

      . . . How great,
How glorious, then, appears the mind of man,
When in it all the stars and planets roll!
And what it seems, it is: great objects make
Great minds, enlarging as their views enlarge;
Those still more godlike, as these more divine.
And more divine than these, thou canst not see.
Dazzled, o'erpowered, with the delicious
    draught
Of miscellaneous splendors, how I reel
From thought to thought, inebriate, without end!

An Eden, this; a Paradise unlost!
I meet the Deity in every view,
And tremble at my nakedness before him.
O that I could but reach the tree of life!
For here it grows, unguarded from our taste;
No flaming sword denies our entrance here:
Would man but gather, he might live for ever.
Nor think thou seest a wild disorder here:
Through this illustrious chaos to the sight,
Arrangement neat and chastest order reign.
The path prescribed, inviolably kept,
Upbraids the lawless sallies of mankind.
Worlds, ever thwarting, never interfere:
What knots are tied! how soon are they
        dissolved,
And set the seeming married planets free!
They rove for ever, without error rove;
Confusion unconfused. Nor less admire
This tumult untumultuous; all on wing,
In motion, all; yet what profound repose!

Leaves so much wonder greater wonder still?
Where are the pillars that support the skies?
What more than Atlantean shoulder props
The incumbent load? What magic, what
        strange art,
In fluid air these ponderous orbs sustains?

Who would not think them hung in golden
    chains?
And so they are, in the high will of Heaven,
Which fixes all . . .
How distant some of these nocturnal suns!
So distant (says the sage) 'twere not absurd
To doubt if beams, set out at nature's birth,
Are yet arrived at this so foreign world,
Though nothing half so rapid as their flight.
An eye of awe and wonder let me roll,
And roll for ever.   Who can satiate sight
In such a scene, in such an ocean wide
Of deep astonishment, where depth, height,
    breadth
Are lost in their extremes; and where, to count
The thick-sown glories in this field of fire,
Perhaps a seraph's computation fails?
Now, go, ambition; boast thy boundless might
In conquest, o'er the tenth part of a grain.
In ardent contemplation's rapid car,
From earth, as from my barrier, I set out.
How swift I mount! Diminished earth recedes;
I pass the moon; and, from her farther side,
Pierce heaven's blue curtain; strike into remote;
Where, with his lifted tube, the subtile sage
His artificial, airy journey takes,
And, to celestial, lengthens human sight.

I pause at every planet on my road,
And ask for him who gives their orbs to roll,
Their foreheads fair to shine. From Saturn's
    ring,
In which, of earths an army might be lost,
With the bold comet, take my bolder flight
Amid those sovereign glories of the skies,
Of independent, native lustre proud;
The souls of systems, and the lords of life,
Through their wide empires.—What behold I
    now?
A wilderness of wonders burning round;
Where larger suns inhabit higher spheres.

    . . . On nature's Alps I stand,
And see a thousand firmaments beneath:
A thousand systems, as a thousand grains!
    . . . Here human effort ends;
And leaves me still a stranger to his throne.
Full well it might. · I quite mistook my road,—
Born in an age more curious than devout,
More fond to fix the place of heaven or hell
Than studious this to shun, or that secure.
'Tis not the curious, but the pious, path
That leads me to my point, Lorenzo. Know,
Without or star or angel for their guide,
Who worship God shall find him. Humble
    love,

And not proud reason, keeps the door of heaven;
Love finds admission where proud science fails.

Night Thoughts

HYMN TO THE SUN *
Amen-hotep IV
King of Egypt, reign 1375–1358 b. c.

Thy dawning is beautiful in the horizon of the
    sky,
O living Aton, Beginning of life!
When thou risest in the eastern horizon,
Thou fillest every land with thy beauty.
Thou art beautiful, great, glittering, high above
    every land;
Thy rays, they encompass the lands, even all
    that thou hast made.
Though thou art far away, thy rays are upon the
    earth;
Though thou art on high, thy (footprints are
    the day).

Bright is the earth when thou risest in the
    horizon.
When thou shinest as Aton by day
Thou drivest away the darkness.
When thou sendest forth thy rays,
The Two Lands (Egypt) are in daily festivity,

Awake and standing upon their feet
When thou hast raised them up.
Their limbs bathed, they take their clothing,
Their arms uplifted in adoration to thy dawn-
　　ing.
(Then) in all the world they do their work:
All cattle rest upon their pasturage,
The trees and the plants flourish,
The birds flutter in their marshes,
Their wings uplifted in adoration to thee.
All the sheep dance upon their feet,
All winged things fly,
They live when thou hast shone upon them.

Thou makest the Nile in the nether world,
Thou bringest it as thou desirest,
To preserve alive the people.
Thou hast set a Nile in the sky;
When it falleth for them,
It maketh waves upon the mountains,
Like the great green sea,
Watering their fields in their towns.

Thy rays nourish every garden:
When thou risest they live,
They grow by thee.
Thou makest the seasons

In order to create all thy work.
Thou alone, shining in thy form as living Aton,
Dawning, glittering, going afar and returning,
Thou makest millions of forms
Through thyself alone;
Cities, towns, and tribes, highways and rivers.
All eyes see thee before them,
For thou art Aton of the day over the earth.

Trans. J. H. Breasted
Development of Religion and Thought
in Ancient Egypt
J. H. Breasted

THE CANTICLE OF THE SUN *
St. Francis of Assisi
Italian monk and preacher, 1182–1226

Most high, most great and good Lord, to
thee belong praises, glory, and every blessing!

Blessed be thou, my Lord, for the gift of all
thy creatures; and specially for our brother,
(the) sun, by whom the day is enlightened. He
is radiant and bright, of great splendor, bearing
witness to thee, O my God.

Blessed be thou, my Lord, for our sister the
moon, and (for) the stars; thou hast formed
them in the heavens, fair and clear.

Blessed be thou, my Lord, for our brother the

wind, for the air, for cloud, and calm, for every kind of weather, for by them thou dost sustain all creatures.

Blessed be my Lord for our sister water, which is very useful, humble, chaste, and precious.

Blessed be thou, my Lord, for our brother fire, gay, noble and beautiful, untamable and strong; by whom thou dost illumine the night.

Blessed be thou, my Lord, for our mother the earth, who sustains and nourishes us, who brings forth all kinds of fruit, herbs, and bright-hued flowers.

Blessed be thou, my Lord, for those who pardon for love of thee, who patiently bear infirmity and tribulation. Happy are those who abide in peace, for by thee, Most High, they will be crowned.

Blessed be thou, my Lord, for our sister death of body, from whom no living man can escape.

Happy are they who at the hour of death are found in obedience to thy holy will.

Praise ye and bless ye my Lord; give him thanks, and serve him with great humility.

The Writings of St. Francis of Assisi
Trans. Constance de la Warr

TO FATHER SUN

FROM THE HAKO CEREMONY

(a prayer for children)

Pawnee Indian

Now behold: hither comes the ray of our father
sun; it cometh over all the land, passeth
in the lodge, us to touch, and give us
strength.

Now behold: where alights the ray of our
father sun; it touches lightly on the rim,
the place above the fire, whence the smoke
ascends on high.

Now behold: softly creeps the ray of our father
sun; now o'er the rim it creeps to us, climbs
down within the lodge; climbing down, it
comes to us.

Now behold: nearer comes the ray of our father
sun; it reaches now the floor and moves
within the open space, walking there, the
lodge about.

Now behold where has passed the ray of our
father sun; around the lodge the ray has
passed and left its blessing there, touching
us, each one of us.

Now behold: softly climbs the ray of our father
sun; it upward climbs, and o'er the rim it

passes from the place whence the smoke
ascends on high.

Now behold on the hills the ray of our father
sun; it lingers there as loath to go, while
all the plain is dark. Now has gone the
ray from us.

Now behold: lost to us the ray of our father
sun; beyond our sight the ray has gone,
returning to the place whence it came to
bring us strength.

Rhythmic rendering
*Annual Reports of the United States
Bureau of American Ethnology*

TO EARTH,
THE MOTHER OF ALL
GREEK HYMN,
about 750-500 B.C.

I will sing of well-founded Earth, mother of
all, eldest of all beings. She feeds all creatures that are in the world, all that go upon the
goodly land, and all that are in the paths of
the seas, and all that fly: all these are fed of
her store. Through you, O queen, men are
blessed in their children and blessed in their
harvests, and to you it belongs to give means

of life to mortal men and to take it away.
Happy is the man whom you delight to honor!
He has all things abundantly: his fruitful land
is laden with corn, his pastures are covered
with cattle, and his house is filled with good
things. Such men rule orderly in their cities of
fair women; great riches and wealth follow
them; their sons exult with ever fresh delight,
and their daughters in flower-laden bands play
and skip merrily over the soft flowers of the
field. Thus is it with those whom you honor,
O holy goddess, bountiful spirit.

Hail, mother of the gods, wife of starry
heaven!

The Homeric Hymns
Trans. H. A. Evelyn White

PARABLES FROM NATURE *
Christian, first century

"Behold, the sower went forth to sow: and
it came to pass, as he sowed, some seed fell
by the wayside, and the birds came and devoured it. And other fell on the rocky ground,
where it had not much earth; and straightway it
sprang up, because it had no deepness of earth:

and when the sun was risen, it was scorched: and because it had no root, it withered away. And other fell among the thorns, and the thorns grew up and choked it, and it yielded no fruit. And others fell into the good ground, and yielded fruit, growing up and increasing; and brought forth, thirtyfold, and sixtyfold, and a hundredfold." And he said, "Who hath ears to hear, let him hear."

And he said: "So is the kingdom of God, as if a man should cast seed upon the earth; and should sleep and rise night and day, and the seed should spring up and grow, he knoweth not how. The earth beareth fruit of herself: first the blade, then the ear, then the full corn in the ear. But when the fruit is ripe, straightway he putteth forth the sickle, because the harvest is come."

From *The Gospel According to Mark*
New Testament

TO MOTHER CORN *

FROM THE HAKO CEREMONY

(A prayer for children)

Pawnee Indian

Mother with the life-giving power now comes,
Stepping out of far distant days she comes,
Days wherein to our fathers gave she food;
As to them, so now 'unto us she gives:
Thus she will to our children faithful be.
Mother with the life-giving power now comes!

Mother with the life-giving power is here.
Stepping out of far distant days she comes,
Now she forward moves, leading as we walk
Toward the future, where blessings she will
    give:
Gifts 'for which we have prayed granting to us.
Mother with the life-giving power is here!

The Mother leads and we follow on,
Her devious pathway before us lies.
She leads us as were our fathers led
Down through the ages.
The Mother leads and we follow on,
Her pathway straight, where a stage each **day**

We forward walk, as our fathers walked
Down through the ages.[1]

------

[1] *"Everything speaks: the eagle, Kwas, speaks; the corn speaks; so we say Hako, the voice of all these things."*

> Rhythmic rendering
> *Annual Reports of the United States*
> *Bureau of American Ethnology*

THE LEGEND OF THE CORNSTALK *
HENRY WADSWORTH LONGFELLOW
American poet, 1807–1882

You shall hear how Hiawatha
Prayed and fasted in the forest,
Not for greater skill in hunting,
Not for greater craft in fishing,
Not for triumphs in the battle,
And renown among the warriors,
But for profit of the people,
For advantage of the nations

  First he built a lodge for fasting,
Built a wigwam in the forest,
And, with dreams and visions many,
Seven whole days and nights he fasted.

  On the fourth day of his fasting
In his lodge he lay exhausted:

  And he saw a youth approaching.

Dressed in garments green and yellow,
Plumes of green bent o'er his forehead,
And his hair was soft and golden.

"From the Master of Life descending,
I, the friend of man, Mondamin,
Come to warn you and instruct you,
How by struggle and by labor
You shall gain what you have prayed for.
Rise up from your bed of branches,
Rise, O youth, and wrestle with me!"

So they wrestled there together
In the glory of the sunset,
And the more they strove and struggled,
Stronger still grew Hiawatha:

Then he smiled, and said: "To-morrow
Is the last day of your conflict,
Is the last day of your fasting,
You will conquer and o'ercome me;
Make a bed for me to lie in,
Where the rain may fall upon me,
Where the sun may come and warm me;
Strip these garments, green and yellow,
Strip this nodding plumage from me,
Lay me in the earth, and make it
Soft and loose and light above me."

But the place was not forgotten
Where he wrestled with Mondamin;

Nor forgotten nor neglected
Was the grave where lay Mondamin,
Sleeping in the rain and sunshine,
Where his scattered plumes and garments
Faded in the rain and sunshine.

Day by day did Hiawatha
Go to wait and watch beside it;
Kept the dark mould soft above it,
Kept it clean from weeds and insects,
Drove away, with scoffs and shoutings,
Kahgahgee, the king of ravens.

Till at length a small green feather
From the earth shot slowly upward,
Then another and another,
And before the summer ended
Stood the maize in all its beauty,
With its shining robes about it,
And its long, soft, yellow tresses:
And in rapture Hiawatha
Cried aloud, "It is Mondamin!
Yes, the friend of man, Mondamin!"

Then he called to old Nokomis
And Iagoo, the great boaster,
Showed them where the maize was growing,
Told them of his wondrous vision,
Of his wrestling and his triumph,
Of this new gift to the nations,
Which should be their food forever.

And still later, when the autumn
Changed the long, green leaves to yellow,
And the soft and juicy kernels
Grew like wampum hard and yellow,
Then the ripened ears he gathered,
Stripped the withered husks from off them,
As he once had stripped the wrestler;
Gave the first feast of Mondamin,
And made known unto the people
This new gift of the Great Spirit.

From *Hiawatha*

A DAY IN JUNE

JAMES RUSSELL LOWELL
American poet and essayist, 1819-1891

What is so rare as a day in June?
Then, if ever, come perfect days;
Then heaven tries earth if it be in tune,
And over it softly her warm ear lays;
Whether we look or whether we listen,
We hear life murmur, or see it glisten;
Every clod feels a stir of might,
An instinct within it that reaches and towers,
And, groping blindly above it for light,
Climbs to a soul in grass and flowers;

The flush of life may well be seen
Thrilling back over hills and valleys;
The cowslip startles in meadows green,
The buttercup catches the sun in its chalice,
And there's never a leaf nor a blade too mean
To be some happy creature's palace;
The little bird sits at his door in the sun,
Atilt like a blossom among the leaves,
And lets his illumined being o'errun
With the deluge of summer it receives;
His mate feels the eggs beneath her wings,
And the heart in her dumb breast flutters and
    sings;
He sings to the wide world, and she to her
    nest,—
In the nice ear of nature, which song is the
    best?

Now is the high-tide of the year,
And whatever of life hath ebbed away
Comes flooding back with a ripply cheer,
Into every bare inlet and creek and bay;
Now the heart is so full that a drop over-
    fills it;
We are happy now because God wills it;
No matter how barren the past may have been,
'Tis enough for us now that the leaves are
    green;

We sit in the warm shade and feel right well
How the sap creeps up and the blossoms swell;
We may shut our eyes, but we cannot help
    knowing
That skies are clear and grass is growing;
The breeze comes whispering in our ear
That dandelions are blossoming near,
That maize has sprouted, that streams are
    flowing,
That the river is bluer than the sky,
That the robin is plastering his house hard by;
And if the breeze kept the good news back,
For other couriers we should not lack;
We could guess it all by yon heifer's lowing,—
And hark! how clear bold chanticleer,
Warmed with the new wine of the year,
Tells all in his lusty crowing!

Joy comes, grief goes, we know not how;
Everything is happy now,
Everything is upward striving;
'Tis as easy now for the heart to be true
As for grass to be green or skies to be blue,—
'Tis the natural way of living.

        From *The Vision of Sir Launfal*

COMMUNION WITH NATURE

GEORGE GORDON, LORD BYRON

English poet, 1788–1824

There is a pleasure in the pathless woods,
There is a rapture on the lonely shore,
There is society where none intrudes
By the deep sea, and music in its roar:
I love not man the less but nature more
From these our interviews, in which I steal
From all I may be or have been before
To mingle with the universe and feel.
What I can ne'er express, yet cannot all conceal.

Childe Harold, Canto 4, clxxviii

MY GARDEN

THOMAS EDWARD BROWN

English poet, 1830–1897

A garden is a lovesome thing, God wot!
Rose plot,
Fringed pool,
Ferned grot—
The veriest school
Of peace; and yet the fool
Contends that God is not—

Not God! in gardens! when the eve is cool?
    Nay, but I have a sign:
    'Tis very sure God walks in mine.

THE EVER-PRESENT SPIRIT
RICHARD REALF
British-American poet, 1834–1878

O earth! thou hast not any wind that blows
Which is not music; every weed of thine
Pressed rightly flows in aromatic wine;
And every humble hedgerow flower that grows,
And every little brown bird that doth sing,
Hath something greater than itself, and bears
A living word to every living thing,
Albeit it holds the message unawares.
All shapes and sounds have something which is
    not
Of them: a Spirit broods amid the grass;
Vague outlines of the Everlasting Thought
Lie in the melting shadows as they pass;
The touch of an Eternal Presence thrills
The fringes of the sunsets and the hills.

Symbolisms, Sonnet 3

THE ANNUAL DRAMA
WALT WHITMAN
American poet, 1819-1892

Ever upon this stage
Is acted God's calm annual drama:
Gorgeous processions, songs of birds,
Sunrise that fullest feeds and freshens most the
    soul;
The heaving sea, the waves upon the shore, the
    musical, strong waves,
The woods, the stalwart trees, the slender,
    tapering trees;
The liliput countless armies of the grass;
The heat, the showers, the measureless
    pasturages,
The scenery of the snows, the winds' free
    orchestra;
The stretching light-hung roof of clouds, the
    clear cerulean and the silvery fringes,
The high dilating stars, the placid beckoning
    stars,
The moving flocks and herds, the plains and
    emerald meadows,—
The shows of all the varied lands and all the
    growths and products.

              From *The Return of the Heroes*

MIRACLES *

WALT WHITMAN
American poet, 1819–1892

Why, who makes much of a miracle?
As to me I know of nothing else but miracles,
Whether I walk the streets of Manhattan,
Or dart my sight over the roofs of houses
    toward the sky,
Or wade with naked feet along the beach just
    in the edge of the water,
Or stand under the trees in the woods,
Or sit at table at dinner with the rest,
Or look at strangers opposite me riding in the
    car,
Or watch honey-bees busy around the hive of a
    summer forenoon,
Or animals feeding in the fields,
Or birds, or the wonderfulness of insects in the
    air,
Or the wonderfulness of the sundown, or of
    stars shining so quiet and bright,
Or the exquisite delicate thin curve of the new
    moon in spring;
These with the rest, one and all, are to me
    miracles,
The whole referring, yet each distinct and in
    its place.

To me every hour of the light and dark is a
    miracle,
Every cubic inch of space is a miracle,
Every square yard of the surface of the earth
    is spread with the same,
Every foot of the interior swarms with the
    same.
To me the sea is a continual miracle,
The fishes that swim—the rocks—the motion of
    the waves—the ships with men in them.
What stranger miracles are there?

TIDINGS OF INVISIBLE THINGS

WILLIAM WORDSWORTH
English poet, 1770–1850

                  I have seen
A curious child, who dwelt upon a tract
Of inland ground, applying to his ear
The convolutions of a smooth-lipped shell;
To which, in silence hushed, his very soul
Listened intensely; for from within were heard
Murmurings, whereby the monitor expressed
Mysterious union with its native sea.
Even such a shell the universe itself
Is to the ear of faith; and there are times,

I doubt not, when to you it doth impart
Authentic tidings of invisible things,
Of ebb and flow, and ever-during power,
And central peace, subsisting at the heart
Of endless agitation.

The Excursion, Book iv

THE WORSHIP OF NATURE *
JOHN GREENLEAF WHITTIER
American poet and reformer, 1807–1892

The harp at Nature's advent strung
Has never ceased to play;
The song the stars of morning sung
Has never died away.

And prayer is made, and praise is given
By all things near and far;
The ocean looketh up to heaven
And mirrors every star.

The green earth sends her incense up
From many a mountain shrine;
From folded leaf and dewy cup
She pours her sacred wine.

The blue sky is the temple's arch,
Its transept, earth and air;
The music of its starry march,
The chorus of a prayer.

So Nature keeps the reverent frame
With which her years began;
And all her signs and voices shame
The prayerless heart of man.

Studies in the Book of Nature

THE UNIVERSAL POINT OF VIEW
Henri Frédéric Amiel
Swiss scholar and writer, 1821–1881

It gives liberty and breadth to thought to learn to judge our own epoch from the point of view of universal history, history from the point of view of geological periods, geology from the point of view of astronomy. When the duration of a man's life or of a people's life appears to us as microscopic as that of a fly, and inversely the life of a gnat as infinite as that of a celestial body, with all its dust of nations, we feel ourselves at once very small and very great; and we are able, as it were, to survey from the height of the spheres our own existence and the little whirlwinds which agitate our little Europe.

Journal
Trans. Mrs. Humphry Ward

SCIENCE [*]

J. ARTHUR THOMSON
British: professor of natural history,
editor and author; 1861–1933

THE AIM OF SCIENCE

Many of the misunderstandings that have arisen in regard to "science and religion," "science and philosophy," and similar questions are due to a failure to recognize what science aims at—the formulation of things as they are and as they have come to be. The primary aim of science is not to "explain," except in the sense of saying, "This is the outcome of that." It does not inquire into the "why" of things, the purpose or significance of the cosmos.

THE METHODS OF SCIENCE

In any scientific inquiry the first step is to get at the facts, and this requires precision, patience, impartiality, watchfulness against the illusions of the senses and the mind, and carefulness to keep inferences from mingling with observations. The second step is accurate registration of the data. A third step is arranging the data in workable form. The fourth step is when a whole series of occurrences is seen to have a uniformity, which is called their law.

SCIENCE AND FEELING

Truly, science as science is unemotional and impersonal, and its analytic, atomizing, or anatomizing methods are apt, in their matter-of-factness, to seem antagonistic to artistic unities and poetical interpretations. But here must be learned the lesson of patience and open-mindedness, and here the limitations of science must be borne in mind. The poetry of the man of feeling must not contradict the formulations of the man of science, but they are speaking different languages, and we may know by feeling some aspect of reality which eludes us in scientific analysis. Our delight in fine scenery is not less real than our knowledge of the geology. Both are pathways to reality. When science makes minor mysteries disappear, greater mysteries stand confessed. For one object of delight whose emotional value science has inevitably lessened—as Newton damaged the rainbow for Keats—science gives back double. Science widens and clears the emotional window. There are great vistas to which science alone can lead, and they make for elevation of mind.

SCIENCE AND RELIGION

Science seeks to discover the laws of concrete being and becoming and to state these in the simplest possible terms. These terms are either the immediate data of experience or verifiably derived from these. Religion, on the other hand, implies a recognition—practical, emotional, and intellectual—of a higher order of reality than is reached in sense-experience. It sees an unseen universe, which throws light on the riddles of the observed world. Its language is not scientific language and the two cannot be spoken at once. The concepts of religion are transcendental, those of science empirical. The aim of religion is interpretation, not description. Religious interpretation and scientific description must not be inconsistent, but they are incommensurable. This is not falling back on the impossible solution of having idea-tight compartments: what is meant is that while the form of a religious idea, of creation, let us say, must be congruent with the established scientific system, scientific description and religious interpretation work in two quite different "universes of discourse."

SCIENCE AND PHILOSOPHY

The philosophical outlook is synoptic; an all-round view. Science and philosophy are complementary. To the scientific thinker philosophy is of service in helping him to recognize the limitations of his task. On the other side, a modern philosophy must take account of all the far-reaching results of scientific inquiry. Thus an adequate interpretative system must have been receptive to all the influences of such conclusions as the principle of the conservation of energy, the doctrine of organic evolution, and the outstanding facts of heredity. Philosophy begins where the experimental and observational sciences leave off, but it does not follow that philosophy in its edifice must use the building-stones just as science hands them over. Thus the results of modern study of heredity need not be accepted in a form so crude that the inevitable outcome is fatalism. Similarly, when philosophy takes over from the biologist the formula of organic evolution that the present is the child of the past and the parent of the future, it is bound to scrutinize the concept of evolution and to show that it is no easy one. The general *fact* of evolution stands firmer than ever; but inquiry into the *factors* is still relatively young.

SCIENCE AND LIFE

The old discouragement expressed in the saying that increase of knowledge is increase of sorrow has been replaced by a more robust confidence in what science may achieve in the control of life. The modern outlook is expressed in Herbert Spencer's pithy sentence: "Science is for life, not life for science," or in Comte's well-known saying: "Knowledge is foresight, and foresight is power."

Bacon had the idea clearly in mind when he wrote in *The Advancement of Learning:* "This is that which will indeed dignify and exalt knowledge if contemplation and action be more nearly and straitly conjoined and united together than they have been." And the passage ends by declaring that what is sought in science should be "a rich storehouse for the glory of the Creator and the relief of man's estate." But what is distinctively modern is the ideal of bringing the light of science to bear on man's problems all along the line, on health of mind as well as of body, on education as well as on agriculture, on ethical development as well as on the more economical exploitation and usage of natural resources, on eugenics as well as on eutopias. Just as many ills that the flesh is heir to are met no longer with folded hands but by confident therapeutics, so over a wide range there is a promiseful application of all kinds of science to the amelioration of the conditions of human life. Great stores of wealth are awaiting the scientific "Open Sesame"; a great heightening of the standard of health will be attainable in a few generations if men of good-will take science as their torch. But wealth and health are the pre-conditions of true progress, which means a fuller embodiment of the true, the beautiful, and the good in lives which are increasingly a satisfaction in themselves.

The Outline of Science, Vol. iv, p. 1165

NATURE'S IMPARTIAL PROVIDENCE *

JOHN BURROUGHS
American naturalist, 1837–1921

I see the Nature Providence going its impartial way. I see drought and flood, heat and cold, war and pestilence, defeat and death, besetting man at all times, in all lands. I see hostile germs in the air he breathes, in the water he drinks, in the soil he tills. I see the elemental forces as indifferent toward him as toward ants and fleas. I see pain and disease and defeat and failure dogging his footsteps. I see the righteous defeated and the ungodly triumphant—this and much more I see; and yet I behold through the immense biological vista behind us the race of man slowly, oh, so slowly! emerging from its brute or semi-human ancestry into the full estate of man, from blind instinct and savage passion into the light of reason and moral consciousness. I behold the great scheme of evolution unfolding despite all the delays and waste and failures, and the higher forms appearing upon the scene. I see on an immense scale, and as clearly as in a demonstration in a laboratory, that good comes out of evil; that the impartiality of the Nature Providence is best; that we are made strong by what we overcome; that man is man because he is as free to do evil as to do good; that life is as free to develop hostile forms as to develop friendly; that power waits upon him who earns it; that disease, wars, the unloosened, devastating elemental forces have each and all played their part in developing and hardening man and giving him the heroic fiber.

The celestial laws are here underfoot and our treading upon them does not obliterate or vulgarize them. Chemistry is incorruptible and immortal, it is the handmaid of God; the yeast works in the elements of our bread of life while we sleep; the stars send their influences, the earth renews itself, the brooding heaven gathers us under its wings, and all is well with us if we have the heroic hearts to see it.

In the curve of the moon's or of the planets'

disks, all broken or irregular lines of the surface
are lost to the eye—the wholeness of the sphere
form subordinates and obliterates them all; so
all the failures and cross-purposes and dishar-
monies in nature and life do not suffice to break
or mar the vast general beneficence; the flowing universal good is obvious above all.

God is the fact of the fact, the life of the life,
the soul of the soul, the incomprehensible, the
sum of all contradictions, the unit of all diversity; he who knows him, knows him not; he who
is without him, is full of him; turn your back
upon him, then turn your back upon gravity,
upon air, upon light. He cannot be seen; but
by him all seeing comes. He cannot be heard,
yet by him all hearing comes. He is not a being, yet apart from him there is no being—there
is no apart from him.

Accepting the Universe

SUCCESSIVE INCARNATIONS *

Giuseppe Mazzini
Italian patriot, and defender of
republicanism, 1805–1872

God incarnates himself successively in humanity. Humanity is the living word of God.

Eternal God! Thy word is not finished; thy thought, the thought of the world, is not yet all revealed. It still creates, and will continue to create, for long ages beyond all human calculation. The ages that have run their course have revealed to us only a few fragments. Our mission is not ended. We scarcely know its origin; we know nothing of its final end: time and our discoveries do but extend its confines. It ascends from century to century, towards destinies unknown to us; it seeks its own law, of which we possess but the first few lines. From initiative to initiative through the series of thy successive incarnations it purifies and extends the formula of self-sacrifice, pursues its own path, learns thy ever-widening law. Forms are altered and dissolved. Religions die. The human spirit leaves them behind, as the wayfarer leaves the fires that warmed him in the night, and goes in search of other suns; but religion remains Thought is immortal: it survives all forms and is born again from its own ashes. The idea frees itself from the shrunken symbol, escapes from the chrysalis which prisoned it, which criticism had eaten through. It shines forth pure and bright, a new star in the firmament of humanity. How many has faith yet to add that the whole way of the future may be il-

lumined? Who can say how many stars,
thoughts of the ages, have yet to rise in cloudless splendor and shine in the firmament of mind
that man may become a living epitome of the
Word on the earth?

The Duties of Man and Other Essays

THE BOOK OF NATURE *

RALPH WALDO EMERSON
American philosopher, poet and essayist, 1803–1882

The book of nature is the book of fate. She
turns the gigantic pages, leaf after leaf, never
re-turning one. One leaf she lays down, a floor
of granite; a thousand ages, and a bed of slate;
a thousand ages, and a measure of coal; a thousand ages, and a layer of marl and mud; vege-
table forms appear; her first misshapen animals, zoöphyte, trilobium, fish; then saurians,—
rude forms, in which she has only blocked her
future statue, concealing under these unwieldy
monsters the fine type of her coming king. The
face of the planet cools and dries, the races
meliorate, and man is born. But when a race
has lived its term, it comes no more again.

We learn what patient periods must round
themselves before the rock is broken, and the

first lichen race has disintegrated the thinnest external plate into soil, and opened the door for the remote Flora, Fauna, Ceres, and Pomona to come in. How far off yet is the trilobite, how far the quadruped, how inconceivably remote is man! All duly arrive, and then race after race of men. It is a long way from granite to the oyster; farther yet to Plato and the preaching of the immortality of the soul.

We call these millions men; but they are not yet men. Half engaged in the soil, pawing to get free, man needs all the music that can be brought to disengage him. If love, red love, with tears and joy, if want with his scourge, if war with its cannonade, if Christianity with its charity, if trade with its money, if art with its portfolios, if science with her telegraphs through the deeps of space and time, can set his dull nerves throbbing and by loud taps on the tough chrysalis can break its walls and let the new creature emerge erect and free,—make way and sing pæan! The age of the quadruped is to go out, the age of the brain and of the heart is to come in. And if one shall read the future of the race hinted in the organic effort of nature to mount and meliorate, and the corresponding impulse to the Better in the human being, we shall dare affirm that there is nothing he will not overcome and convert, until at last culture shall absorb the chaos and gehenna. He will convert the furies into muses, and the hells into benefit.

Essays on Fate, Nature, Culture

THE SUBLIME MEANING OF EVOLUTION

HENRY DRUMMOND
Scottish writer, 1854–1897

Those who know the Cathedral of St. Mark's will remember how this noblest of the *Stones of Venice* owes its greatness to the patient hands of centuries and centuries of workers, how every quarter of the globe has been spoiled of its treasures to dignify this single shrine. But he who ponders over the more ancient temple of the human body will find imagination fail him as he tries to think from what remote and mingled sources, from what lands, seas, climates, atmospheres, its various parts have been called together, and by what innumerable contributory creatures, swimming, creeping, flying, climbing, each of its several members was wrought and perfected.

How these things came to be, biology is one

long record. The architects and builders of this mighty temple are not anonymous. Their names, and the work they did, are graven for ever on the walls and arches of the human embryo. For this is a volume of that book in which man's members were written, which in continuance were fashioned, when as yet there was none of them.

The descent of man from the animal kingdom is sometimes spoken of as a degradation. It is an unspeakable exaltation. Recall the vast antiquity of that primal cell from which the human embryo sets forth. Compass the nature of the potentialities stored up in its plastic substance. Watch all the busy processes, the multiplying energies, the mystifying transitions, the inexplicable chemistry of this living laboratory. Observe the variety and intricacy of its metamorphoses, the exquisite gradation of its ascent, the unerring aim with which the one type unfolds—never pausing, never uncertain of its direction, refusing arrest at intermediate forms, passing on to its flawless maturity without waste or effort or fatigue. See the sense of motion at every turn, of purpose and of aspiration. Discover how, with identity of process and loyalty to the type, a hair-breadth of deviation is yet secured to each, so that no two forms come out the same, but each arises an original creation, with features, characteristics, and individualities of its own.

Remember, finally, that even to make the first cell possible, stellar space required to be swept of matter, suns must needs be broken up and planets cool, the agents of geology labor millennium after millennium at the unfinished earth to prepare a material resting-place for the coming guest. Consider all this, and judge if creation could have a sublimer meaning, or the human race possess a more splendid genesis.

Natural Law in the Spiritual World

EVOLUTION
J. Arthur Thomson
British: professor of natural history, editor and author; 1861–1933

The evolution-idea is a master-key that opens many doors. It is a luminous interpretation of the world, throwing the light of the past upon the present. Everything is seen to be an antiquity, with a history behind it—a natural history, which enables us to understand in some measure how it has come to be as it is. We cannot say more than "understand in some measure," for while the *fact* of evolution is certain, we are only beginning to discern the *factors* that have been at work.

The evolution-idea is very old, going back to some of the Greek philosophers, but it is only in modern times that it has become an essential part of our mental equipment. It is now an everyday intellectual tool. It was applied to the origin of the solar system and to the making of the earth before it was applied to plants and animals; it was extended from these to man himself; it spread to language, to folk-ways, to institutions. Within recent years the evolution-idea has been applied to the chemical elements, for it appears that uranium may change into radium, that radium may produce helium, and that lead is the final stable result when the changes of uranium are complete. Perhaps all the elements may be the outcome of an inorganic evolution. Not less important is the extension of the evolution-idea to the world within as well as to the world without. For alongside of the evolution of bodies and brains is the evolution of feelings and emotions, ideas and imagination.

Organic evolution means that the present is the child of the past and the parent of the future. It is not a power or a principle; it is a process—a process of becoming. It means that the present-day animals and plants and all the subtle inter-relations between them have arisen in a natural, knowable way from a preceding state of affairs on the whole somewhat simpler, and that again from forms and inter-relations simpler still, and so on backwards and backwards for millions of years till we lose all clues in the thick mist that hangs over life's beginnings.

Our solar system was once represented by a nebula of some sort, and we may speak of the evolution of the sun and the planets. But since it has been the same material throughout that has changed in its distribution and forms, it might be clearer to use some word like genesis. Similarly, our human institutions were once very different from what they are now, and we may speak of the evolution of government or of cities. But man works with a purpose, with ideas and ideals in some measure controlling his actions and guiding his achievements, so that it is probably clearer to keep the good old word history for all processes of social becoming in which man has been a conscious agent. Now between the genesis of the solar system and the history of civilization there comes the vast process of organic evolution. The word development should be kept for the becoming of the individual,—the chick out of the egg, for instance.

Organic evolution is a continuous natural process of racial change by successive steps in a definite direction, whereby distinctively new individualities arise, take root, and flourish, sometimes alongside of, and sometimes, sooner or later, in place of the originative stock. Our domesticated breeds of pigeons and poultry are the results of evolutionary change whose origins are still with us in the rock dove and the jungle fowl; but in most cases in wild nature the ancestral stocks of present-day forms are long since extinct, and in many cases they are unknown. Evolution is a long process of coming and going, appearing and disappearing, a long-drawn-out sublime process like a great piece of music.

The Outline of Science, Vol. i, p. 55

THE CONSTANT LAW OF NATURE *
John Tyndall
British physicist, 1820–1893

Presented rightly to the mind, the discoveries and generalizations of modern science constitute a poem more sublime than has ever yet been addressed to the imagination. The natural philosopher of today may dwell amid conceptions which beggar those of Milton. So great and grand are they that in the contemplation of them a certain force of character is requisite to preserve us from bewilderment. Look at the integrated energies of our world,—the stored power of our coal-fields; our winds and rivers; our fleets, armies, and guns. What are they? They are all generated by a portion of the sun's energy which does not amount to $\frac{1}{2,300,000,000}$ of the whole. This is the entire fraction of the sun's force intercepted by the earth, and we convert but a small fraction of this fraction into mechanical energy. Multiplying all our powers by millions of millions, we do not reach the sun's expenditure. And still, notwithstanding this enormous drain, in the lapse of human history we are unable to detect a diminution of his store. Measured by our largest terrestrial standards, such a reservoir of power is infinite; but it is our privilege to rise above these standards, and to regard the sun himself as a speck in infinite extension—a mere drop in the universal sea. We analyze the space in which he is immersed, and which is the vehicle of his power. We pass to other systems and other suns, each pouring forth energy like our own, but still without infringement of the law, which reveals immutability in the midst of change, which recognizes incessant transference or conversion, but neither final gain nor loss.

To nature nothing can be added; from nature nothing can be taken away: the sum of her energies is constant, and the utmost man can do in the pursuit of physical truth, or in the applications of physical knowledge, is to shift the constituents of the never-varying total. The law of conservation rigidly excludes both creation and annihilation. Waves may change to ripples, and ripples to waves; magnitude may be substituted for number, and number for magnitude; asteroids may aggregate to suns, suns may resolve themselves into florae and faunae, and florae and faunae melt in air,—the flux of power is eternally the same: it rolls in music through the ages, and all terrestrial energy, the manifestations of life as well as the display of phenomena, are but the modulations of its rhythm.

Heat, Considered as a Mode of Motion

THE RECONCILIATION OF SCIENCE AND RELIGION

Henri Frédéric Amiel
Swiss scholar and writer, 1821–1881

Every fresh cosmical conception demands a religion which corresponds to it. Our age of transition stands bewildered between the two incompatible methods, the scientific method and the religious method, and between the two certitudes, which contradict each other.

Surely the reconciliation of the two must be sought for in the moral law, which is also a fact, and every step of which requires for its explanation another cosmos than the cosmos of necessity. Who knows if necessity is not a particular case of liberty, and its condition? Who knows if nature is not a laboratory for the fabrication of thinking beings who are ultimately to become free creatures? Biology protests, and indeed the supposed existence of souls, independently of time, space, and matter, is a fiction of faith, less logical than the Platonic dogma. But the question remains open. We may eliminate the idea of purpose from nature; yet, as the guiding conception of the highest being of our planet, it is a fact, and a fact which postulates a meaning in the history of the universe.

Journal
Trans. Mrs. Humphry Ward

MAN'S PLACE IN NATURE [*]
Edwin Grant Conklin
American biologist, 1863–

One of the greatest results of the doctrine of organic evolution has been the determination of man's place in nature. For many centuries it has been known that in bodily structure man is an animal, that he is born, nourished, and developed, that he matures, reproduces, and dies just as does the humblest animal or plant.

The many undoubted resemblances between man and the lower animals, and the discovery of the remains of lower types of man, real "missing links," have inevitably led to the conclusion that man also is a product of evolution, that he is a part of the great world of living things and not a being who stands apart in solitary grandeur in some isolated sphere.

We hear much nowadays about man's control over nature, though in no single instance has he ever changed any law or principle of nature.

What he can do is to put himself into such relations to natural phenomena that he may profit by them, and all that can be done toward the improvement of the human race is consciously and purposively to apply to man those great principles of development and evolution which have been at work, unknown to man, through the ages.

Heredity and Environment in the
Development of Man

THE MORAL SENSE EVER NEW *
RALPH WALDO EMERSON
American philosopher, poet, and essayist; 1803–1882

The moral sense reappears to-day with the same morning newness that has been from of old the fountain of beauty and strength. You say there is no religion now. 'Tis like saying in rainy weather, There is no sun, when at that moment we are witnessing one of his superlative effects. We have learned the manners of the sun and of the moon, of the rivers and the rain, of the mineral and elemental kingdoms, of plants and animals. Man has learned to weigh the sun. The next lesson taught is the continuation of the inflexible law of matter into the subtile kingdom of will and of thought. The primordial atoms are prefigured and predetermined to moral issues. Those laws do not stop where our eyes lose them, but push the same geometry and chemistry up into the invisible plane of social and rational life, so that, look where we will, in a boy's game, or in the strifes of races, a perfect reaction, a perpetual judgment keeps watch and ward. That only which we have within, can we see without. If we meet no gods, it is because we harbor none. If there is grandeur in you, you will find grandeur in porters and sweeps. Every man's task is his life-preserver. The conviction that his work is dear to God and cannot be spared defends him.

And so I think that the last lesson of life, the choral song which rises from all elements and all angels, is a voluntary obedience, a necessitated freedom. Man is made of the same atoms as the world is, he shares the same impressions, predispositions, and destiny. When his mind is illuminated, when his heart is kind, he throws himself joyfully into the sublime order and does, with knowledge, what the stones do by structure.

The laws are his consolers: the good laws

themselves are alive, they know if he have kept them, they animate him with the leading of great duty, and an endless horizon. Honor and fortune exist to him who always recognizes the neighborhood of the great,—always feels himself in the presence of high causes.

Worship

STUDIES IN THE BOOK OF NATURE

Intimations of Immortality

THE DIVINE NATURE OF MAN[*]
EPICTETUS
Greek philosopher, born about 60 A.D.

You travel to Olympia that you may see the work of Phidias, and each of you thinks it a misfortune to die without visiting these sights; and will you have no desire to behold and to comprehend those things for which there is no need of travel, in the presence of which you stand here and now, each one of you? Will you not realize then who you are, and to what end you are born, and what that is which you have received power to see?

When a man therefore has learned to understand the government of the universe and has realized that there is nothing so great or sovereign or all-inclusive as this frame of things wherein men and God are united, and that from it come the seeds from which are sprung not only my own father or grandfather, but all things that grow upon the earth, and rational

creatures in particular—for these alone are by
nature fitted to share in the society of God,
being connected with him by the bond of reason
—why should he not call himself a citizen of
the universe and son of God? Why should he
fear anything that can happen to him among
men?

Discourses and Manual of Epictetus
Trans. P. E. Matheson

IMMORTALITY

PTOLEMY
Egyptian astronomer and
geographer, about 139–161

Mortal though I be, yea, ephemeral, if but a
moment
I gaze up to the night's starry domain of
heaven,
Then no longer on earth I stand; I touch the
Creator,
And my lively spirit drinketh immortality.

Trans. Robert Bridges
The Spirit of Man
Ed. Robert Bridges

INTIMATIONS OF IMMORTALITY *

WILLIAM WORDSWORTH

English poet, 1770–1850

Our birth is but a sleep and a forgetting:
The soul that rises with us, our life's star,
 Hath had elsewhere its setting,
 And cometh from afar:
 Not in entire forgetfulness,
 And not in utter nakedness,
But trailing clouds of glory do we come
 From God, who is our home.
Heaven lies about us in our infancy.
Shades of the prison-house begin to close
 Upon the growing boy,
But he beholds the light, and whence it flows
 He sees it in his joy;
The youth, who daily farther from the east
 Must travel, still is nature's priest,
 And by the vision splendid
 Is on his way attended;
At length the man perceives it die away,
And fade into the light of common day.

 O joy, that in our embers
 Is something that doth live,
 That nature yet remembers
 What was so fugitive!

The thought of our past years in me doth breed
    Perpetual benediction,
    For those first affections,
    Those shadowy recollections,
    Which, be they what they may,
Are yet the fountain-light of all our day,
Are yet a master-light of all our seeing;
Uphold us, cherish, and have power to make
Our noisy years seem moments in the being
Of the eternal silence: truths that wake
    To perish never;
Which neither listlessness, nor mad endeavor,
    Nor man nor boy,
Nor all that is at enmity with joy,
Can utterly abolish or destroy.
    Hence, in a season of calm weather
    Though inland far we be,
Our souls have sight of that immortal sea
    Which brought us hither,
    Can in a moment travel thither
And see the children sport upon the shore,
And hear the mighty waters rolling evermore.

Then sing, ye birds, sing, sing a joyous song!
    And let the young lambs bound
    As to the tabor's sound!
I love the brooks which down their channels
    fret,
Even more than when I tripped lightly as they;

The innocent brightness of a new-born day
     Is lovely yet.

The clouds that gather round the setting sun
Do take a sober coloring from an eye
That hath kept watch o'er man's mortality:
Another race hath been, and other palms are
     won.
Thanks to the human heart by which we live,
Thanks to its tenderness, its joys and fears,
To me the meanest flower that blows can give
Thoughts that do often lie too deep for tears.

    From *Ode on Intimations of Immortality*

THE GRANDEUR OF THE SOUL

RALPH WALDO EMERSON

American philosopher, poet, and essayist; 1803–1882

We cannot describe the natural history of
the soul, but we know that it is divine. I cannot tell if these wonderful qualities which
house to-day in this mortal frame shall ever
re-assemble in equal activity in a similar frame,
or whether they have before had a natural history like that of this body you see before you;

but this one thing I know, that these qualities did not now begin to exist, cannot be sick with my sickness, nor buried in any grave; but that they circulate through the universe: before the world was, they were. Nothing can bar them out, or shut them in, but they penetrate the ocean and land, space and time, form an essence, and hold the key to universal nature. I draw from this faith courage and hope. All things are known to the soul. It is not to be surprised by any communication. Nothing can be greater than it. Let those fear and those fawn who will. The soul is in her native realm, and it is wider than space, older than time, wide as hope, rich as love. Pusillanimity and fear she refuses with a beautiful scorn; they are not for her who puts on her coronation robes and goes out through universal love to universal power.

The Method of Nature

THE TESTIMONY OF THE IDEALISTS *
WILLIAM OSLER
British physician, scholar, and author; 1849–1919

On the question of the immortality of the soul, the only people who have ever had perfect satisfaction are the idealists, who walk by faith and not by sight. "Many are the wand bearers, few are the mystics," said Plato. Children of Light, children of the Spirit, whose ways are foolishness to the children of this world, mystics, idealists with no strong reason for the faith that is in them, yet they compel admiration and imitation by the character of the life they lead and the beneficence of the influence they exert. The serene faith of Socrates with the cup of hemlock at his lips, the heroic devotion of a St. Francis or a St. Theresa, but more often for each one of us the beautiful life of some good woman whose—

"Eyes are homes of silent prayer,
   Whose loves in higher love endure,"
do more to keep alive a belief in immortality than all the preaching in the land.

Science and Immortality

THE CHOIR INVISIBLE *
GEORGE ELIOT
English novelist, 1819–1880

Oh, may I join the choir invisible
Of those immortal dead who live again
In minds made better by their presence; live

In pulses stirred to generosity,
In deeds of daring rectitude, in scorn
For miserable aims that end with self,
In thoughts sublime that pierce the night like
    stars,
And with their mild persistence urge man's
    search
To vaster issues!

             This is life to come,
Which martyred men have made more glorious
For us who strive to follow. May I reach
That purest heaven, be to other souls
The cup of strength in some great agony,
Enkindle generous ardor, feed pure love,
Beget the smiles that have no cruelty,
Be the sweet presence of a good diffused,
And in diffusion ever more intense.
So shall I join the choir invisible
Whose music is the gladness of the world.

THEIR SILENT MINISTRY
FREDERICK LUCIAN HOSMER
American preacher and hymn writer, 1840-1929

I cannot think of them as dead
  Who walk with me no more

Along the path of life I tread;
    They have but gone before.

The Father's house is mansioned fair
    Beyond my vision dim;
All souls are his, and here or there
    Are living unto him.

And still their silent ministry
    Within my heart hath place,
As when on earth they walked with me
    And met me face to face.

Their lives are made forever mine;
    What they to me have been
Hath left henceforth its seal and sign
    Engraven deep within.

Mine are they by an ownership
    Nor time nor death can free;
For God hath given to love to keep
    Its own eternally.

The Thought of God

THEY SOFTLY WALK

Hugh Robert Orr
American: teacher of religion, 1887—

They are not gone who pass
Beyond the clasp of hand,
Out from the strong embrace.
They are but come so close
We need not grope with hands,
Nor look to see, nor try
To catch the sound of feet.
They have put off their shoes
Softly to walk by day
Within our thoughts, to tread
At night our dream-led paths
Of sleep.

They are not lost who find
The sunset gate, the goal
Of all their faithful years.
Not lost are they who reach
The summit of their climb,
The peak above the clouds
And storms. They are not lost
Who find the light of sun
And stars and God.

They are not dead who live
In hearts they leave behind.
In those whom they have blessed
They live a life again,
And shall live through the years
Eternal life, and grow
Each day more beautiful
As time declares their good,
Forgets the rest, and proves
Their immortality.

Harp of My Heart and Other Poems

NATURAL AND SPIRITUAL
The Apostle Paul
Christian, first century

If there is a natural body, there is also a
spiritual body. So also it is written, The first
man Adam became a living soul: the last Adam
became a life-giving spirit. Howbeit that is
not first which is spiritual, but that which is
natural; then that which is spiritual. The first
man is of the earth, earthy: the second man is
of heaven. As is the earthy, such are they also
that are earthy: and as is the heavenly, such
are they also that are heavenly. And as we

have borne the image of the earthy, we shall
also bear the image of the heavenly.

From *The First Epistle to the Corinthians*
New Testament

WHAT IS EXCELLENT IS
PERMANENT*

RALPH WALDO EMERSON

American philosopher, essayist, and poet, 1803–1882

When frail nature can no more,
Then the Spirit strikes the hour:
My servant death, with solving rite,
Pours finite into infinite.

What is excellent,
As God lives, is permanent;
Hearts are dust, hearts' loves remain;
Heart's love will meet thee again.

From *Threnody*

IN MEMORIAM
MARGARITÆ SORORIS

WILLIAM E. HENLEY

English poet, 1849–1903

A late lark twitters from the quiet skies;
And from the west,

Where the sun, his day's work ended,
Lingers as in content,
There falls on the old, gray city
An influence luminous and serene,
A shining peace.

The smoke ascends
In a rosy-and-golden haze.   The spires
Shine, and are changed.   In the valley
Shadows rise.   The lark sings on.   The sun
Closing his benediction,
Sinks, and the darkening air
Thrills with a sense of the triumphing night—
Night with her train of stars
And her great gift of sleep.

So be my passing!
My task accomplished and the long day done,
My wages taken and in my heart
Some late lark singing,
Let me be gathered to the quiet west,
The sundown splendid and serene,
Death.

THE LARGER HOPE *
Alfred Tennyson
English poet, 1809–1892

O yet we trust that somehow good
  Will be the final goal of ill,
  To pangs of nature, sins of will,
Defects of doubt, and taints of blood;

That nothing walks with aimless feet;
  That not one life shall be destroyed,
  Or cast as rubbish to the void,
When God hath made the pile complete;

That not a worm is cloven in vain;
  That not a moth with vain desire
  Is shriveled in a fruitless fire,
Or but subserves another's gain!

Behold, we know not anything:
  I can but trust that good shall fall
  At last—far off—at last, to all,
And every winter change to spring.

So runs my dream; but what am I?
  An infant crying in the night;

An infant crying for the light
And with no language but a cry.

I falter where I firmly trod,
    And falling with my weight of cares
    Upon the great world's altar-stairs
That slope through darkness up to God,

I stretch lame hands of faith, and grope,
    And gather dust and chaff, and call
    To what I feel is Lord of all,
And faintly trust the larger hope.

In Memoriam, liv, lv

THIS LIFE AND THE NEXT *
EDWARD YOUNG
English clergyman and author, 1683–1765

A truth it is, few doubt but fewer trust,
"He sins against this life who slights the next."
What is this life? How few their favorite
    know!
Fond in the dark, and blind in our embrace,
By passionately loving life, we make
Loved life unlovely, hugging her to death.
We give to time eternity's regard;

And, dreaming, take our passage for our port.
Life has no value as an end, but means;
An end, deplorable—a means, divine.
When 'tis our all, 'tis nothing; worse than
    nought;
A nest of pains; when held as nothing, much:
Like some fair humorists, life is most enjoyed
When courted least; most worth, when
    disesteemed;
Then 'tis the seat of comfort, rich in peace;
In prospect richer far; important, awful;
Not to be mentioned but with shouts of praise;
Not to be thought on but with tides of joy:
The mighty basis of eternal bliss.

Vain is the world, but only to the vain.
To what compare we then this varying scene,
Whose worth ambiguous rises, and declines,
Waxes and wanes? (In all propitious, night
Assists me here.) Compare it to the moon,
Dark in herself and indigent, but rich
In borrowed lustre from a higher sphere.

                    Night Thoughts

ENTERING INTO THE HALL OF TRUTH *

Egyptian, from about 4500 B.C.

[That which is said on reaching the Hall of Truth, when X (the deceased's name) is purged from all evil that he has done and he beholds the face of the god.]

Hail to thee, great god, lord of truth! I have come to thee, my lord, and I am led (thither) in order to see thy beauty. Behold, I come to thee, I bring to thee righteousness and I expel for thee sin. I have committed no sin against people. I have not done evil in the place of truth. I knew no wrong. I did no evil thing. I did not do that which the god abominates. I did not report evil of a servant to his master. I allowed no one to hunger. I caused no one to weep. I did not murder. I did not command to murder. I caused no man misery. I did not diminish food in the temples. I did not decrease the offerings of the gods. I did not commit adultery. I did not diminish the grain measure. I did not diminish the span. I did not diminish the land measure. I did not load the weight of the balances. I did not deflex the index of the scales. I did not take milk from the mouth of the child. I did not drive away the cattle from their pasturage. I did not snare the fowl of the gods. I did not catch the fish in their pools. I did not hold back the water in its time. I did not dam the running water. I did not quench the fire in its time. I did not withhold the herds of the temple endowment. I am purified four times.

I did not slay men, I did not rob, I did not steal, I did not rob one crying for his possessions, my fortune was not great but by my (own) property, I did not take away food, I did not stir up fear, I did not stir up strife. I did not speak lies, I did not make falsehood in the place of truth, I was not deaf to truthful words. I did not diminish the grain measure, I was not avaricious, my heart devoured not, my heart was not hasty, I did not multiply words in speaking, my voice was not overloud, my mouth did not wag, I did not wax hot, I did not revile, I was not an eavesdropper, I was not puffed up. I did not revile the king, I did not blaspheme the god.

Hail to you, ye gods who are in the Hall of Truth, in whose bodies are neither sin nor falsehood, who live on truth in Heliopolis! Behold, I come to you without sin, without evil, without wrong. I have satisfied the god with

that which he desires. I gave bread to the
hungry, water to the thirsty, clothing to the
naked, and a ferry to him who was without a
boat. I made divine offerings for the gods and
food-offerings for the dead. Save ye me; protect ye me. Enter no complaint against me
before the great god. For I am one of pure
worth and pure hands, to whom was said "Welcome, welcome" by those who saw him.

The Book of the Dead,
Trans. J. H. Breasted
Development of Religion and Thought
in Ancient Egypt
J. H. Breasted

NIRVANA

Attributed to Buddha
Founder of Buddhism, India, 568?–488? B. C.

Earnestness is the path of immortality
(Nirvana), thoughtlessness the path of death.
Those who are in earnest do not die, those who
are thoughtless are as if dead already.

These wise people, meditative, steady, always
possessed of strong powers, attain to Nirvana,
the highest happiness.

He whose appetites are stilled, who is not absorbed in enjoyment, who has perceived void and unconditioned freedom (Nirvana), his path is difficult to understand, like that of birds in the air.

His thought is quiet, quiet are his word and deed, when he has obtained freedom by true knowledge, when he has thus become a quiet man.

The man who is free from credulity but knows the uncreated, who has cut all ties, removed all temptations, renounced all desires, he is the greatest of men.

Looking for the maker of this tabernacle, I have run through a course of many births, not finding him; and painful is birth again and again. But now, maker of the tabernacle, thou hast been seen; thou shalt not make up this tabernacle again. All thy rafters are broken, thy ridge-pole is sundered; the mind, approaching the Eternal (Nirvana), has attained to the extinction of all desires.

Look upon the world as you would on a bubble, look at it as you would on a mirage:

the king of death does not see him who thus looks down upon the world.

Come, look at this world, glittering like a royal chariot: the foolish are immersed in it, but the wise do not touch it.

Better than sovereignty over the earth, better than going to heaven, better than lordship over all worlds is the reward of the first step in holiness.

We live happily indeed, not hating those who hate us. Among men who hate us we dwell free from hatred.

We live happily indeed, free from greed among the greedy. Among men who are greedy, let us dwell free from greed.

We live happily indeed, though we call nothing our own. We shall be like the bright gods, feeding on happiness!

Victory breeds hatred, for the conquered is unhappy. He who has given up both victory and defeat, he, the contented, is happy.

There is no fire like passion; there is no losing throw like hatred; there is no pain like this body; there is no happiness higher than rest.

"All created things perish." He who knows and sees this becomes passive in pain: this is the way to purity.

"All created things are grief and pain." He who knows and sees this becomes passive in pain; this is the way that leads to purity.

"All forms are unreal." He who knows and sees this becomes passive in pain; this is the way that leads to purity.

The gift of the law exceeds all gifts; the sweetness of the law exceeds all sweetness; the delight in the law exceeds all delights; the extinction of thirst overcomes all pain.

Dhammapada (Path of Virtue,
or Footstep of the Law)
Trans. Max Müller, *The Sacred Books of the East*

THE HEAVENLY MAIDEN *

Yasts,
Zoroastrian liturgics,
fifth century B. C. or later

Zarathustra asked Ahura Mazda: "O Ahura Mazda, most beneficent Spirit, Maker of the material world, thou Holy One! When one of the faithful departs this life, where does his soul abide on that night?" Ahura Mazda answered: (Here follows an account of the experiences of the first two nights of the journey. Ed.) "At the end of the third night, when the dawn appears, it seems to the soul of the faithful one as if it were brought amidst plants and scents; it seems as if a wind were blowing from the region of the south. And it seems to him as if his own conscience were advancing to him in that wind, in the shape of a maiden.

"And the soul of the faithful one addressed her, asking: 'What maid art thou, who art the fairest maid I have ever seen?'

"And she, being his own conscience, answers him, 'O thou youth of good thoughts, good words, and good deeds, of good religion, I am thy own conscience! Everybody did love thee for that greatness, goodness, sweet-scentedness, victorious strength, and freedom from sorrow, in which thou dost appear to me. And so thou, O youth of good thoughts, good words and good deeds, of good religion, didst love me for that greatness, goodness, fairness, sweet-scentedness, victorious strength, and freedom from sorrow, in which I appear to thee. I was lovely, and thou madest me still lovelier; I was fair, and thou madest me still fairer; I was desirable, and thou madest me still more desirable; I was sit-

ting in a forward place, and thou madest me sit
in a foremost place, through this good thought,
through this good speech, through this good
deed of thine.'"

The Zend-Avesta
Trans. James Darmesteter, *The Sacred Books*
of the East.

A BLEST ABODE *
VIRGIL
Latin epic poet, 70–19 B. C.

         "Behold yon arching doors,
Yon walls in furnace of the Cyclops forged!"
    . . . So, side by side,
Swift through the intervening dark they strode,
And, drawing near the portal arch, made pause.
Aeneas, taking station at the door,
Pure, lustral waters o'er his body threw,
And hung for garland there the Golden Bough.
At last within a land delectable
Their journey lay, through pleasurable bowers
Of groves where all is joy,—a blest abode!
An ampler sky its roseate light bestows
On that bright land, which sees the cloudless
    beam
Of suns and planets to our earth unknown.

On smooth green lawns, contending limb with
    limb,
Immortal athletes play, and wrestle long
'Gainst mate or rival on the tawny sand;
With sounding footsteps and ecstatic song
Some thread the dance divine: among them
    moves
The bard of Thrace, in flowing vesture clad,
Discoursing seven-noted melody,
Who sweeps the numbered strings with change-
    ful hand,
Or smites with ivory point his golden lyre.
Here Trojans be of eldest, noblest race,
Great-hearted heroes, born in happier times,
Ilus, Assaracus, and Dardanus,
Illustrious builders of the Trojan town.
Their arms and shadowy chariots he views,
And lances fixed in earth, while through the
    fields
Their steeds without a bridle graze at will.
For if in life their darling passion ran
To chariots, arms, or glossy-coated steeds,
The self-same joy, though in their graves, they
    feel.
Lo! on the left and right at feast reclined
Are other blessed souls, whose chorus sings
Victorious pæans on the fragrant air
Of laurel groves: and hence to earth outpours

Eridanus, through forests rolling tree.
Here dwell the brace who for their native land
Fell wounded on the field; here holy priests
Who kept them undefiled their mortal day;
And poets, of whom the true-inspired song
Deserved Apollo's name; and all who found
New arts, to make man's life more blest or fair;
Yea! here dwell all those dead whose deeds
    bequeath
Deserved and grateful memory to their kind;
And each bright brow a snow-white fillet wears.

The Æneid, Book vi
Trans. Theodore C. Williams

THE CELESTIAL COUNTRY *

BERNARD OF CLUNY
French monk, twelfth century

Brief life is here our portion,
    Brief sorrow, short-lived care;
The life that knows no ending,
    The tearless life, is there.

For thee, O dear, dear Country,
    Mine eyes their vigils keep;
For very love, beholding
    Thy happy name they weep.

The mention of thy glory
    Is unction to the breast,
And medicine in sickness,
    And love, and life, and rest.

Jerusalem the Golden,
    With milk and honey blest,
Beneath thy contemplation
    Sink heart and voice oppressed.
I know not, O I know not,
    What social joys are there!
What radiancy of glory,
    What light beyond compare!

There is the throne of David,
    And there, from care released,
The song of them that triumph,
    The shout of them that feast;
And they who, with their Leader,
    Have conquered in the fight,
For ever and for ever
    Are clad in robes of white.

O fields that know no sorrow!
    O state that fears no strife!
O princely bowers! O land of flowers!
    O realm and home of Life!

The Seven Great Hymns of
the Mediæval Church

The Light of Faith

WISDOM *
Hebrew, first century B. C.

I called upon God, and there came to me a spirit of wisdom. I preferred her before sceptres and thrones, and riches I esteemed nothing in comparison of her; neither did I liken to her any priceless gem, because all the gold of the earth in her presence is a little sand, and silver shall be accounted as clay before her. Above health and comeliness I loved her; and I chose to have her rather than light, because her bright shining is never laid to sleep.

But with her there came to me all good things together, and in her hands innumerable riches. And I rejoiced over them all because Wisdom leadeth them; though I knew not that she was the mother of them. As I learned without guile, I impart without grudging; I do not hide her riches. For she is unto men a treasure that faileth not; and they that use it obtain friendship with God.

There is in her a spirit quick of understanding, holy, alone in kind, manifold, subtile, freely moving, clear in utterance, unpolluted, distinct, unharmed, loving what is good, keen, unhindered, beneficent, loving toward man, steadfast, sure, free from care, all-powerful, all-surveying, and penetrating through all spirits that are quick of understanding, pure, most subtile. For Wisdom is more mobile than any motion; yea, she pervadeth and penetrateth all things by reason of her pureness. For she is a breath of the power of God, and a clear effluence of the glory of the Almighty; therefore can nothing defiled find entrance into her. For she is an effulgence from everlasting light, and an unspotted mirror of the working of God, and an image of his goodness. And she, being one, hath power to do all things; and remaining in herself, reneweth all things; and from generation to generation, passing into holy souls, she maketh men friends of God and prophets.

From *The Wisdom of Solomon*
Old Testament Apocrypha

REVELATIONS OF GOD

JOHN ROBINSON, 1575–1625

(From an address to his congregation just before the Pilgrims, who were members, sailed to America, July 21, 1620.)

We are now ere long to part asunder, and the Lord knoweth whether I shall live to see your faces again. But whether the Lord hath appointed it or not, I charge you before God and his blessed angels to follow me no further than I have followed Christ; and if God should reveal anything to you by any other instrument of his, to be as ready to receive it as ever you were to receive any truth by my ministry; for I am very confident the Lord hath more truth and light yet to break forth out of his holy Word.

I bewail the condition of the reformed churches who are come to a period in religion and will go no further than the instruments of their reformation. The Lutherans cannot be drawn to go beyond what Luther saw; for whatever part of God's will has been imparted and revealed to Calvin, they will rather die than embrace it. And the Calvinists, as you see, stick where Calvin left them. This is a misery much to be lamented; for though Luther and

Calvin were precious shining lights in their
times, yet God did not reveal his whole will to
them; and were they living now they would
be as ready and willing to embrace further light
as that that they had received. I beseech you
to remember your church covenant, at least that
part of it whereby you promise and covenant
with God and one with one another to receive
whatsoever light or truth shall be made known
to you from the written Word of God.

Old South Leaflets, Vol. vi
(Put into direct discourse from the account
by Edward Winslow.)

TRUTH AND LIBERTY *
John Milton
English Puritan poet, 1608–1674

Truth is compared in Scripture to a stream-
ing fountain: if her waters flow not in a perpetual progression, they sicken into a muddy
pool of conformity and tradition.

We boast our light; but if we look not wisely
on the sun itself, it smites us into darkness.
The light which we have gained was given us,
not to be ever staring on, but by it to discover
onward things more remote from our knowledge.

To be still searching what we know not by

what we know, still closing up truth as we find it, this is the golden rule in theology as well as in arithmetic, and makes up the best harmony in a church; not the forced and outward union of cold and natural and inwardly divided minds. Where there is much desire to learn, there of necessity will be much arguing, much writing, many opinions; for opinion in good men is but knowledge in the making. A little generous prudence, a little forbearance of one another, and some grain of charity, might win all these diligences to join, and unite in one general and brotherly search after truth, could we but forego this prelatical tradition of crowding free consciences and Christian liberties into canons and precepts of men. Give me the liberty to know, to utter, and to argue freely according to conscience, above all liberties. The Temple of Janus with his two controversial faces might now not unsignificantly be set open. And though all the winds of doctrine were let loose to play upon the earth, so truth be in the field, we do injuriously by licensing and prohibiting to misdoubt her strength. Let her and falsehood grapple: who ever knew truth put to the worse, in a free and open encounter? Her confuting is the best and surest suppressing.

Areopagitica

TRUTH STRENGTHENED BY OPPOSITION

WILLIAM ELLERY CHANNING
American preacher
and religious reformer, 1780–1842

In the long run, truth is aided by nothing so much as by opposition, and by the opposition of those who can give the full strength of the argument on the side of error. In an age of authority and spiritual bondage, the opinions of an individual are often important,—sometimes decisive. One voice may determine the judgment of a country. But, in an age of free discussion, little is to be feared from great names, on whatever side arrayed. When I hear a man complaining that some cause which he has at heart will be put back for years by a speech or a book, I suspect that his attachment to it is prejudice, that he has no consciousness of standing on a rock. The more discussion the better, if passion and personality be eschewed; and discussion, even if stormy, often winnows truth from error, a good never to be expected in an unenquiring age.

On the Slavery Question

DOUBTING CASTLE *

JOHN BUNYAN
English preacher and writer, 1628–1688

Now there was, not far from where they (Christian and Hopeful) lay, a castle, called Doubting Castle, the owner whereof was Giant Despair, and it was in his grounds they were now sleeping; wherefore he, getting up in the morning early and walking up and down in his fields, caught Christian and Hopeful asleep in his grounds. Then with a grim and surly voice he bid them awake and asked them whence they were, and what they did in his grounds. They told him they were pilgrims and that they had lost their way.

Then said the giant, "You have this night trespassed on me by trampling and lying on my grounds, and therefore you must go along with me."

So they were forced to go, because he was stronger than they. They had also but little to say, for they knew themselves in a fault. The giant, therefore, drove them before him, and put them into his castle, into a very dark dungeon, nasty and stinking to the spirits of these two men. Here then they lay from

Wednesday morning until Saturday night, without one bit of bread or drop of drink, or light.

Well, on Saturday, about midnight, they began to pray, and continued in prayer till almost break of day. Now, a little before it was day, good Christian, as one half amazed, brake out into this passionate speech: "What a fool," quoth he, "am I, thus to lie in a stinking dungeon when I may as well walk at liberty! I have a key in my bosom called Promise that will I am persuaded open any lock in Doubting Castle."

Then said Hopeful, "That is good news: good brother, pluck it out of thy bosom and try."

Then Christian pulled it out of his bosom and began to try at the dungeon-door, whose bolt as he turned the key gave back, and the door flew open with ease, and Christian and Hopeful both came out. Then he went to the outward door that leads into the castle-yard, and with his key opened that door also. After that he went to the iron gate, for that must be opened too; but that lock went desperately hard, yet the key did open it. They then thrust open the gate to make their escape with speed; but that gate, as it opened, made such a creaking that it waked Giant Despair, who hastily rising to pursue his prisoners, felt his limbs to fail: for his fits took him again, so that he could by no

means go after them. Then they went on, and
came to the King's highway.

The Pilgrim's Progress, Part i

(Christiana and her companions) went on.
And when they were come to By-path meadow,
to the stile over which Christian went with his
fellow Hopeful when they were taken by Giant
Despair and put into Doubting Castle, they sat
down and consulted what was best to be done.

Mr. Greatheart said, "I have a commandment
to resist sin, to overcome evil, to fight the good
fight of faith: and I pray, with whom should I
fight this good fight, if not with Giant Despair?
I will therefore attempt the taking away of his
life, and the demolishing of Doubting Castle."

Then said he, "Who will go with me?" Then
said old Honest, "I will." "And so will we
too," said Christiana's four sons, Matthew,
Samuel, Joseph, and James; for they were
young men and strong.

So Mr. Greatheart, old Honest, and the four
young men went to go up to Doubting Castle
to look for Giant Despair. When they came
at the castle-gate they knocked for entrance
with an unusual noise. At that the old giant
comes to the gate, and Diffidence his wife follows. Then said he, "Who and what is he that

is so hardy as after this manner to molest the Giant Despair?"

Mr. Greatheart replied, "It is I, Greatheart, one of the King of the Celestial Country's conductors of pilgrims to their place; and I demand of thee that thou open thy gates for my entrance; prepare thyself also to fight, for I am come to take away thy head, and to demolish Doubting Castle."

Now Giant Despair, because he was a giant, thought no man could overcome him; and again thought he, Since heretofore I have made a conquest of angels, shall Greatheart make me afraid? So he harnessed himself and went out. He had a cap of steel upon his head, a breastplate of fire girded to him, and he came out in iron shoes, with a great club in his hand.

Then these six men made up to him and beset him behind and before. They fought for their lives and Giant Despair was brought down to the ground, but was very loth to die. He struggled hard, and had, as they say, as many lives as a cat; but Greatheart was his death, for he left him not till he had severed his head from his shoulders.

Then they fell to demolishing Doubting Castle, and that you know might with ease be done. since the Giant Despair was dead. They

were seven days in destroying of that; and in it
of pilgrims they found one Mr. Despondency,
almost starved to death, and one Muchafraid,
his daughter: these two they saved alive.

The Pilgrim's Progress, Part ii

THE SELECTION OF BELIEFS *

CHARLES W. ELIOT
Eminent American educator, 1834–1926

Here we are living on a little islet of sense
and fact in the midst of a boundless ocean of
the unknown and mysterious. From year to
year and century to century the islet expands,
as new districts are successively lifted from
out the encompassing sea of ignorance; but it
still remains encircled by this prodigious sea.
In this state of things, every inquisitive, truth-
seeking human being is solicited by innumerable
beliefs, old and new. The past generations,
out of which we spring, have been believing
many undemonstrated and undemonstrable
things; and we inherit their beliefs. Every
year new beliefs appeal to us for acceptance,
some of them clashing with the old. Everybody holds numerous beliefs on subjects outside
the realm of knowledge; and, moreover, every-

body has to act on these beliefs from hour to hour. All men of science walk by faith and not by sight in exploring and experimenting, the peculiarity of their walk being that they generally take but one step at a time, and that a short one. All business proceeds on beliefs, or judgments of probabilities, and not on certainties. The very essence of heroism is that it takes adverse chances; so that full foreknowledge of the issue would subtract from the heroic quality. Beliefs, then, we must have and must act on; and they are sure to affect profoundly our happiness in this world. How to treat our old beliefs and choose our new ones, with a view to happiness, is in these days a serious problem for every reflective person.

The first steps toward making a calm choice are to observe strictly the line of demarcation between facts on the one hand and beliefs on the other, and to hold facts as facts and beliefs as nothing more than beliefs. Next we need a criterion or touchstone for beliefs old and new. The surest touchstone is the ethical standard which through inheritance, education, and the experience of daily life has, as a matter of fact, become our standard. It is not for our happiness to believe any proposition about the nature of man, the universe, or God which is really at war with our fundamental instincts of honor and justice, or with our ideals of gentleness and love, no matter how those instincts and ideals have been implanted or arrived at. The man or woman who hopes to attain reflective happiness as he works his strenuous way through the world must bring all beliefs, old and new, to this critical test, and must reject, or refuse to entertain, beliefs which do not stand the test.

We may be sure that cheerful beliefs about the unseen world, framed in full harmony with the beauty of the visible universe and with the sweetness of the domestic affections and joys, and held in company with kindred and friends, will illuminate the dark places on the pathway of earthly life and brighten all the road.

From *The Happy Life*
The Durable Satisfactions of Life

THE RELIGIOUS BELIEF OF ABRAHAM LINCOLN

ABRAHAM LINCOLN

President of the United States during the Civil War; preserver of the Union, and emancipator of the slaves; 1809–1865

I do not see that I am more astray—though perhaps in a different direction—than many others whose points of view differ widely from each other in the sectarian denominations. They all claim to be Christian and interpret their several creeds as infallible ones. Yet they differ and discuss these questionable subjects without settling them with any mutual satisfaction among themselves.

I doubt the possibility, or propriety, of settling the religion of Jesus Christ in the models of man-made creeds and dogmas. It was a spirit in the life that he laid stress on and taught, if I read aright. I know I see it to be so with me.

The fundamental truths reported in the four gospels as from the lips of Jesus Christ and that I first heard from the lips of my mother are settled and fixed moral precepts with me. I have concluded to dismiss from my mind the debatable wrangles that once perplexed me with distractions that stirred up, but never absolutely settled, anything. I have tossed them aside with the doubtful differences which divide denominations—sweeping them all out of my mind among the non-essentials. I have ceased to follow such discussions or be interested in them.

I cannot without mental reservations assent to long and complicated creeds and catechisms.

If the church would ask simply for assent to the Saviour's statement of the substance of the law: "Thou shalt love the Lord thy God with all thy heart, and with all thy soul, and with all thy mind, and thy neighbour as thyself,"—that church would I gladly unite with.

(From the answer to questions asked of Lincoln by the mother of Henry B. Rankin)

Personal Recollections of Abraham Lincoln

Henry B. Rankin

THE LIGHT OF FAITH

GEORGE SANTAYANA

American philosopher and writer, 1863—

O world, thou choosest not the better part!
It is not wisdom to be only wise,
And on the inward vision close the eyes;
But it is wisdom to believe the heart.
Columbus found a world, and had no chart
Save one that faith deciphered in the skies;
To trust the soul's invincible surmise
Was all his science and his only art.
Our knowledge is a torch of smoky pine
That lights the pathway but one step ahead
Across a void of mystery and dread.
Bid, then, the tender light of faith to shine

By which alone the mortal heart is led
Unto the thinking of the thought divine.

IS LIFE WORTH LIVING? *

WILLIAM JAMES
American philosopher and psychologist, 1842–1910

Many of you are students of philosophy and have already felt in your own persons the skepticism and unreality that too much grubbing in the abstract roots of things will breed. This is, indeed, one of the regular fruits of the overstudious career. Too much questioning and too little active responsibility lead, almost as often as too much sensualism does, to the edge of the slope, at the bottom of which lie pessimism and the nightmare view of life. But to the diseases which reflection breeds, still further reflection can oppose effective remedies.

Let me say, immediately, that my final appeal is to nothing more recondite than religious faith. Pessimism is essentially a religious disease. Religion has meant many things in human history; but when from now onward I use the word I mean to use it in the supernatural sense, as declaring that the so-called order of nature, which constitutes this world's experience, is only one portion of the total universe, and that there stretches beyond this visible world an unseen world of which we now know nothing positive, but in its relation to which the true significance of our present mundane life consists. A man's religious faith (whatever more special items of doctrine it may involve) means for me essentially his faith in the existence of an unseen order of some kind in which the riddles of the natural order may be found explained. The bare assurance that this natural order is not ultimate but a mere sign or vision, the external staging of a many storied universe, in which spiritual forces have the last word and are eternal,—this bare assurance is to such men enough to make life seem worth living in spite of every contrary presumption suggested by its circumstances on the natural plane. Destroy this inner assurance, however, vague as it is, and all the light and radiance of existence is extinguished for these persons at a stroke.

In human life, although we only see our world, yet encompassing (it) a still wider world may be there; and to believe in that world may be the most essential function that our lives in this world have to perform. The "scientific" life itself has much to do with maybes, and human life at large has everything to do with them. Not a victory is gained, not a deed of faithfulness or courage is done, except upon a maybe; not a service, not a sally of generosity, not a scientific exploration or experiment or textbook, that may not be a mistake. It is only by risking our persons from one hour to another that we live at all. And often enough our faith beforehand in an uncertified result is the only thing that makes the result come true. Suppose, for instance, that you are climbing a mountain, and have worked yourself into a position from which the only escape is by a terrible leap. Have faith that you can successfully make it, and your feet are nerved to its accomplishment. But mistrust yourself, and you will hesitate so long that, at last, all unstrung and trembling, and launching yourself in a moment of despair, you roll in the abyss. In such a case (and it belongs to an enormous class) the part of wisdom as well as of courage is to believe what is in the line of your needs, for only by such belief is the need fulfilled. Refuse to believe, and you shall indeed be right, for you shall irretrievably perish. But believe, and again you shall be right, for you shall save yourself. You make one or the other of two possible universes true to your trust or mistrust,—both universes having been only maybes, in this particular, before you contributed your act. Now, it appears to me that the question whether life is worth living is subject to conditions logically much like these.

I confess that I do not see why the very existence of an invisible world may not in part depend on the personal response which any one of us may make to the religious appeal. God himself, in short, may draw vital strength and increase of very being from our fidelity. For my own part, I do not know what the sweat and blood and tragedy of this life mean, if they mean anything short of this. If this life be not a real fight, in which something is eternally gained for the universe by success, it is no better than a game of private theatricals from which one may withdraw at will. But it feels like a real fight,—as if there were something really wild in the universe which we, with all our idealities and faithfulnesses, are needed to redeem; and first of all to redeem our own hearts from atheisms and fears. For such a half-wild, half-saved universe our nature is adapted. The deepest thing in our nature is this dumb region of the heart in which we dwell alone with our willingnesses and unwillingnesses, our faiths and fears. As through the cracks and crannies of caverns those waters exude from the earth's bosom which then form the fountain-heads of springs, so in these crepuscular depths of personality the sources of all our outer deeds and decisions take their rise. Here is our deepest organ of communication with the nature of things; and compared with these concrete movements of our soul all abstract statements and scientific arguments—the veto, for example, which the strict positivist pronounces upon our faith—sound to us like mere chatterings of the teeth.

These then are my last words to you: Be not afraid of life. Believe that life is worth living, and your belief will help create the fact. The "scientific proof" that you are right may not be clear before the day of judgment (or some stage of being which that expression may serve to symbolize) is reached. But the faithful fighters of this hour, or the beings that then and there will represent them, may then turn to the faint-hearted, who here decline to go on, with words like those with which Henry IV greeted the tardy Crillon after a great victory had been gained: "Hang yourself, brave Crillon! We fought at Arques, and you were not there."

From *Is Life Worth Living?*
The Will to Believe and Other Essays

THE HIDDEN CHILD *
Henri Frédéric Amiel
Swiss scholar and writer, 1821–1881

I have finished Schopenhauer. My mind has been a tumult of opposing systems—Stoicism, Quietism, Buddhism, Christianity. What then do I believe in? I do not know. And what is it I hope for? It would be difficult to say.

Folly! I believe in goodness, and I hope that good will prevail. Deep within this ironical and disappointed being of mine there is a child hidden—a frank, sad, simple creature, who believes in the ideal, in love, in holiness, and all heavenly superstitions. A whole millennium of idylls sleeps in my heart; I am a pseudo-skeptic, a pseudo-scoffer.

Let mystery have its place in you; do not be always turning up your whole soil with the plowshare of self-examination, but leave a little fallow corner in your heart ready for any seed the winds may bring, and reserve a nook of shadow for the passing bird; keep a place in your heart for the unexpected guests, an altar for the unknown God. Then if a bird sing among your branches, do not be too eager to take it. If you are conscious of something new

—thought or feeling, wakening in the depths of your being—do not be in a hurry to let in light upon it, to look at it; let the springing germ have the protection of being forgotten, hedge it round with quiet, and do not break in upon its darkness; let it take shape and grow, and not a word of your happiness to any one! Sacred work of nature as it is, all conception should be enwrapped by the triple veil of modesty, silence, and night.

Journal

Trans. **Mrs. Humphry Ward**

THE CHIEF FACT WITH REGARD TO MAN

Thomas Carlyle
Scottish essayist and historian, 1795-1881

It is well said, in every sense, that a man's religion is the chief fact with regard to him. A man's, or a nation of men's— By religion I do not mean here the church-creed which he professes, the articles of faith which he will sign and, in words or otherwise, assert; not this wholly, in many cases not this at all. We see men of all kinds of professed creeds attain to almost all degrees of worth or worthlessness under each or any of them. This is not what I call religion, this profession and assertion, which is often only a profession and assertion from the outworks of the man, from the mere argumentative region of him, if even so deep as that. But the thing a man does practically believe (and this is often enough without asserting it even to himself, much less to others); the thing a man does practically lay to heart, and know for certain, concerning his vital relations to this mysterious universe, and his duty and destiny there, that is in all cases the primary thing for him, and creatively determines all the rest. That is his religion; or, it may be, his mere skepticism and no-religion: the manner it is in which he feels himself to be spiritually related to the unseen world or no world; and I say, if you tell me what that is, you tell me to a very great extent what the man is, what the kind of things he will do is. Of a man or of a nation we inquire, therefore, first of all, what religion they had.

Heroes and Hero-Worship

THE TIDES OF FAITH

GEORGE ELIOT

English novelist, 1819–1880

The faith that life on earth is being shaped
To glorious ends, that order, justice, love
Mean man's completeness, mean effect as sure
As roundness in the dew-drop—that great faith
Is but the rushing and expanding stream
Of thought, of feeling, fed by all the past.
Our finest hope is finest memory,
As they who love in age think youth is blest
Because it has a life to fill with love.
Full souls are double mirrors, making still
An endless vista of fair things before
Repeating things behind: so faith is strong
Only when we are strong, shrinks when we
    shrink.
It comes when music stirs us, and the chords
Moving on some grand climax shake our souls
With influx new that makes new energies.
It comes in swellings of the heart and tears
That rise at noble and at gentle deeds—
At labors of the master-artist's hand
Which, trembling, touches to a finer end,
Trembling before an image seen within.
It comes in moments of heroic love,
Unjealous joy in joy not made for us—

In conscious triumph of the good within
Making us worship goodness that rebukes.
Even our failures are a prophecy,
Even our yearnings and our bitter tears
After that fair and true we cannot grasp;
As patriots who seem to die in vain
Make liberty more sacred by their pangs.

Presentiment of better things on earth
Sweeps in with every force that stirs our souls
To admiration, self-renouncing love,
Or thoughts, like light, that bind the world in
     one;
Sweeps like the sense of vastness when at night
We hear the roll and dash of waves that break
Nearer and nearer with the rushing tide,
Which rises to the level of the cliff
Because the wide Atlantic rolls behind,
Throbbing respondent to the far-off orbs.

From *A Minor Prophet*

THE RELIGIOUS SENTIMENT
GIUSEPPE MAZZINI
Italian patriot, and defender of
republicanism, 1805–1872

The religious sentiment is the divine fount of
all religions, of all beliefs that have God for

their beginning and humanity for their end, and which are animated by the spirit, without which every belief is passive and barren, every religion no more than a sect, every faith but a tradition, a habit and outward profession.

It is the religious sentiment which hallows the thoughts and actions of man, that ennobles the human creature in his own eyes, and gives him the consciousness of a mission to fulfil. It gives him the sense that God has not cast him at a venture upon this earth of trial, but that his existence is a function of universal life and harmony, a link in the great chain of beings, a necessary point in the line that connects man with God, and our earth with his universe: it is that which makes all his life a scene of self-sacrifice and charity.

The religious sentiment is brotherhood, and association, and love. From it flow strength and constancy in the struggle for these great principles, indifference to danger, noble resignation in persecution and misfortune.

Such is the religious sentiment, by means of which alone you can advance along the path of progress; for materialism—be assured—however you may desire to consider it, will verily give nothing but the consciousness of your own individuality, the certainty of a few rights, the

power to use them or not at will, or the habit
of seeking your own material success even at the
cost of your brother's weal, wherever society
does not rebel, and allow(s) it with impunity.
But you will never draw from materialism
either capacity for progress, or the virtue of
self-sacrifice and martyrdom.

Now, this religious sentiment is the foundation
and bond of all social fellowship, the only
pledge of security for the continuous and pa-
cific progress of every people that desires to be
a nation, since it unites the souls of men in one
purpose, and refers to a superior law what rival
theories make the result of chance and the
moment's ebb and flow, thus placing under God's
own tutelage the rights and happiness and independence and improvement of the peoples.

From The Patriots and the Clergy
The Duties of Man and Other Essays

FOR RELIGION'S SAKE
WALT WHITMAN
American poet, 1819–1892

I say the whole earth and all the stars in the sky
    are for religion's sake.

I say no man has ever yet been half devout
enough,
None has ever yet adored or worshiped half
enough,
None has begun to think how divine he himself
is, and how certain the future is.
I say that the real and permanent grandeur of
these States must be their religion,
Otherwise there is no real and permanent
grandeur;
Nor character nor life worthy the name without
religion,
Nor land nor man or woman without religion.

From *Starting from Paumanok*

The Thought of God

TO THE UNKNOWN GOD
VEDIC HYMNS,
religious poetry of India,
several centuries B. C.

In the beginning there arose the Golden Child; as soon as born he alone was the lord of all that is. He established the earth and this heaven:— Who is the God to whom we shall offer sacrifice?

He who gives strength, whose command all the bright gods revere, whose shadow is immortality, whose shadow is death:— Who is the God to whom we shall offer sacrifice?

He who through his might became the sole king of the breathing and twinkling world, who governs all this, man and beast:— Who is the God to whom we shall offer sacrifice?

He through whose might these snowy mountains are, and the sea, they say, with the distant river, he of whom these regions are the two arms:— Who is the God to whom we shall offer sacrifice?

He through whom the awful heaven and the earth were made fast, he through whom the ether was established, and the firmament; he who measured the air in the sky:— Who is the God to whom we shall offer sacrifice?

He to whom heaven and earth, standing firm by his will, look up trembling in their mind; he over whom the risen sun shines forth:— Who is the God to whom we shall offer sacrifice?

He who by his might looked even over the waters which held power (the germ) and generated the sacrifice (light), he who alone is God above all gods:— Who is the God to whom we shall offer sacrifice?

May he not hurt us, he who is the begetter of the earth, or he, the righteous, who begat the heaven; he who also begat the bright and mighty waters:— Who is the God to whom we shall offer sacrifice?

Mandala x, Hymn 121, The Rig-Vedas
Trans. Max Müller, *The Sacred Books of the East*

REVERENCE TO PRĀNA

Vedic Hymns,
religious poetry of India,
several centuries B. C.

Reverence to Prāna, to whom all this (universe) is subject, who has become the lord of the all, on whom the all is supported!

Reverence, O Prāna, to thy roaring (wind); reverence, O Prāna, to thy thunder; reverence, O Prāna, to thy lightning; reverence, O Prāna, to thy rain!

When Prāna calls aloud to the plants with his thunder, they are fecundated, they conceive, and then are produced abundant (plants).

When the season has arrived, and Prāna calls aloud to the plants, then everything rejoices, whatsoever is upon the earth.

When Prāna has watered the great earth with rain, then the beasts rejoice; (they think): "Strength, forsooth, we shall now obtain."

When they had been watered by Prāna, the plants spake in concert: "Thou hast, forsooth, prolonged our life, thou hast made us all fragrant."

Reverence be, O Prāna, to thee coming, reverence to thee going; reverence to thee standing, and reverence, too, to thee sitting!

Reverence be to thee, O Prāna, when thou breathest in, reverence when thou breathest out! Reverence be to thee when thou art turned away, reverence to thee when thou art turned hither: to thee, entire, reverence be here!

Of thy dear form, O Prāna, of thy very dear form, of the healing power that is thine, give unto us, that we may live! [1]

---

[1] (Prāna; life or breath, personified as the Supreme Spirit.)

The Tenth Hymn of the Atharva-Veda
Trans. Maurice Blomfield
The Sacred Books of the East

O GREAT CREATOR

GATHA,
Zoroastrian hymn,
about 1000 B. C.

This I ask thee, O Ahura! tell me aright: Who by generation was the first father of the righteous order (within the world)? Who gave the (recurring) sun and stars their (undeviating) way? Who established that whereby the moon waxes, and whereby she wanes, save thee? These things, O Great Creator! would I know, and others likewise still.

This I ask thee, O Ahura! tell me aright:

Who from beneath hath sustained the earth and the clouds above that they do not fall? Who made the waters and the plants? Who to the wind has yoked on the storm-clouds, the swift and fleetest two? Who, O Great Creator! is the inspirer of the good thoughts (within our souls)?

This I ask thee, O Ahura! tell me aright: Who, as a skilful artisan, hath made the lights and the darkness? Who, as thus skilful, hath made sleep and the zest (of waking hours)? Who (spread) the auroras, the noontides and midnight, monitors to discerning (man), duty's true (guides)?

The Zend-Avesta
Trans. L. H. Mills
The Sacred Books of the East

THE CREATOR *

Hebrew; this passage, fifth century B.C.

In the beginning God created the heavens and the earth. And the earth was without form, and void; and darkness was upon the face of the deep. And the Spirit of God moved upon the face of the waters. And God said, Let there be light: and there was light. And God saw the light, that it was good: and God divided the light from the darkness.

And God said, Let the waters under the heavens be gathered together unto one place, and let the dry land appear: and it was so. And God saw that it was good.

And God said, Let the earth put forth grass, the herb yielding seed after its kind, and the fruit tree yielding fruit after its kind, whose seed is in itself, upon the earth: and it was so. And God saw that it was good.

And God said, Let there be lights in the firmament of heaven. And God made the two great lights; the greater light to rule the day, and the lesser light to rule the night: he made the stars also. And God set them in the firmament of heaven to give light upon the earth, and to rule over the day and over the night, and to divide the light from the darkness: and God saw that it was good.

And God said, Let the waters bring forth abundantly the moving creature that hath life, and let fowl fly above the earth in the open firmament of heaven. And God created great sea-monsters, and every living creature that moveth, which the waters brought forth abundantly after their kinds, and every winged fowl after its kind: and God saw that it was good.

And God said, Let the earth bring forth the living creature after his kind, cattle, and creeping thing, and beast of the earth after his kind: and it was so: and God saw that it was good.

And God said, Let us make man in our image, after our likeness: and let them have dominion over the fish of the sea, and over the fowl of the air, and over the cattle, and over all the earth, and over every creeping thing that creepeth upon the earth. And God created man in his own image, in the image of God created he him; male and female created he them. And God blessed them.

And God saw everything that he had made, and, behold, it was very good.

From *The Book of Genesis*
Old Testament

BRAHMAN—THE SELF *
UPANISHADS,
ancient religious literature of India,
probably within 1000 B. C.

The knowing (Self) is not born, it dies not; it sprang from nothing, nothing sprang from it. The Ancient is unborn, eternal, everlasting; he is not killed, though the body is killed.

The Self, smaller than small, greater than

great, is hidden in the heart of that creature. A man who is free from desires and free from grief sees the majesty of the self by the grace of the Creator.

Though sitting still, he walks far; though lying down he goes everywhere. Who, save myself, is able to know that God who rejoices and rejoices not?

The wise who knows the Self as bodiless within the bodies, as unchanging among changing things, as great and omnipresent, does never grieve.

But he who has not first turned away from his wickedness, who is not tranquil, and subdued, or whose mind is not at rest, he can never obtain the Self (even) by knowledge.

No mortal lives by the breath that goes up and by the breath that goes down. We live by another, in whom these two repose.

He, the highest Person, who is awake in us while we are asleep, shaping one lovely sight after another, that indeed is the Bright, that is Brahman, that alone is called the Immortal. All worlds are contained in it, and no one goes beyond. This is that.

As the one fire, after it has entered the world, though one, becomes different according to whatever it burns; thus the one Self within all things becomes different, according to whatever it enters, and exists also without.

As the sun, the eye of the whole world, is not contaminated by the external impurities seen by the eyes, thus the one Self within all things is never contaminated by the misery of the world, being himself without.

There is one ruler, the Self within all things, who makes the one form manifold. The wise who perceive him within their Self, to them belongs eternal happiness, not to others.

There is one eternal thinker, thinking non-eternal thoughts, who, though one, fulfils the desires of many. The wise who perceive him within their Self, to them belongs eternal peace, not to others.

Katha-Upanishad
Trans. Max Müller
The Sacred Books of the East

AHURA MAZDA *

ORMAZD YAST,
Zoroastrian daily liturgic,
fifth century B. C. or later

Zarathustra said: "Reveal unto me that name of thine, O Ahure Mazda, that is the greatest, the best, the fairest, the most effective, the best healing."

Ahura Mazda replied unto him: "My name is the One of whom questions are asked, O holy Zarathustra!

My second name is the Herd-giver.

My third name is the Strong One.

My fourth name is Perfect Holiness.

My fifth name is All Good Things created by Mazda, the offspring of the holy principle.

My sixth name is Understanding;

My seventh name is the One with Understanding.

My eighth name is Knowledge;

My ninth name is the One with Knowledge.

My tenth name is Weal;

My eleventh name is He Who Produces Weal.

My twelfth name is Ahura (the Lord).

My thirteenth name is the Most Beneficent.

My fourteenth name is He in Whom there is No Harm.

My fifteenth name is the Unconquerable One.

My sixteenth name is He Who Makes the True Account.

My seventeenth name is the All-seeing One.

My eighteenth name is the Healing One.

My nineteenth name is the Creator.

My twentieth name is Mazda (the All-
Knowing One).

Worship me, O Zarathustra, by day and by
night, with offerings of libations well accepted.
I will come unto thee for help and joy, I, Ahura
Mazda; the good, holy Sraosha (priest-god)
will come unto thee for help and joy; the waters,
the plants, and the Fravishas (angelic guard-
ians) of the holy ones will come unto thee for
help and joy."

The Zend-Avesta
Trans. James Darmesteter
The Sacred Books of the East

ALLAH

Teachings of Mohammed,
prophet of Islam, 571?–632

PRAYER FOR GUIDANCE

In the name of the merciful and compassionate God.

Praise belongs to God, the Lord of the worlds,
the merciful, the compassionate, the ruler of
the day of judgment! Thee we serve and thee
we ask for aid. Guide us in the right path,
the path of those thou art gracious to; not of

those thou art wroth with; nor of those who err.

THE VERSE OF THE THRONE

God, there is no God but him, the living, the self-subsistent. Slumber takes him not, nor sleep. His is what is in the heavens and what is in the earth. Who is it that intercedes with him save by his permission? He knows what is before them and what behind them, and they comprehend not aught of his knowledge but of what he pleases. His throne extends over the heavens and the earth, and it tires him not to guard them both, for he is high and grand.

ALMSGIVING

Be ye steadfast in prayer and give alms. Here are ye called upon to expend in God's cause, and among you are some who are niggardly; and he who is niggardly is but niggardly against his own soul.

Whatsoever good ye send before for your own souls, ye shall find it with God; for God, in all ye do, doth see.

FATE AND JUDGMENT

If God were to punish men for their wrong-doing, he would not leave upon the earth a single beast, but he respites them until a stated time; and when their time comes they cannot put it off an hour, nor can they bring it on.

Every nation has its appointed time, and when their appointed time comes they cannot keep it back an hour, nor can they bring it on.

He will bring forth for (man) on the resurrection day a book offered to him wide open. Read thy book. Thou art accountant enough against thyself this day.

GOD IS ONE

God's is the east and the west, and wherever ye turn, there is the face of God. Verily, God comprehends and knows.

Your God is one God; there is no God but him, the merciful, the compassionate.

He is God, the creator, the maker, the fashioner, his are the excellent names. His praises, whatever are in the heavens and the earth do celebrate; for God is the mighty, the wise.

O ye who believe! Remember God with frequent remembrance, and celebrate his praises morning and evening.

The Koran: Sacred Book of the Mohammedans
Trans. E. H. Palmer
The Sacred Books of the East

LIFE OF AGES

Samuel Johnson
American preacher, 1822–1882

Life of ages, richly poured,
Love of God, unspent and free,
Flowing in the prophet's word
And the people's liberty,—

Never was to chosen race
That unstinted tide confined;
Thine is every time and place,
Fountain sweet of heart and mind.

Breathing in the thinker's creed,
Pulsing in the hero's blood,
Nerving simplest thought and deed,
Freshening time with truth and good,

Consecrating art and song,
Holy book and pilgrim track,
Hurling floods of tyrant wrong
From the sacred limits back,—

Life of ages, richly poured,
Love of God, unspent and free,
Flow still in the prophet's word
And the people's liberty!

Hymns of the Spirit

THE HIGHER PANTHEISM

ALFRED TENNYSON
English poet, 1809–1892

The sun, the moon, the stars, the seas, the hills,
    and the plains,—
Are not these, O soul, the vision of Him who
    reigns?

Is not the vision He, though He be not that
    which He seems?
Dreams are true while they last, and do we not
    live in dreams?

Earth, these solid stars, this weight of body
    and limb,
Are they not sign and symbol of thy division
    from Him?

Dark is the world to thee: thyself art the reason
    why,
For is He not all but that which has power to
    feel "I am I"?

Glory about thee, without thee; and thou ful-
    fillest thy doom,
Making Him broken gleams, and a stifled
    splendor and gloom.

Speak to Him, thou, for He hears, and Spirit
    with Spirit can meet—
Closer is He than breathing, and nearer than
    hands and feet.

God is law, say the wise; O soul, and let us
    rejoice,
For if He thunder by law the thunder is yet
    His voice.

Law is God, say some; no God at all, says the
    fool:
For all we have power to see is a straight staff
    bent in a pool:

And the ear of man cannot hear, and the eye
    of man cannot see;
But if we could see and hear, this vision—were
    it not He?

FLOWER IN THE CRANNIED WALL
ALFRED TENNYSON
English poet, 1809–1892

Flower in the crannied wall,
I pluck you out of the crannies:
I hold you here, root and all, in my hand,

Little flower—but if I could understand
What you are, root and all, and all in all,
I should know what God and man is.

Appearing after The Voice and the Peak

BEHOLDING GOD

WALT WHITMAN
American poet, 1819–1892

Why should I wish to see God better than this
   day?
I see something of God each hour of the
   twenty-four, and each moment then;
In the faces of men and women I see God, and
   in my own face in the glass;
I find letters from God dropped in the street,
   and every one is signed by God's name;
And I leave them where they are, for I know
   that wheresoe'er I go
Others will punctually come for ever and ever.

From Song of Myself

CONSIDER THE LILIES

WILLIAM CHANNING GANNETT
American preacher and hymn writer, 1840–1923

He hides within the lily
    A strong and tender care,
That wins the earth-born atoms
    To glory of the air;
He weaves the shining garments
    Unceasingly and still,
Along the quiet waters,
    In niches of the hill.

We linger at the vigil
    With him who bent the knee
To watch the old-time lilies
    In distant Galilee;
And still the worship deepens
    And quickens into new,
As brightening down the ages
    God's secret thrilleth through.

O Toiler of the lily,
    Thy touch is in the man!
No leaf that dawns to petal
    But hints the angel-plan:
The flower-horizons open,
    The blossom vaster shows;

We hear thy wide worlds echo,
  "See how the lily grows!"

Shy yearnings of the savage,
  Unfolding, thought by thought,
To holy lives are lifted,
  To visions fair are wrought:
The races rise and cluster,
  And evils fade and fall,
Till chaos blooms to beauty,
  Thy purpose crowning all!

The Thought of God

HUMANISM—THE GIFT OF GREECE *

PERCY GARDNER

English: professor of classical archæology, 1846–1937

The discovery of man and his capacities is the great gift of Greece to the world. There were epics before the *Iliad,* but no epic full of charm, of tragedy, of tears and laughter. There were philosophers before Socrates; but they were busied in trying to find the physical constituents of the world. Socrates took up the motto of Delphi, "Know thyself," and became the progenitor of all who study the nature of duty and of happiness. In the same way there was much art in the world before the rise of Greece, in Egypt, in Mesopotamia, in Crete. But it was not a humanist art. It represented the worship of the gods, battles and sieges, the life of the fields. But the human figures in these scenes were conventional: there was nothing in them to stir the finer feelings, to produce a love of beauty, to raise man above the ordinary daily level.

It was quite natural that as the Greek thinkers interpreted all experience in relation to human powers and faculties, so the artists of Greece thought of all nature in terms of the human body. Thus while the stern monotheism of later Israel absolutely prohibited the representation in art of any living thing, and especially of man, Greek artists entirely devoted themselves to such representation. The great result of the working of the spirit of humanism in Greek art was the representation of the gods in human form.

Our religion comes not only from Judea, but also from Greece. The Jewish passion for the divine righteousness lies at its roots. But that passion is consistent with narrowness, bigotry, inhumanity. For the modifications of it which come from the working of the spirit of humanism we have to turn to the Hellenes, for the feeling of the likeness in nature between God and man, the love of the beauty of the created works of God, the joy in whatever is sweet, whatever is comely, whatever is charming. The beauty and majesty of God appealed to the Greek, as the unapproachable transcendence of God inspired the Jew. There is a sweet reasonableness in the words of Maximus of Tyre: "The Greek custom is to represent the gods by the most beautiful things on earth—pure material, the human form, consummate art. The idea of those who make divine images in human shape is quite reasonable, since the spirit of man is nearest of all things to God and most godlike."

The whole history of Greek sculpture, from its rise in the sixth century to its decline in the third (B.C.), is inspired by this desire to represent the divine by the most beautiful things on earth.

From *The Lamps of Greek Art*
Greek Art and Architecture
Gardner and Blomfield

THE BOOK OF GOD

GIUSEPPE MAZZINI

Italian patriot and defender of
republicanism, 1805–1872

The Book of God is not closed. The coming
generations are not disinherited; they who preceded Jesus were not accursed. Revelation,
which is, as Lessing says, the education of the
human race, descends continuously from God
to man.

From epoch to epoch the pages of that eternal
gospel are turned; each fresh page disclosed,
by the ever-renovating Spirit of God, indicates
a period of the progress marked out for us by
the providential plan, and corresponds, his-
torically, to a religion. Each religion sets before mankind a new educational idea as its
aim; each is a fragment, enveloped in symbols,
of eternal truth. So soon as that idea, compre-
hended by the intelligence and incarnated in the
hearts of mankind, has become an inalienable
part of the universal tradition, even as the
mountain traveler on reaching one summit beholds another rising above him, so is a new idea
or aim presented to the human mind, and a new
conception of life, a faith, arises to consecrate
that idea, and unite the powers and activity of

mankind in the fulfilment of that aim. Having accomplished its mission, that religion disappears, leaving behind the portion of truth it contained, the unknown quantity disengaged by it from its symbol, a new immortal star in humanity's heaven.

The Duties of Man and Other Essays

EACH IN HIS OWN TONGUE
William H. Carruth
American educator, 1859–1924

A fire-mist and a planet,
    A crystal and a cell,
A jelly-fish and a saurian,
    And caves where the cave-men dwell;
Then a sense of law and beauty
    And a face turned from the clod,—
Some call it Evolution,
    And others call it God.

A haze on the far horizon,
    The infinite, tender sky,
The ripe, rich tint of the cornfields,
    And the wild geese sailing high;
And all over upland and lowland
    The charm of the golden-rod,—

Some of us call it Autumn,
  And others call it God.

Like tides on a crescent sea-beach,
  When the moon is new and thin,
Into our hearts high yearnings
  Come welling and surging in:
Come from the mystic ocean
  Whose rim no foot has trod,—
Some of us call it Longing,
  And others call it God.

A picket frozen on duty,
  A mother starved for her brood,
Socrates drinking the hemlock,
  And Jesus on the rood;
And millions who, humble and nameless,
  The straight, hard pathway plod,—
Some call it Consecration,
  And others call it God.

  Each in His Own Tongue and Other Poems

THE RULING PASSION

FRANCIS WILLIAM NEWMAN
English scholar and author, 1805–1897

Heart-worship, not head-worship, makes a
man's religion.

Devotion to an ideal is worship; the higher the ideal, the nobler the worship.

By devotion to our highest ideal we expand our minds to embrace what is still higher. By devotion to self we quench idealism and become base.

There is no higher idea of God than righteousness and perfection; to follow these is virtue and spirituality, and is the only reasonable service of God.

Whatever each man worships inwardly is his God, whether he know it or not.

He who has a ruling passion worships one God, good or evil.

He who is carried at random by many impulses has many gods; perhaps as shiftless, as shapeless, as unworthy, as any heathen divinities.

Religion is a free service: each chooses his God for himself.

Those who in head are atheists yet worship God in the heart, if they are votaries of goodness; and those who in head are theists are but pagans and devil-worshipers, when they are votaries of wickedness or folly.

Religion is a powerful passion of the soul; a vehement mover to good or evil.

Religious theories have improved, and have

depraved, morals: no mere theory of religion marks the line between good men and bad.

From *Theism*

ON THE NATURE OF GOD *
IMMANUEL KANT
German: founder of critical philosophy, 1724–1804

For the purely speculative use of reason, the Supreme Being remains, no doubt, an ideal only, but an ideal without a flaw, a notion which finishes and crowns the whole of human knowledge, and the objective reality of which, though it cannot be proved, can neither be disproved.

The Critique of Pure Reason

THE IDEAL TRINITY *
RALPH WALDO EMERSON
American philosopher, poet, and essayist, 1803–1882

The universe has three children, born at one time, which reappear under different names in every system of thought. These stand respectively for the love of truth, for the love of good, and for the love of beauty. These three are equal. Each is that which he is essentially so that he cannot be surmounted or analyzed, and each of these three has the power of the others latent in him, and his own patent. The world is not painted or adorned, but is from the beginning beautiful; and God has not made some beautiful things, but Beauty is the creator of the universe.

In the eternal trinity of truth, goodness, and beauty, each in its perfection (includes) the three.

Beauty in its largest and profoundest sense is one expression for the universe. God is the all-fair. Truth, and goodness, and beauty are but different faces of the same All.

Beauty, truth, and goodness are not obsolete; they spring eternal in the breast of man; they are as indigenous in Massachusetts as in Tuscany or the Isles of Greece. And that Eternal Spirit whose triple face they are moulds from them forever, for his mortal child, images to remind him of the Infinite and Fair.

From the essays, *The Poet, The Transcendentalist,*
Nature, Art

O LOVE THAT WILT NOT LET
ME GO

GEORGE MATHESON
Scottish preacher, 1842–1906

O Love that wilt not let me go,
I rest my weary soul in thee;
I give thee back the life I owe,
That in thine ocean depths its flow
    May richer, fuller be.

O Light that followest all my way,
I yield my flickering torch to thee;
My heart restores its borrowed ray,
That in thy sunshine's blaze its day
    May brighter, fairer be.

O Joy that seekest me through pain,
I cannot close my heart to thee;
I trace the rainbow through the rain,
And feel the promise is not vain
    That morn shall tearless be.

O Cross that liftest up my head,
I dare not ask to fly from thee;
I lay in dust life's glory dead,
And from the ground there blossoms red
    Life that shall endless be.

Sacred Songs

THE THOUGHT OF GOD

FREDERICK LUCIAN HOSMER
American preacher and hymn writer, 1840-1929

One thought I have, my ample creed,
　So deep it is and broad,
And equal to my every need,—
　It is the thought of God.

Each morn unfolds some fresh surprise,
　I feast at Life's full board;
And rising in my inner skies
　Shines forth the thought of God.

At night my gladness is my prayer;
　I drop my daily load,
And every care is pillowed there
　Upon the thought of God.

I ask not far before to see,
　But take in trust my road;
Life, death, and immortality
　Are in my thought of God.

To this their secret strength they owed
　The martyr's path who trod;
The fountains of their patience flowed
　From out their thought of God.

Be still the light upon my way,
My pilgrim staff and rod,
My rest by night, my strength by day,
O blessed thought of God!

The Thought of God

The Sustaining Strength

THE EVERLASTING ARMS
Hebrew; this passage, sixth or fifth century B. C.

The eternal God is thy dwelling place,
And underneath are the everlasting arms.

From *The Book of Deuteronomy, Old Testament*

POWER TO THE FAINT
Hebrew; this passage, sixth or fifth century B. C.

Hast thou not known? hast thou not heard? the everlasting God, the Lord, the Creator of the ends of the earth fainteth not, neither is weary; there is no searching of his understanding. He giveth power to the faint; and to him that hath no might he increaseth strength. Even the youths shall faint and be weary, and the young men shall utterly fall: but they that wait upon the Lord shall renew their strength;

they shall mount up with wings as eagles; they shall run, and not be weary; they shall walk, and not faint.

From *The Book of Isaiah, Old Testament*

THE PSALM OF THE SHEPHERD
Hebrew, fourth to second century B. C.

The Lord is my shepherd;
I shall not want.
    He maketh me to lie down in green pastures;
    He leadeth me beside the still waters;
    He restoreth my soul;
    He leadeth me in the paths of righteousness
        for his name's sake.

    Yea, though I walk through the valley of the
        shadow of death,
    I will fear no evil,
    For thou art with me;
    Thy rod and thy staff, they comfort me.

    Thou preparest a table before me
    In the presence of mine enemies;
    Thou hast anointed my head with oil;
    My cup runneth over.

Surely goodness and mercy shall follow me all
    the days of my life;
And I will dwell in the house of the Lord
    forever.

            The Twenty-third Psalm, Old Testament

THE SEARCHER OF HEARTS*
Hebrew, perhaps second century B.C.

O Lord, thou hast searched me, and known me.
    Thou knowest my downsitting and mine
        uprising,
    Thou understandest my thought afar off.
Thou searchest out my path and my lying down,
    And art acquainted with all my ways.
For there is not a word in my tongue,
    But, lo, O Lord, thou knowest it altogether.
Thou hast beset me behind and before,
    And laid thine hand upon me.
Such knowledge is too wonderful for me;
    It is high, I cannot attain unto it.
Whither shall I go from thy spirit?
    Or whither shall I flee from thy presence?
If I ascend up into heaven, thou art there:
    If I make my bed in Sheol, behold, thou art
        there.

If I take the wings of the morning,
    And dwell in the uttermost parts of the sea,
Even there shall thy hand lead me,
    And thy right hand shall hold me.
If I say, Surely the darkness shall overwhelm
        me,
    And the light about me shall be night;
Even the darkness hideth not from thee,
    But the night shineth as the day:
    The darkness and the light are both alike to
        thee.
Search me, O God, and know my heart:
    Try me, and know my thoughts;
And see if there be any way of wickedness in
        me,
    And lead me in the way everlasting.

From *the 139th Psalm, Old Testament*

WHO GOD POSSESSETH

Santa Teresa
Spanish mystic, 1515–1582

Let nothing disturb thee,
Nothing affright thee;
All things are passing;
God never changeth;

Patient endurance
Attaineth to all things.
Who God possesseth
In nothing is wanting:
Alone God sufficeth.
Trans. Henry Wadsworth Longfellow

O GOD, OUR HELP IN AGES PAST
ISAAC WATTS
English preacher and hymn writer, 1674–1748

O God, our help in ages past,
Our hope for years to come,
Our shelter from the stormy blast,
And our eternal home,

Before the hills in order stood,
Or earth received her frame,
From everlasting thou art God,
To endless years the same.

A thousand ages in thy sight
Are like an evening gone,
Short as the watch that ends the night
Before the rising sun.

Time, like an ever-rolling stream,
Bears all its sons away:
They fly forgotten, as a dream
Dies at the opening day.

O God, our help in ages past,
Our hope for years to come,
Be thou our guard while troubles last,
And our eternal home.

Hymns and Spiritual Songs

A SUPPLICATION

MICHELANGELO
Italian sculptor, painter, poet, and
architect; 1475–1564

The prayers I make will then be sweet indeed
If thou the spirit give by which I pray;
My unassisted heart is barren clay,
That of its native self can nothing feed:
Of good and pious works thou art the seed
That quickens only where thou sayest it may.
Unless thou show to us thine own true way,
No man can find it.   Father, thou must lead:
Do thou then breathe those thoughts into my
      mind
By which such virtue may in me be bred

That in thy holy footsteps I may tread;
The fetters of my tongue do thou unbind
That I may have the power to sing of thee
And sound thy praises everlastingly.

Trans. William Wordsworth

SHELTER, FOOD, AND COMPANY
Roger Williams
English colonist and preacher; founder of
the State of Rhode Island; 1604–1684

As the same sun shines on the wildernesse
that doth on a garden! so the same faithfull and
all sufficient God can comfort, feede, and safely
guide even through a desolate howling wildernesse.

More particular:

1. God makes a path, provides a guide,
   And feeds in wildernesse!
His glorious name while breath remains,
   O that I may confesse.

2. Lost many a time, I have had no guide,
   No house but hollow tree!
In stormy winter night no fire,
   No food, no company.

3. In him I have found a house, a bed,
  A table, company;
No cup so bitter but's made sweet
  When God shall sweetning be.

Rhode Island Historical Society
Collections, Vol. i

LORD OF THE BRAVE AND STRONG
Russian Hymn

Lord of the brave and strong,
Armed for the ceaseless fight,
Fired with the love of right,
Filled with a hate of wrong,—
Thine is the might they wield,
Lord of the brave and strong.

Lord of the weak and faint,
Faint yet pursuing still,
Bowing to thy sweet will,
Bearing without complaint,—
Thine is their power to bear,
Lord of the weak and faint.

Lord of the good and true,
Souls that the rays entwine
Shot from the orb divine,

Lives that their tasks pursue,—
Thine is the life they live,
Lord of the good and true.

Lord of the souls that love,
Seeking the lives that roam,
Bringing the wanderers home,
Pointing to bliss above,—
Thine is the love, O Christ,
Lord of the souls that love.

Lord of all souls that live!
Grant us thy grace, we pray,
Humbly from day to day,
Ever our best to give,—
Thou wilt our souls befriend,
Lord of all souls that live.

Hymns of the Russian Church
Trans. John Brownlie

FAITH
FROM THE HAKO CEREMONY
(A prayer for children)
Pawnee Indian

I know not if the voice of man can reach to
the sky;

I know not if the mighty one will hear as I
   pray;
I know not if the gifts I ask will all granted be;
I know not if the word of old we truly can hear;
I know not what will come to pass in our future
   days;
I hope that only good will come, my children,
   to you.

I now know that the voice of man can reach
   to the sky;
I now know that the mighty one has heard as I
   prayed;
I now know that the gifts I asked have all
   granted been;
I now know that the word of old we truly have
   heard;
I now know that Tira'wa harkens unto man's
   prayer;
I know that only good has come, my children, to
   you.

Rhythmic rendering
Annual reports of the United States
Bureau of American Ethnology

THE ETERNAL GOODNESS *

JOHN GREENLEAF WHITTIER
American poet and reformer, 1807–1892

O friends, with whom my feet have trod
    The quiet aisles of prayer,
Glad witness to your zeal for God
    And love of man I bear.

I trace your lines of argument;
    Your logic linked and strong
I weigh as one who dreads dissent,
    And fears a doubt as wrong.

But still my human hands are weak
    To hold your iron creeds:
Against the words ye bid me speak
    My heart within me pleads.

I walk with bare, hushed feet the ground
    Ye tread with boldness shod;
I dare not fix with mete and bound
    The love and power of God.

I see the wrong that round me lies,
    I feel the guilt within;
I hear, with groan and travail-cries,
    The world confess its sin.

Yet, in the maddening maze of things,
    And tossed by storm and flood,
To one fixed trust my spirit clings;
    I know that God is good!

I know not what the future hath
    Of marvel or surprise,
Assured alone that life and death
    His mercy underlies.

And so beside the Silent Sea
    I wait the muffled oar;
No harm from him can come to me
    On ocean or on shore.

DEAR LORD AND FATHER OF MANKIND *

JOHN GREENLEAF WHITTIER
American poet and reformer, 1807-1892

Dear Lord and Father of mankind,
    Forgive our foolish ways!
Reclothe us in our rightful mind,
In purer lives thy service find,
    In deeper reverence, praise.

In simple trust like theirs who heard,
   Beside the Syrian sea,
The gracious calling of the Lord,
Let us, like them, without a word,
   Rise up and follow thee.

O Sabbath rest by Galilee!
   O calm of hills above,
Where Jesus knelt to share with thee
The silence of eternity
   Interpreted by love!

With that deep hush subduing all
   Our words and works that drown
The tender whisper of thy call,
As noiseless let thy blessing fall
   As fell thy manna down.

Drop thy still dews of quietness,
   Till all our strivings cease;
Take from our souls the strain and stress,
And let our ordered lives confess
   The beauty of thy peace.

          From *The Brewing of Soma*

BECAUSE OF THEE

RABINDRANATH TAGORE

Philosopher and poet of India, 1861–1941

Life of my life, I shall ever try to keep my body pure, knowing that thy living touch is upon all my limbs.

I shall ever try to keep all untruths out from my thoughts, knowing that thou art that truth which has kindled the light of reason in my mind.

I shall ever try to drive all evils away from my heart and keep my love in flower, knowing that thou hast thy seat in the inmost shrine of my heart.

And it shall be my endeavor to reveal thee in my actions, knowing it is thy power gives me strength to act.

Gitanjali

PRAYER

RICHARD C. TRENCH

British prelate and author, 1807–1886

Lord, what a change within us one short hour
Spent in thy presence will avail to make—

What heavy burdens from our bosoms take,
What parchéd grounds refresh as with a shower!
We kneel, and all around us seems to lower;
We rise, and all, the distant and the near,
Stands forth in sunny outline, brave and clear;
We kneel, how weak; we rise, how full of
    power!
Why, therefore, should we do ourselves this
    wrong,
Or others—that we are not always strong;
That we are overborne with care,
That we should ever weak or heartless be,
Anxious or troubled, when with us is prayer,
And joy and strength and courage are with
    thee?

THE RENEWING OF STRENGTH *

J. ARTHUR HADFIELD
) English psychotherapist, 1882–

The Mental Factor in Fatigue. If we are to
discover the sources of strength we must first
investigate the causes of fatigue. There is a
fatigue that comes from the body and a fatigue
that is of the mind. This is the type of fatigue
from which most of us normally suffer. I

would not have it assumed that, in emphasizing mental fatigue, I am denying there is such a thing as physical fatigue. But the greater part of the fatigue from which we suffer is of mental origin; in fact, exhaustion of purely physical origin is rare. Purely mental fatigue is chiefly due to the conflict in the mind between the instincts and the will, or between the instincts themselves, and is of the greatest importance not only in the study of the causes of fatigue but for the acquisition of power. The powerful instincts crave for free expression; the will attempts to hold them down: the house is divided against itself and cannot stand. To call fatigue mental rather than physical is not to suggest that it is "unreal." Mental fatigue is the most real and the most important for our lives.

The Infirmity of the Will. It is generally considered that it is only by force of will that we exercise power. My own hospital ward, as well as those of every physician of the mind, is full of examples of will that fails to accomplish what it wills. I have only to appeal to the reader to look into his own life to realize how futile is the will to help us in many of our difficulties. Our attempts to prevent blushing produce only a deeper crimson; the effort to be at our ease produces a strained attitude; and in moral actions how often does our greatest determination to do right end in failure! Will and determination are, of course, essential to moral endeavor, and without them the instincts would run riot. But the futility of looking to the will alone for our source of strength is obvious. For practical action the will is dependent on some other power. As long as it acts in conformity with this power all is well. The function of the will is to direct and work in conformity with the potent forces derived from the instinctive emotions, and to regulate the release of these forces waiting ready for action.

To Give is to Receive. Nature is economic in her gifts: she will not give strength to those who will not expend it. These remain uninspiring and uninspired. She is lavish in her gifts to those who will use them, and especially to those who will devote them to nature's altruistic ends, for such ends harmonize the soul. The Sea of Galilee is fresh and blue and gives life to living creatures within its sunlit waters —not because it receives waters, but because it gives of them freely. The Dead Sea is dead, not because there is no supply of fresh water, but because it permits no outlet. It is a law of nature—a law of life—that only by giving shall we receive.

Rest. Weakness results from the wastage caused by restlessness of mind; power comes from a condition of mental quietude. The secret of energy is to learn to keep the mind at rest, even in the multitude of life's activities. To attempt to stimulate a restless and worried mind with energetic suggestions is as futile as whipping a dying horse. When the mind is quiet and rested, only then suggest thoughts of vigor of mind, strength of body, and determination of will. Inspiring, stimulating thoughts, falling on a mind calm and receptive, draw from its silent depths ample resources of strength which produce calmness and peace.

The Dynamic of Religion. The psychology of power has a very direct bearing on the question of the dynamic of religion. In its fundamental doctrine of love to God and man, Christianity harmonizes the emotions of the soul into one inspiring purpose, thereby abolishing all conflict, and liberating instead of suppressing the free energies of men. "They that *wait* on the Lord shall *renew* their strength." Christianity also teaches that to learn to rest, not only in moments snatched from our work but by keeping a mind free from worry and anxiety, neither caring for the morrow nor fearful of the forgiven past, is to give ourselves the opportunity of drawing on that "ample re-supply" which comes to those who do not fear to expend their energy for others. Life will throb within and through us, but our souls will be in repose. The fact that so many seek for power and yet do not receive it suggests that piety is not the only requisite of power. To obtain it we must obey the higher laws of nature, and in particular make use of the forces we already find at our human disposal; and fearlessly expending them in a spirit of confidence for the fulfilment of our ideals, we shall harmonize mind, will, and emotion in one throbbing impulse of life and power.

From *The Psychology of Power*
The Spirit
Ed. B. H. Streeter

Communion with God

PRAYER

JAMES MONTGOMERY
Scottish hymn writer, 1771–1854

Prayer is the soul's sincere desire,
Uttered or unexpressed,
The motion of a hidden fire
That trembles in the breast.

Prayer is the burden of a sigh,
The falling of a tear,
The upward glancing of an eye,
When none but God is near.

Prayer is the simplest form of speech
That infant lips can try,
Prayer, the sublimest strains that reach
The Majesty on high.

O thou by whom we come to God—
The life, the truth, the way—
The path of prayer thyself hast trod,
Lord, teach us how to pray!

Original Hymns

PRIVAT PRAYER
JOHN KNOX
Scottish preacher and reformer, 1505–1572

Privat prayer, suche as men secreitlie offer unto God by thame selves, requyres no speciall place; althocht that Jesus Chryst commandeth when we pray to enter into our chamber, and to clois the dur, and sa to pray secretlie unto our Father. Whairby he wald that we suld chuse to oure prayeris sic places as mycht offer leist occasioun to call us back from prayer; and also, that we suld expell furth of oure myndis in tyme of our prayer all vane cogitatiounis. For utherwayis Jesus Chryst himself doith observe no speciall place of prayer; for we find him sumtyme pray in Mont Olivet, sumtyme in the Desert, sumtyme in the Tempill, and in the Garden. And Peter covetteth to pray upon the top of the house. Paule prayed in prisone, and was hard of God. Who also commandeth men to pray in all places, lifting up unto God pure and cleane handis; as we find that the Propheitis and maist Holie men did, whensoever danger or necessitie requyrit.

Appoyntit places to Pray in may not be Neglectit. But publict and commoun prayeris suld be useit in place appcyntit for the As-

semblie, from whence whosoever negligentlie
extracteth thame selves is in no wyse excusabill.
I meane not that to absent from that place is
syn, because that place is more holie than another; for the haill earth creatit be God is
equallie holie.

Works, Vol. iii

RELIGION IN ACT *
AUGUSTE SABATIER
French preacher, 1839–1901

The essence of religion is a commerce, a conscious and willed relation into which the soul
enters with the mysterious power on which it
feels that it and its destiny depend. This act
is prayer, by which I mean not an empty utterance of words, not the repetition of certain
sacred formulas, but the movement of the soul
putting itself into personal relation and contact
with the mysterious power whose presence it
feels even before it is able to give it a name.
Where this inward prayer is wanting there is no
religion; on the other hand, wherever this
prayer springs up in the soul and moves it,
even in the absence of all form and doctrine

clearly defined, there is true religion, living piety.

The living expression of the relations of man to his God, prayer is the very soul of religion. It brings back to man the communion and help of God.

From this point of view, perhaps a history of prayer would be the best history of the religious development of mankind. That history would be seen to commence in the crudest cry for help and to complete itself in perfect prayer which, on the lips of Christ, is simply submission to and confidence in the Father's will.

Progress is more apparent here than anywhere else. The savage beats his fetish when it is not complacent enough. The Christian in his greatest distresses repeats the prayer of Jesus in the garden: "Father, not my will, but thine, be done!" What a long road man has traveled between these two extreme points of religion!

Outlines of a Philosophy of Religion

WORSHIP *

WILLIAM ERNEST HOCKING
American philosopher, 1873—

Worship is indeed a reasonable act, even when instinctive and momentary: it is informed of God; it uses and contains all available knowledge of the Being whom it addresses. But in worship the universality of thought is overcome, and God is appropriated uniquely to the individual self. Worship brings the experience of God to pass in self-consciousness with a searching valency not obligatory upon the pure thinker: in some way it *enacts* the presence of God, sets God into the will to work there. In the nature of the case, the aspect of deity which reason discovers is an unconditional, inevitable, universal presence; from such a presence there can be no escape—and so no drawing near—save by the movements of deliberate attention. But the drawing-near of worship is more than a movement of attention.

Worship may be regarded as an attempt to detach oneself from everything else in uniting with God. It seeks God first as an object, that Other of all worldly objects; and it seeks to join itself to that absolute Other. The mystic proceeds by negation: this and that, he says, are not

God; it is not these that I seek. The effort of
worship measures the soul's power of detachment. And my power of detachment measures
the whole of my freedom, the whole of my possibility of happiness, the whole of my possible
originality, the whole depth and reach of my
morality and of my human contribution.

The Meaning of God in Human Experience

CONCERNING PRAYER *

JOHN TYNDALL
British physicist, 1820–1893

It may be interesting to some of my readers
if I glance at a few cases illustrative of the
history of the human mind in relation to this
and kindred questions. Lactantius was irritated because in his mind, by education and
habit, cosmogony and religion were indissolubly
associated, and therefore simultaneously disturbed. In the early part of the seventeenth
century the notion that the earth was fixed and
that the sun and stars revolved round it daily
was interwoven with religious feeling, the
separation then attempted by Galileo rousing
the animosity and kindling the persecution of
the Church. Men still living can remember the

indignation excited by the first revelations of geology regarding the age of the earth, the association between chronology and religion being for the time indissoluble. In our day however the best informed theologians are prepared to admit that our views of the universe and its Author are not impaired, but improved, by the abandonment of the Mosaic account of the creation. Look, finally, at the excitement caused by the publication of the "Origin of Species"; and compare it with the calm attendant on the appearance of the far more outspoken and from the old point of view more impious "Descent of Man."

Thus religion survives after the removal of what had been long considered essential to it. In our day the antipodes are accepted; the fixity of the earth is given up; the period of creation and the reputed age of the world are alike dissipated; evolution is looked upon without terror, and other changes have occurred in the same direction too numerous to be dwelt upon here.

In fact, from the earliest times to the present, religion has been undergoing a process of purification, freeing itself slowly and painfully from the physical errors which the active but uninformed intellect mingled with the aspirations of the soul. Some of us think that a final act of purification is needed, while others oppose this notion with the confidence and the warmth of ancient times. The bone of contention at present is the physical value of prayer. It is not my wish to excite surprise, much less to draw forth protest, by the employment of this phrase. I would simply ask any intelligent person to look the problem honestly in the face, and then to say whether, in the estimation of the great body of those who sincerely resort to it, prayer does not, at all events upon special occasions, invoke a Power which checks and augments the descent of rain, which changes the force and direction of winds, which affects the growth of corn and the health of men and cattle—a Power, in short, which, when appealed to under pressing circumstances, produces the precise effects caused by physical energy in the ordinary course of things. To any person who deals sincerely with the subject, and refuses to blur his moral vision by intellectual subtleties, this, I think, will appear a true statement of the case. It is under this aspect alone that the scientific student, so far as I represent him, has any wish to meddle with prayer.

It is not my habit of mind to think otherwise than solemnly of the feeling which prompts prayer. It is a power which I should like to see guided, not extinguished—devoted to practicable objects instead of wasted upon air. In some form or other, not yet evident, it may as alleged be necessary to man's highest culture. Certain it is that, while I rank many persons who resort to prayer low in the scale of being, —natural foolishness, bigotry, and intolerance being in their case intensified by the notion that they have access to the ear of God—I regard others who employ it as forming part of the very cream of the earth. The faith that adds to the folly and ferocity of the one is turned to the enduring sweetness, holiness, abounding charity, and self-sacrifice by the other. Religion, in fact, varies with the nature upon which it falls. Often unreasonable, if not contemptible, prayer in its purer forms hints at disciplines which few of us can neglect without moral loss.

On Prayer as a Form of Physical Energy

SEEKING GOD

EDWARD DOWDEN

English poet, 1843–1913

I said, "I will find God"; and forth I went
To seek him in the clearness of the sky.

But over me stood unendurably
Only a pitiless, sapphire firmament
Ringing the world,—blank splendor; yet intent
Still to find God, "I will go and seek," said I,
"His way upon the waters," and drew nigh
An ocean marge weed-strewn and foam-besprent;
And the waves dashed on idle sand and stone,
And very vacant was the long, blue sea.
But in the evening as I sat alone,
My window open to the vanishing day,
Dear God! I could not choose but kneel and
    pray,
And it sufficed that I was found of thee.

The Inner Life, iii

THE QUEST

Eliza Scudder
American, 1821–1896

I cannot find thee! Still on restless pinion
    My spirit beats the void where thou dost
        dwell;
I wander lost through all thy vast dominion,
    And shrink beneath thy light ineffable.

I cannot find thee! E'en when most adoring
    Before thy throne I bend in lowliest prayer,

Beyond these bounds of thought, my thought
    upsoaring,
  From farthest quest comes back: thou art not
    there.

Yet high above the limits of my seeing,
  And folded far within the inmost heart,
And deep below the deeps of conscious being,
    Thy splendor shineth: there, O God, thou
    art.

I cannot lose thee! Still in thee abiding
  The end is clear, how wide soe'er I roam;
The hand that holds the worlds my steps is
    guiding,
  And I must rest at last, in thee, my home.
                 Hymns and Sonnets

THE SEARCH FOR GOD *

St. Anselm

Italian by birth, generally considered the
founder of Scholasticism; 1033–1109

Enter the inner chamber of thy mind; shut
out all thoughts save that of God, and such as
can aid thee in seeking him; close thy door and
seek him.

Lord, my heart is made bitter by its desolation: sweeten thou it, I beseech thee, with thy consolation. Lord, in hunger I began to seek thee; I beseech thee that I may not cease to hunger for thee. In hunger I have come to thee; let me not go unfed. I have come in poverty to the rich, in misery to the compassionate; let me not return empty and despised.

Teach me to seek thee and reveal thyself to me when I seek thee, for I cannot seek thee except thou teach me, nor find thee except thou reveal thyself. Let me seek thee in longing, let me long for thee in seeking; let me find thee in love, and love thee in finding. Lord, I acknowledge and I thank thee that thou hast created me in this thine image in order that I may be mindful of thee, may conceive of thee, and love thee; but that image has been so consumed and wasted away by vices and obscured by the smoke of wrong doing that it cannot achieve that for which it was made except thou renew it and create it anew. I do not endeavor, O Lord, to penetrate thy sublimity, for in no wise do I compare my understanding with that; but I long to understand in some degree thy truth, which my heart believes and loves.

Is the eye of the soul darkened by its infirmity, or dazzled by thy glory? Surely it is both darkened in itself and dazzled by thee.

Truly, O Lord, this is the unapproachable light in which thou dwellest; for truly there is nothing else which can penetrate this light, that it may see thee there. Truly, I see it not, because it is too bright for me. And yet, whatever I see, I see through it, as the weak eye sees what it sees through the light of the sun, which in the sun itself it cannot look upon.

O Supreme and Unapproachable Light! O Whole and Blessed Truth, how far art thou from me, who am so near to thee! How far art thou removed from my vision, though I am so near to thine! Everywhere thou art wholly present, and I see thee not. In thee I move, and in thee I have my being, and I cannot come to thee: thou art within me, and about me, and I feel thee not.

Proslogium
Trans. S. N. Deane

WHAT DO I LOVE WHEN I LOVE THEE? *

St. Augustine

Latin Church Father, 354–430

Thou madest us for thyself, and our heart is restless until it find rest in thee.

Not with doubting but with assured consciousness do I love thee, O Lord. Thou hast stricken my heart with thy word and I loved thee. And the heavens, too, and the earth and all that therein is, behold, on every side they bid me love thee, nor cease to say so unto all.

But what do I love when I love thee? Not grace of bodies nor the fair harmony of time, nor the brightness of the light, so gladsome to our eyes; nor sweet melodies of varied songs, nor the fragrant smell of flowers, of ointments and spices, not manna and honey. None of these love I when I love my God; and yet I love a kind of light, and melody, and fragrance, a food, when I love my God, the light. melody, fragrance, food of my inner man: where there shineth unto my soul what space cannot contain, and there soundeth what time beareth not away, and there smelleth what breath disperseth not, and there tasteth what eating diminisheth not, and there clingeth what satiety divorceth not. This is what I love when I love my God.

And what is this? I asked the earth and it answered me, "I am not he." And whatsoever is in it confessed the same. I asked the sea and the deeps, and the living creeping things, and they answered, "We are not thy God; seek above us." I asked the moving air; and the whole air with his inhabitants spoke, "Anaximenes was deceived; I am not God." I asked the heavens, sun, moon, stars, "Nor," say they, "are we the God whom thou seekest." And I replied unto all the things that encompass the door of my flesh: "Ye have told me of my God, that ye are not he; tell me something of him." And they cried out with a loud voice, "He made us." What then do I love when I love my God? By my soul will I ascend to him. See, I am mounting up through my mind toward thee. I will pass beyond this power of mind which is called memory, desirous to arrive at thee, and to cleave unto thee.

How then do I seek thee, O Lord? For when I seek thee, I seek a happy life. I will seek thee that my soul may live. For my body liveth by my soul, and my soul by thee. Nor is it I alone nor some few besides, but we all would fain be happy. Happy then will (the soul of man) be when, no distraction interposing, it shall joy in that only Truth, by whom all things are true.

Too late I loved thee, O thou Beauty of Ancient Days, yet ever new! Behold, thou wert within,—and I abroad, and there I searched for thee. Thou wert with me, but I was not with thee. When I shall with my whole self cleave to thee, I shall nowhere have sorrow or labor, and my life shall wholly live as wholly full of thee.

Confessions
Translation after E. B. Pusey

THE FOUR DEGREES OF LOVE *
St. Bernard, Abbott of Clairvaux
French ecclesiastic influential in Europe, 1091–1153

Because we are born of the flesh, it must needs be that our desire, or love, begins from the flesh; and if it is directed by right order, advancing by its several degrees under guidance of grace, it will at last be consummated by spirit: for "that was not first which is spiritual, but that which is natural; afterwards that which is spiritual." And first we must bear "the image of the earthly," afterwards "the image of the heavenly."

First, then, man loves himself for his own sake; he is flesh, forsooth, and can have no taste for aught beyond himself. And when he sees that he cannot subsist of himself, he begins by faith to seek God as necessary to him, and to love him. Thus he loves God in the second degree, but for his own sake, not for Himself.

But when by occasion of his own necessity, he has begun to worship and approach him, by meditation, reading, prayer, obedience; by a certain familiarity of this kind, little by little and gradually, God becomes known and consequently grows sweet; and thus, having tasted how sweet is the Lord, he passes on to the third degree, so that he loves God, not now for his own sake, but for Himself.

Assuredly the abiding is long in this degree; and I know not if the fourth is perfectly attained by any man in this life, so that, that is, a man love himself only for the sake of God. Let those, if any, who have experienced, tell us; to me, I confess it seems impossible. But it will be beyond question when the good and faithful servant is brought into the joy of his Lord, and inebriated with the plenty of the house of God. For in a certain wondrous fashion oblivious of himself, and as it were utterly abandoning himself, he will wholly pass on into God; and henceforth, joined to the Lord, will be one in spirit with him.

On the Love of God
Trans. Edmund G. Gardner

UNION WITH THE ETERNAL *

Bhagavad-Gita,

most widely known and used religious poem in India; in present form, first century B. C.

The soul of him who is self-conquered and full of peace is fixed on the Supreme, in cold and heat, in pleasure and pain, in honor and dishonor.

With soul at peace, with fear gone, standing firm in the vow of service of the Eternal, controlling the mind, with heart set on me, let him dwell in union intent on me.

The seeker for union, thus ever joining himself in union, his darkness gone, happily attains the infinite joy of union with the Eternal.

He sees his soul as one with all beings, and all beings as one with his soul; his soul joined in union, beholding oneness everywhere.

Who sees me everywhere, and sees all in me, him I lose not, nor will he lose me.

They who strive for freedom from age and death, taking refuge in me, know the Eternal, the all, the highest self, the perfect work.

They who know me as the highest being, the highest divinity, the highest sacrifice, even in death perceive me, their hearts united to me.

I am equal toward all beings: nor is any

hated or favored of me; but they who love me with dear love, they are in me and I in them.

I am the offering, I am the sacrifice, I am the oblation, I am the libation; I am the chant, I am the holy oil, I am the fire, I am what is offered.

I am the father of this world, the mother, the guardian, the father's father; I am the end of knowledge, the purifier, the sacred syllable, the hymn, the chant, the sacred sentence.

I am the way, the supporter, the lord, the witness, the home, the refuge, the beloved; the forthcoming and withdrawing, the place, the treasure, the everlasting seed.

Bhagavad-Gita (Divine Lay, or Song of the Deity)
Trans. Charles Johnston

LORD OF ALL BEING
Oliver Wendell Holmes
American poet and essayist, 1809-1894

Lord of all being, throned afar,
  Thy glory flames from sun and star;
Center and soul of every sphere,
  Yet to each loving heart how near!

Sun of our life, thy quickening ray
Sheds on our path the glow of day:
Star of our hope, thy softened light
Cheers the long watches of the night.

Our midnight is thy smile withdrawn;
Our noontide is thy gracious dawn;
Our rainbow arch, thy mercy's sign:
All, save the clouds of sin, are thine.

Lord of all life, below, above,
Whose light is truth, whose warmth is love,
Before thy ever-blazing throne
We ask no luster of our own.

Grant us thy truth to make us free,
And kindling hearts that burn for thee,
Till all thy living altars claim
One holy light, one heavenly flame.

THE SONG OF PRAISE *
EPICTETUS
Greek philosopher, born about 60 A. D.

What words are enough to praise the works
of Providence in us or bring them home to us?

Ought we not, as we dig and plough and eat, to sing the hymn to God, "Great is God?" At every moment we ought to sing these praises, and above all the greatest and divinest praise, that God gave us the faculty to comprehend these gifts and to use the way of reason.

What else can a lame old man, as I am, do but chant the praise of God? If indeed I were a nightingale, I should sing as a nightingale; if a swan, as a swan; but as I am a rational creature, I must praise God. This is my task, and I do it, and I will not abandon this duty so long as it is given me; and I invite you all to join in this same song.

Discourses and Manual of Epictetus
Trans. P. E. Matheson

MORNING HYMN IN PARADISE
John Milton
English Puritan poet, 1608–1674

These are thy glorious works, Parent of good,
Almighty! Thine this universal frame,
Thus wondrous fair; thyself how wondrous
    then,
Unspeakable! Who sit'st above these heavens
To us invisible, or dimly seen

In these thy lowest works; yet these declare
Thy goodness beyond thought, and power
    divine.
Speak, ye who best can tell, ye sons of light,
Angels—for ye behold him, and with songs
And choral symphonies, day without night
Circle his throne rejoicing—ye in heaven;
On earth join, all ye creatures, to extol
Him first, him last, him midst, and without end.
Fairest of stars, last in the train of night,
If better thou belong not to the dawn,
Sure pledge of day, that crown'st the smiling
    morn
With thy bright circlet, praise him in thy
    sphere
While day arises, that sweet hour of prime.
Thou sun, of this great world both eye and soul,
Acknowledge him thy greater; sound his praise
In thy eternal course, both when thou climb'st
And when high noon hast gained, and when
    thou fall'st.
Moon, that now meet'st the orient sun, now
    fliest
With the fixed stars, fixed in their orb that flies;
And ye five other wandering fires, that move
In mystic dance, not without song, resound
His praise who out of darkness called up light.
Air, and ye elements, the eldest birth

Of nature's womb, that in quaternion run
Perpetual circle, multiform, and mix
And nourish all things, let your ceaseless change
Vary to our great Maker still new praise.
Ye mists and exhalations, that now rise
From hill or steaming lake, dusky or gray;
Till the sun paint your fleecy skirts with gold,
In honor to the world's great Author rise;
Whether to deck with clouds the uncolored sky,
Or wet the thirsty earth with falling showers,
Rising or falling, still advance his praise.
His praise, ye winds, that from four quarters
    blow,
Breathe soft or loud; and wave your tops, ye
    pines,
With every plant, in sign of worship wave.
Fountains, and ye that warble, as ye flow,
Melodious murmurs, warbling, tune his praise,
Join voices all ye living souls. Ye birds,
That, singing, up to heaven-gate ascend,
Bear on your wings and in your notes his praise.
Ye that in waters glide, and ye that walk
The earth, and stately tread, or lowly creep,
Witness if I be silent, morn or even,
To hill or valley, fountain, or fresh shade,
Made vocal by my song, and taught his praise.
Hail, universal Lord! Be bounteous still
To give us only good; and, if the night

Have gathered aught of evil or concealed,
Disperse it, as now light dispels the dark.

Paradise Lost, Book v

THE ETERNAL
Isaac Watts
English preacher and hymn writer, 1674–1748

From all that dwell below the skies
Let the Creator's praise arise;
Let the Redeemer's name be sung
Through every land, by every tongue.

Eternal are thy mercies, Lord;
Eternal truth attends thy word;
Thy praise shall sound from shore to shore
Till suns shall rise and set no more.

Hymns and Spiritual Songs

A PRAYER
Theodore Parker
American preacher and reformer, 1810–1860

O Thou Eternal One, may I commune
With thee, and for a moment bathe my soul

In thy infinity, Mother and Sire
Of all that are?   In all that is art thou;
Being is but by thee, of thee, in thee;
Yet far thou reachest forth beyond the scope
Of space and time, or verge of human thought.
Transcendent God!   Yet, ever immanent
In all that is, I flee to thee, and seek
Repose and soothing in my Mother's breast.
O God, I cannot fear, for thou art love,
And wheresoe'er I grope I feel thy breath!
Yea, in the storm which wrecks an argosy,
Or in the surges of the sea of men
When empires perish, I behold thy face,
I hear thy voice, which gives the law to all
The furies of the storm, and law proclaims,
"Peace, troubled waves, serve ye the right,—be
        still!"
From all this dusty world thou wilt not lose
A molecule of earth nor spark of light.
I cannot fear a single flash of soul
Shall ever fail, outcast from thee, forgot.
Father and Mother of all things that are,
I flee to thee, and in thy arms find rest.
My God! how shall I thank thee for thy love?
Tears must defile my sacramental words,
And daily prayer be daily penitence
For actions, feelings, thoughts, which are amiss:
Yet will I not say, "God forgive!" for thou

Hast made the effect to follow cause, and bless
The erring, sinning man. Then let my sin
Continual find me out, and make me clean
From all transgression, purified and blest.

Autobiography, Poems, and Prayers

PARABLE OF THE PHARISEE AND THE PUBLICAN
Christian, first century

Two men went up into the temple to pray;
the one a Pharisee, and the other a publican.
The Pharisee stood and prayed thus with himself: God, I thank thee that I am not as the rest
of men, extortioners, unjust, adulterers, or even
as this publican. I fast twice in the week; I
give tithes of all that I get. But the publican,
standing afar off, would not lift up so much as
his eyes unto heaven, but smote his breast, saying, God, be merciful to me a sinner. I say
unto you, This man went down to his house
justified rather than the other: for everyone
that exalteth himself shall be humbled; but he
that humbleth himself shall be exalted.

From *The Gospel According to Luke*
New Testament

TWO WENT UP INTO THE TEMPLE TO PRAY

RICHARD CRASHAW
English clergyman and poet, 1613?–1649

Two went to pray?   O rather say,
One went to brag, th' other to pray:

One stands up close and treads on high,
Where th' other dares not lend his eye.

One nearer to God's altar trod,
The other to the altar's God.

Steps to the Temple

THE ACCEPTABLE SACRIFICE
Hebrew; date unknown

Wherewith shall I come before the Lord, and bow myself before the high God?   Shall I come before him with burnt offerings, with calves of a year old?   Will the Lord be pleased with thousands of rams, or with ten thousands of rivers of oil?   Shall I give my first born for my transgression, the fruit of my body for the sin of my soul?

He hath showed thee, O man, what is good;

and what doth the Lord require of thee but to
do justly, and to love mercy, and to walk humbly
with thy God?

From *The Book of Micah, Old Testament*

THE PRACTICE OF THE PRESENCE OF GOD *

BROTHER LAWRENCE (NICHOLAS HERMAN)
Admitted a lay brother among the barefooted
Carmelites at Paris, 1666.

Brother Lawrence told me that God had done
him a singular favor, in his conversion at the
age of eighteen. That in the winter, seeing
a tree stripped of its leaves, and considering
that within a little time the leaves would be
renewed and after that the flowers and fruit
appear, he received a high view of the providence and power of God. which has never since
been effaced from his soul.

That we should establish ourselves in a sense
of God's presence, by continually conversing
with him. That we ought to give ourselves up
to God, with regard both to things temporal and
spiritual, and seek our satisfaction only in the
fulfilling of his will. That in order to form

a habit of conversing with God continually, and referring all we do to him, we must at first apply to him with some diligence; but that after a little care we should find his love inwardly excite us to it without any difficulty. That we ought to act with God in the greatest simplicity, speaking to him frankly and plainly, and imploring his assistance in our affairs, just as they happen.

In his business in the kitchen (to which he had naturally a great aversion) having accustomed himself to do everything there for the love of God, he had found everything easy, during fifteen years that he had been employed there.

That with him the set times of prayer were not different from other times; that he retired to pray, according to the directions of his superior, but that he did not want such retirement, nor ask for it, because his greatest business did not divert him from God. That all bodily mortifications and other exercises are useless, except as they serve to arrive at the union with God by love; that he had well considered this, and found it the shortest way to go straight to him by a continual exercise of love, and doing all things for his sake.

That he was more united to God in his outward employments than when he left them for devotion in retirement.

That many do not advance in the Christian progress because they stick in penances, and particular exercises, while they neglect the love of God, which is the end. That there needed neither art nor science for going to God, but only a heart resolutely determined to apply itself to nothing but him, or for his sake, and to love him only.

He discoursed with me very frequently and with great openness of heart concerning his manner of going to God, whereof some part is related already. He told me that all consists in one hearty renunciation of everything which we are sensible does not lead to God; that we might accustom ourselves to continual conversation with him, with freedom and in simplicity.

That it was a great delusion to think that the times of prayer ought to differ from other times: that we are as strictly obliged to adhere to God by action in the time of action, as by prayer in the season of prayer. That his prayer was nothing else but a sense of the presence of God, his soul being at that time insensible to everything but Divine love; and that when the appointed times of prayer were past, he found no difference, because he still continued with God.

That all things are possible to him who believes, that they are less difficult to him who hopes, that they are more easy to him who loves, and still more easy to him who perseveres in the practice of these three virtues.

As Brother Lawrence had found such an advantage in walking in the presence of God, it was natural for him to recommend it earnestly to others; but his example was a stronger inducement than any arguments he could propose. His very countenance was edifying, such a sweet and calm devotion appearing in it as could but affect the beholders. And it was observed that in the greatest hurry of business in the kitchen, he still preserved his recollection and heavenly-mindedness. He was never hasty nor loitering, but did each thing in its season, with an even, uninterrupted composure and tranquillity of spirit. "The time of business," said he, "does not with me differ from the time of prayer; and in the noise and clatter of my kitchen, while several persons are at the same time calling for different things, I possess God in as great tranquillity as if I were upon my knees at the blessed sacrament.

"As for what passes in me at present, I can

not express it. I have no pain or difficulty about my state, because I have no will but that of God, which I endeavor to accomplish in all things.

"I have quitted all forms of devotion and set prayers but those to which my state obliges me. And I make it my business only to persevere in his holy presence, wherein I keep myself by a simple attention, and a general fond regard to God, which I may call an actual presence of God; or, to speak better, an habitual, silent, and secret conversation of the soul with God. A little lifting up of the heart suffices. A little remembrance of God, one act of inward worship, are prayers, however short.

"Were I a preacher, I should, above all things, preach the practice of the presence of God."

The Practice of the Presence of God
Conversations and Letters of Nicholas
Herman of Lorraine (Brother Lawrence)

THE ELIXIR *
GEORGE HERBERT
English writer of religious poetry, 1593–1633

Teach me, my God and King,
   In all things thee to see;

And what I do in any thing,
    To do it as for thee.

All may of thee partake;
    Nothing can be so mean
Which with his tincture (for thy sake)
    Will not grow bright and clean.

A servant with this clause
    Makes drudgerie divine;
Who sweeps a room as for thy laws,
    Makes that and th' action fine.

This is the famous stone
    That turneth all to gold;
For that which God doth touch and **own**
    Cannot for lesse be told.

THY BROTHER

Theodore Chickering Williams
American preacher and writer, 1855–1915

When thy heart, with joy o'erflowing
    Sings a thankful prayer,
In thy joy, O let thy brother
    With thee share.

When the harvest-sheaves ingathered
　　Fill thy barns with store,
To thy God and to thy brother
　　Give the more.

If thy soul, with power uplifted,
　　Yearn for glorious deed,
Give thy strength to serve thy brother
　　In his need.

Hast thou borne a secret sorrow
　　In thy lonely breast?
Take to thee thy sorrowing brother
　　For a guest.

Share with him thy bread of blessing,
　　Sorrow's burden share;
When thy heart enfolds a brother,
　　God is there.

CONTEMPLATION *

HENRI FRÉDÉRIC AMIEL

Swiss scholar and writer, 1821–1881

The whole secret of remaining young in spite
of years, and even of gray hairs, is to cherish
enthusiasm in one's self by poetry, by contemplation, by charity—that is, in fewer words, by

the maintenance of harmony in the soul. The problem set before us is to bring our daily task into the temple of contemplation and ply it there, to act as in the presence of God, to interfuse one's little part with religion. So only can we inform the detail of life, all that is passing, temporary, and insignificant, with beauty and nobility. So may we dignify and consecrate the meanest of occupations. So may we feel that we are paying our tribute to the universal work and the eternal will. So are we reconciled with life and delivered from the fear of death. So are we in order and at peace.

Journal
Trans. Mrs. Humphry Ward

THE ALMIGHTY WILL
ROBERT LOUIS STEVENSON
Scottish novelist, essayist, and poet, 1850–1894

The child, the seed, the grain of corn,
    The acorn on the hill,
Each for some separate end is born
    In season fit, and still
Each must in strength arise to work the Almighty will.

From *"It is not yours, O mother, to complain"*

123

CALL TO GOD'S SERVICE

Francis William Newman
English scholar and author, 1805–1897

Consecrate yourselves to God, all ye youths
and maidens,

Ere the world benumb your fresh feeling or
sin harden your conscience.

Know that others have found God, as ye have
not yet found him;

But seek ye after him, and ye shall find him
also:

Delight yourselves in him, and he shall give
you the desire of your hearts.

Seek him in the open field or in the shrouded
wood,

Under the evening sky or in the solitary chamber.

Take with you words, and turn to him and say:

"O Author of our spirits, Perfector of Souls,

With thee strength dwelleth in repose, and no
passion is in disharmony:

But the passions of youth are untamed, and
we do but move toward perfection,

And desire often seduces from goodness, or
ease deters from duty.

Yet wisely were we made by thee, and thy will
must be best for us;

Early to submit were our prudence, and sweetly
    to obey, our happiness;
And when we know that we seek thy will, we
    know that we become thy servants.
Lo! here we resign all baser desire, we con-
    secrate ourselves to be thine.
We will struggle to be as thou approvest; to
    be pure as thou art pure,
Unwarped by perverse passion, unspoiled by
    selfishness,
Active for every good work, sympathizing with
    every good cause,
Haters and scorners of the wrong, lovers of
    good and of good men.
So will we aspire to thee, that we may be thine
    now and always,
To live before thine open eye, and to die into
    thy secret bosom."

Speak to him thus, or to this effect, knowing
    that he reads all your heart;
Knowing that his light searches your dark
    corners, and sees your unknown faults.
Fear not to meet his piercing gaze, shrink not
    from his eyes of flame,
But stand before them true-heartedly, to let
    them burn up your sin.

Oh, how will it cleanse your conscience and
    strengthen your best purposes!

How will it put to shame all unkindness, all
    impurity, all worldliness and pride!

Ye who admire heroism shall grow heroic, and
    the compassionate more tender,

And the generous more self-sacrificing, and the
    prudent more self-possessed.

Every virtue shall be strengthened, and every
    vice shall be crippled

From the day that ye solemnly consecrate your
    all to the Ever-Present God.

For every impulse shall fall into its own place
    and learn its due subordination,

And become the meek minister of the soul, or
    the pleasant amuser of its weariness,

The strong combatant for the right, or the
    sharp hunter after the true.

And your natures shall become enlarged, as they
    expand towards God:

Your insight shall be deeper and your survey
    broader,

Your selfishness shall become prudence, and your
    prudence unselfish,

Loving your neighbors, loving your country,
    and mankind, and the right.

When the faithless trembles at truth, your faith
    shall but grow stronger,

And where the hypocrite is feeble, your sound
    heart shall be mighty.

Only aspire after perfection, and tell this out
    to God,

And ere long ye shall find him and know his
    exceeding great joy.

He shall make with you a covenant of grace
    and of truth,

And shall fill you of his own fulness and visit
    you with his Spirit,

And he shall be your well-known Lord, and ye
    shall be his conscious servants,

Equipped for life and careless of death, aspir-
    ing after eternity,

Sighing over your own unworthiness, yet certain
    of Almighty Love.

                      From *Theism*

BOOK II

THE CONDUCT OF LIFE

Self-Mastery

EDUCATION AND ENVIRONMENT
Edwin Grant Conklin
American biologist, 1863—

The essence of all education is self-discovery and self-control. When education helps an individual to discover his own powers and limitations and shows him how to get out of his heredity its largest and best possibilities, it will fulfil its real function; when children are taught not merely to know things but particularly to know themselves, not merely how to do things but especially how to compel themselves to do things, they may be said to be really educated. For this sort of education there is demanded rigorous discipline of the powers of observation, of the reason, and especially of the will.

Heredity and Environment in the
Development of Man

205

KNOW THYSELF
Abraham Myerson
American neurologist, 1881—

Character growth, in each individual human being, is a growth in likeness to others and a growth in unlikeness, as well. As we move from childhood to youth, and thence to middle and old age, qualities appear and recede, and the personality passes along to unity and harmony, or else there is disintegration. He who believes as I do that the Grecian sage was immortally right when he enjoined man to know himself will agree that though understanding character is a difficult discipline it is the principal science of life. We are only starting such a science; we need to approach our subject with candor and without prejudice. Though our subject brings us in direct contact with the deepest of problems, the meaning of life, the nature of the ego and the source of consciousness, these we must ignore as out of our knowledge. Limiting ourselves to a humble effort to know our fellow men and our own selves, we shall find that our efforts not only add to our knowledge but add unmeasurably to our sympathy with and our love for our fellows.

The Foundations of Personality

SELF-REALIZATION *

J. Arthur Hadfield
English psychotherapist, 1882–

There is no instinct in man but has been of value in the biological development of the race, and may be of value in the higher ethical development of civilized life. It is true there are activities which appear in themselves evil—conceit, vanity, avarice, hypocrisy, or lust. But it cannot be too strongly emphasized that these vices are not primary impulses but are only the perversions of primary instincts in themselves valuable.

But what of evil? Evil, like dirt, is misplaced matter, or, rather, misdirected function, valuable in itself, noxious if out of place. The instinctive impulse is misplaced if it persists beyond its phase; it is misplaced if it is directed to wrong ends; it is misplaced if attached to wrong objects. All complexes are evil, though not in the sense of being sins, for they are the attachment of our emotions to objects that the self cannot accept as conducive to its happiness. Evil is the discarded good of yesterday. Pugnacity, as such, is an evil in the man of forty, though a valuable and necessary impulse in the boy of twelve. As in the individual, so in the race, pugnacity has served its purpose, which was the development of the race morally as well as physically. It succeeded in developing courage which even today remains one of the greatest of virtues, a racial disposition accepted as noble. That pugnacity has outlived its use when it leads to the war of nations is equally accepted.

Again, there was a time when slavery was a good thing, being a decided step in advance of the earlier custom of murdering off the victims captured in the war. We have progressed, and the good of yesterday is now admitted an evil.

To the psychotherapist there are no vices in their own right; there are only perverted impulses, which, when wrested from their morbid attachments, may be turned into positive virtues. A very large number of disorders at present considered sins really come under the category of moral disease. The moral disease, in contrast with moral fault, is characterized by the fact that it is undesired, uncontrollable, and its cause is unrecognized. To blame the victims of moral disease produces the most disastrous results. To blame a hysteric for his pains, a neurasthenic for his fatigue, a nervous wreck for his breakdown, or a victim of moral disease for his perversion, is to do him the gravest injustice. He is already fighting a losing battle; it flings him into despair, and adds to his distress the discouragements of blame. He is to be held responsible if, recognizing his condition, he does not seek cure for it. It is true that whilst the pervert cannot control his psychological impulses, he can frequently control the expression of these impulses in outward conduct.

Blame is the expedient of impotence; helpfulness, the expression of power. The ends of justice will never be served by being unjust to the individual.

The will has no direct control over any impulses of the mind, except those which are constituted as part of the self. It may repress those elements it has itself rejected as painful or repugnant, but that is not self-control. Indeed, these repressed forces constantly burst forth as impulses, obsessions, fears, and neuroses, which sweep before them the feebly protesting will. Self-control is the conscious and voluntary direction of the instinctive emotions to the will and service of man. This is the essential and important difference between repression and self-control. Repression excludes the complexes and instincts from the self, whereas self-control admits them as part of itself and thereby brings them under its sway. As long as they are excluded they are like bad boys thrust out from school who continue to torment us by throwing stones; our only hope of controlling them is to accept them back. Peace of mind can never be secured by rejecting passions which are unruly, but only by recognizing, accepting, and sublimating them— the process by which instinctive emotions are diverted from their original ends and redirected to purposes satisfying to the individual and of value to the community.

Of all complexes there are none more important than those which form themselves round the idea of the self, our phantasies of ourselves. But we are asked, is it not right to have high ideals, to aim at perfection, to want to be universally loved, and to aim at doing great things? It is; but ideals are quite different from phantasies, both in origin, nature, and effect, although they are constantly, and, from the point of view of character, disastrously confused, by none more than the so-called "idealist." A very simple test of whether ours is a phantasy or an ideal is to ask, "Does the supposed ideal in question lead to greater efficiency and happiness, or not?" If our desire to be uni-

versally loved makes us happier in ourselves
and of more service to others, it is an ideal; if
it makes us feel depressed and not wanted, we
may take it for certain that it is a morbid phantasy. If our ambition makes us work hard
and effectively, and yields happiness, it may be
regarded as a real ideal; if it leads to disap-
pointment, loss of confidence, and breakdown,
we may be sure that our ambition is morbid.
The very function of an ideal is to stimulate us
to endeavor: if it does not stimulate us it is not
an ideal, but merely a phantasy which feeds
our morbid self-esteem.

When the self chooses rightly, that is to say
when it chooses what actually does make for
the happiness and completeness of the self, it
enlarges the freedom and scope of the self, and
by so doing necessarily gives greater power to
the will.

In self-realization there can be no repression:
it involves the expression of all the instincts.
An ascetic ideal based on self-denial ends in
self-annihilation; a stoical ideal which allows
no place to the pleasurable principle in life
justly deserves to meet its fate; a rationalism
which seeks to rise above the instincts will
achieve form without energy; an ideal without

the instincts is an idea without power; a morality that sets itself against joy will achieve rectitude at the expense of life; a religion which
rules out emotion blights the soul of religion,
which is love. All such ideals, in so far as
they involve repression, fail to secure self-
realization and happiness, and are therefore
false. The happy man is without repressions:
the happy man is he who finds in life a harmo-
nized expression for all his instincts.

It is one of the many paradoxes of psychology
that the pursuit of happiness, like the pursuit
of pleasure, defeats its own purpose. We find
happiness only when we do not directly seek
it. An analogy will make this clear. In listening to music at a concert, we experience pleasurable feelings only so long as our attention is
directed towards the music. But if in order
to increase our happiness we give all our attention to our subjective feeling of happiness,
it vanishes. In other words, the ideal must be
objective. So such ideals as beauty, art, virtue,
and religion are sought for their own sake,
and desired as having an intrinsic and objective
worth.

By thus directing our attention to an objective
ideal, nature maintains the healthy balance between the subjective feelings in us and the ob-

jective world. She contrives to make it impossible for any one to attain happiness by turning into himself. Thus each man who succeeds in the search for happiness must needs add his quota to the world's progress.

Psychology and Morals

ORDER AND FREEDOM *
HENRI FRÉDÉRIC AMIEL
Swiss scholar and writer, 1821–1881

It is astonishing how all of us are generally cumbered up with the thousand and one hindrances and duties which are not such, but which nevertheless wind us about with their spider threads and fetter the movement of our wings. It is the lack of order which makes us slaves; the confusion of to-day discounts the freedom of to-morrow.

What comfort, what strength, what economy there is in order—material order, intellectual order, moral order! To know where one is going and what one wishes—this is order; to keep one's word and one's engagements—again order; to have everything ready under one's hand, to be able to dispose of all one's forces, and to have all one's means of whatever kind under command—still order; to discipline one's habits, one's effort, one's wishes; to organize one's life, to distribute one's time, to take the measure of one's duties and make one's rights respected; to employ one's capital and resources, one's talent and one's chances profitably—all this belongs to and is included in the word order. Order means light and peace, inward liberty and free command over one's self; order is power. Aesthetic and moral beauty consist, the first in a true perception of order, and the second in submission to it, and in the realization of it, by, in, and around one's self. Order is man's greatest need and his true well-being.

Journal
Trans. Mrs. Humphry Ward

THE FREE MIND *

WILLIAM ELLERY CHANNING
American preacher and religious reformer, 1780–1842

I call that mind free which masters the senses, which protects itself against animal appetites, which passes life, not in asking what it shall eat or drink, but in hungering, thirsting, and seeking after righteousness.

I call that mind free which escapes the bondage of matter, which instead of stopping at the material universe and making it a prison wall, passes beyond it to its Author, and finds, in the radiant signatures which it everywhere bears of the Infinite Spirit, helps to its own spiritual enlargement.

I call that mind free which jealously guards its intellectual rights and powers, which calls no man master, which does not content itself with a passive or hereditary faith, which opens itself to light whencesoever it may come, which receives new truth as an angel from heaven, which, whilst consulting others, inquires still more of the oracle within itself, and uses instructions from abroad not to supersede but to quicken and exalt its own energies.

I call that mind free which sets no bounds to its love, which is not imprisoned in itself or in a sect, which recognizes in all human beings the image of God and the rights of his children.

I call that mind free which protects itself against the usurpations of society, which does not cower to human opinion, which feels itself accountable to a higher tribunal than man's.

I call that mind free which, through confidence in God and in the power of virtue, has cast off all fear but that of wrong doing, which no menace or peril can enthrall, which is calm in the midst of tumults, and possesses itself though all else be lost.

I call that mind free which resists the bondage of habit, which does not live on in its old virtues, listens for new and higher monitions of conscience, and rejoices to pour itself forth in fresh and higher exertions.

I call that mind free which is jealous of its own freedom, which guards itself from being merged in others, which guards its empire over itself as nobler than the empire of the world.

Political liberty is of little worth but as it springs from, expresses, and invigorates spiritual freedom. Tyranny does evil by invading men's outward interests, by making property and life insecure, by robbing the laborer to pamper the noble and king. But its worst influence is within. Its chief curse is that it breaks and tames the spirit, sinks man in his own eyes, takes away vigor of thought and action, substitutes for conscience an outward rule, makes him abject, cowardly, a parasite, and a cringing slave. This is the curse of tyranny. It wars with the soul, and thus it wars with God. Civil freedom is a blessing, chiefly as it reverences the human soul and ministers to its growth and power.

Without this inward spiritual freedom, outward liberty is of little worth. What boots it that I am crushed by no foreign yoke, if through ignorance and vice, through selfishness and fear, I want the command of my own mind? The worst tyrants are those which establish themselves in our own breast. Civil institutions are to be estimated by the free and pure minds to which they give birth. The human soul is greater, more sacred, than the state, and must never be sacrificed to it. The human soul is to outlive all earthly institutions. The distinction of nations is to pass away. Thrones, which have stood for ages, are to meet the doom pronounced upon all man's works. But the individual mind survives, and the obscurest subject, if true to God, will rise to a power never wielded by earthly potentates.

RIGHTING THY SELFE *
FRANCIS QUARLES
English poet, 1592–1644

Reade not bookes alone, but men, and amongst them chiefly thy selfe: if thou find any thing questionable there, use the commentary of a severe friend rather than the glosse of a sweetlipt flatterer; there is more profit in a distastefull truth than deceitfull sweetnesse.

If thou art rich, strive to command thy mony, lest she command thee: if thou know how to use her, she is thy servant; if not, thou art her slave.

Bee not censorious, for thou know'st not whom thou judgest; it is a more dextrous error to speak well of an evill man than ill of a good man.

Hath any wronged thee? be bravely reveng'd: sleight it, and the work's begun; forgive it, and 'tis finisht: he is below himselfe that is not above an injury.

Give not thy tongue too great a liberty, lest it take thee prisoner. A word unspoken is, like the sword in thy scabberd, thine; if vented, thy sword is in another's hand: if thou desire to be held wise, be so wise as to hold thy tongue.

Demeane thy selfe more warily in thy study than in the street. If thy publique actions have a hundred witnesses, thy private have a thousand. The multitude lookes but upon thy actions: thy conscience lookes into them.

Enchiridion

FREEDOM THROUGH
SELF-CONTROL *
Abraham Myerson
American neurologist, 1881-

Every human being, no matter how civilized and unified, how modern and social his conduct, has within him a core of uncivilized, disintegrating, ancient, and egoistic desires and purposes. The organic activities of the body, basic in desire of all kinds, are crude and give rise to crude forbidden wishes; but the struggle that goes on is repressed, rebelled against. For most men and women, inhibition is no artificial phenomenon, despite its burdensomeness. It is not only inevitable, it is desirable. A feeling of power appears when one resists: there is mental gain, character growth, as a result.

The forms of relief from inhibition—card playing, sports, the theatre, the thrilling story —grow to be habits and lose their exciting value. They can give no permanent relief from the pain of repression: only a philosophy of life can do that. Such a philosophy would state that strenuous purpose must alternate with quiet relaxation; excitement is to be sought only at periods, and never for any length of time; relief from inhibitions can only be found in legitimate ways, or self-reproach enters. Play, sports, short frequent vacations rather than long ones—and a realization that there is no freedom in self-indulgence—

Out of the welter of conflicts into which the individual is plunged through his own nature and the nature of the life around him, out of the experience of the race and the teaching of its leaders. come ideals. Good, beauty, justice—these are good deeds, beautiful things, true and non-contradictory expressions. And their opposite, misleading experiences and suffering arising from evil deeds, become unified into various forms of evil. Man seeks the good, hates evil, esteems himself when he conforms to the ideal, loathes himself when he violates it.

There is no formula for adjustment. Intelligence, insight into one's powers and capacities, caution, boldness, compromise, firmness, agressiveness, tact—these and a dozen other traits and qualities come into play. Fight hard, be brave, keep your powder dry, have good friends, learn resignation, and cultivate a sense of humor is the best counsel for adjustment.

The Foundations of Personality

FREEDOM OF THE WILL

DANTE
Italian poet, 1265–1321

VIRGIL TO DANTE

"The soul, to love created prone and free,
  Is mobile to all objects of delight
  When roused by pleasure to activity.
From something real your perceptive sight
  Shapes forth an image and displays in you
  So as to make the spirit turn to it;
And if, so turning, she incline thereto,
  That inclination is love, is nature's bent
  Through pleasure striking root in you anew.
Then, even as fire has motion of ascent,
  By virtue of its form which makes it wing
  To where it dwells more in its element:
So the rapt soul doth into longing spring,
  A spiritual motion, never still
  Till she rejoice in the beloved thing.
Now may be evident how very ill
  They view the truth, who would aver to thee
  That all love in itself is laudable,
Because its matter may ideally
  Appear good always: but not every seal
  Is good, however good the wax may be."—

"Thy words, and my wit following, reveal
   Love and its nature to me," answered I,
    "But therefore all the greater doubt I feel;
For if love offer from without, and by
   Another foot the spirit travel not,
    She has no merit, go she straight or wry."—

And he to me: "As far as pierces thought,
   Myself can tell: beyond that fix thy mind
    On Beatrice, that faith in thee be wrought.
Every substantial form that is conjoined
   With matter, and yet from it cut away,
    Holds inward virtue of specific kind,
Which, save in act, is not brought into play,
   By its effect alone in evidence,
    Like life in plant evinced by the green spray.
Thus, whence originates intelligence
   Of first ideas is unknown to thee,
    And bent of the primordial appetence,
Which are in you as study in the bee
   To make its honey: and such primal bent
    Of neither praise nor blame receives the fee.
Now, that with this may all desires consent,
   The power that counsels is innate in you,
    And ought to hold the threshold of assent.
This is the principle wherefrom accrue
   The grounds of your desert, as gathering
    And winnowing the false loves from the true.

Who to the bottom went in reasoning
   Took notice of this inborn liberty,
   Thus morals to the world delivering.
Assuming, then, that from necessity
   All love is kindled rightly or amiss,
   To hinder it ye have ability.
This noble virtue is called by Beatrice
   The Freedom of the Will; take heed aright
   If she begins to speak to thee of this."

                From *Purgatory, Canto xviii*

BEATRICE TO DANTE

"The gift most precious to Creative Thought,
   Most signal of God's bounties, and the one
   After the pattern of his goodness wrought,
Was Freedom of the Will,—a benison
   Wherewith all creatures of intelligence
   Both were and are endowed, and they alone."

                From *Paradise, Canto v*
                    The Divine Comedy
                    Trans. M. B. Anderson

9

CONFORMING TO ONE'S BETTER NATURE *

MARCUS AURELIUS
Roman emperor and Stoic philosopher, 121–180

Every man who errs misses his object and is gone astray. For thou wilt find that no one among those against whom thou art irritated has done anything by which thy mind could be made worse; but that which is evil to thee and harmful has its foundation only in the mind. And what harm is done or what is there strange if the man who has not been instructed does the acts of an uninstructed man? Consider whether thou shouldst not rather blame thyself, because thou didst not expect such a man to err in such a way. For thou hadst means given thee by thy reason to suppose that it was likely that he would commit this error, and yet thou hast forgotten and art amazed that he has erred. But most of all when thou blamest a man as faithless or ungrateful, turn to thyself. For the fault is manifestly thy own, whether thou didst trust that a man who had such a disposition would keep his promise, or when conferring thy kindness thou didst not confer it absolutely, nor yet in such way as to have received from thy very act all the profit. For what more dost thou

want when thou hast done a man a service?
Art thou not content that thou hast done something conformable to thy nature, and dost thou
seek to be paid for it, just as if the eye demanded a recompense for seeing, or the feet for
walking? For as these members are formed for
a particular purpose, and by working according
to their several constitutions obtain what is their
own; so also as man is formed by nature to acts
of benevolence, when he has done anything
benevolent or in any other way conducive to the
common interest, he has acted conformably to
his constitution, and he gets what is his own.

The Thoughts of Marcus Aurelius
Trans. George Long

CONCERNING OLD AGE [*]

MARCUS TULLIUS CICERO
Roman orator; supporter of the
Roman Republic, 106–43 B. C.

Undoubtedly the most suitable weapons of old
age are the attainment and practice of the virtues: these, if cultivated at every time of life,
bring forth wondrous fruits when you have lived
long and well, not only because they never desert a man even in the last period of his life

(although that indeed is a most important matter), but also because the consciousness of a well-spent life and the memory of many good deeds is most delightful.

To every period of life its appropriate character has been assigned, so that both the weakness of boys and the impetuosity of youth, and the steadiness of settled years, and the ripeness of old age, contain in them something natural, which must be gathered in in its proper season.

Remember that I am praising such an old age as has been established upon the foundations of a virtuous youth. Hence follows what I once asserted with the hearty assent of all present, that old age was wretched if it had to defend itself with an apology. Neither gray hairs nor wrinkles can suddenly snatch authority, but early life spent with honor reaps the fruits of authority at the last.

De Senectute
Trans. A. H. Allcroft and W. F. Masom

THE GOOD MAN AT UNITY
IN HIMSELF *

ARISTOTLE
Greek philosopher and scientist, 384–322 B.C.

As for the excess (of anger), it occurs in all forms: men are angry with those with whom, and at things with which, they ought not to be, and more than they ought, and too hastily, and for too great a length of time. I do not mean, however, that these are combined in any one person: that would in fact be impossible, because the evil destroys itself, and if it is developed in its full force it becomes unbearable. The bitter-tempered (or "sulky") are hard to reconcile, and keep their anger for a long while, because they repress their feeling. Sulky men, having no outlet for their temper, keep the weight on their minds; because, as it does not show itself, no one attempts to reason it away, and digesting anger within one's self takes time. Such men are very great nuisances to themselves and to their best friends.

It is clear, therefore, that the mean state is what we are to hold to. Goodness, that is, the good man, seems to be a measure to every one else. For he is at unity in himself, and with every part of his soul he desires the same objects; and he wishes for himself both what is, and what he believes to be, good. Furthermore, the good man wishes to continue to live with himself; for he can do it with pleasure in that his memories of past actions are full of delight and his anticipations of the future are good; and such are pleasurable.

The Nichomachean Ethics
Ed. J. M. Mitchell

THE BEAST AND THE GOD IN MAN *

PLATO

Greek philosopher: disciple of
Socrates and teacher of Aristotle; 427–347 B.C.

Let us make an image of the soul, an ideal image of the soul, like the composite creations of ancient mythology, such as the Chimera or Scylla or Cerberus; and there are many others in which two or more different natures are said to grow into one. Now model the form of a multitudinous, many-headed monster, having a ring of heads of all manner of beasts, tame and wild, which he is able to generate and metamorphose at will. Suppose now that you make a second form as of a lion, and a third of a man, the second smaller than the first, and the third smaller than the second. And now join them, and let the three go into one. Next fashion the outside of them into a single image, as of a man, so that he who is not able to look within, and sees only the outer hull, may believe the beast to be a single human creature.

And now, to him who maintains that it is profitable for the human creature to be unjust and unprofitable to be just, let us reply that if he be right it is profitable for this creature to feast the multitudinous monster and strengthen the lion and the lion-like qualities, but to starve and weaken the man, who is consequently liable to be dragged about at the mercy of either of the other two; and he is not to attempt to familiarize or harmonize them with one another —he ought rather to suffer them to fight and bite and devour one another.

To him the supporter of justice makes answer that he should ever so speak and act as to give the man within him in some way or other the most complete mastery over the entire human creature. He should watch over the many-headed monster like a good husbandman, fostering and cultivating the gentle qualities, and preventing the wild ones from growing; he should be making the lion-heart his ally, and in common care of them all should be uniting the several parts with one another and with himself.

Is not the noble that which subjects the beast to the man, or rather to the god in man; and the ignoble that which subjects the man to the beast? Has not the intemperate been censured of old, because in him the huge multiform monster is allowed to be too much at large? And men are blamed for pride and bad temper when the lion and serpent clement in them disproportionately grows and gains strength? And luxury and softness are blamed, because they relax and weaken this same creature, and make a coward of him? And is not a man reproached for flattery and meanness who subordinates the spirited animal to the unruly monster, and, for the sake of money, of which he can never have enough, habituates him in the days of his youth to be trampled in the mire, and from being a lion to become a monkey?

Therefore, being desirous of placing him under a rule like that of the best, we say that he ought to be the servant of the best, in whom the Divine rules; every one had better be ruled by divine wisdom dwelling within him. His whole soul is perfected and ennobled by the acquirement of justice and temperance and wisdom, more than the body ever is by receiving gifts of beauty, strength, and health, in proportion as the soul is more honorable than the body. To this nobler purpose the man of understanding will devote the energies of his life. And in the first place, he will honor studies which impress these qualities on his soul, and will disregard others. In the next place, he will regulate his bodily habit and training. And in the acquisition of wealth there is a principle of order and harmony which he will also observe; he will not allow himself to be dazzled by the foolish applause of the world, and heap up riches to his own infinite harm. He will look at the city which is within him, and take heed that no disorder occur in it. He will be a ruler in the city of which we are the founders, and which exists in idea only. In heaven there is laid up a pattern of it which he who desires may behold, and beholding, may set his own house to order.

The Republic, Book ix
Trans. Benjamin Jowetɪ

THE GREATEST OF CONQUERORS *
ATTRIBUTED TO BUDDHA
Founder of Buddhism: India, 568?–488? B. C.

He who lives looking for pleasures only, his senses uncontrolled, immoderate in his food, idle, and weak, the tempter will certainly overthrow him, as the wind throws down a weak tree.

He who lives without looking for pleasures, his senses well controlled, moderate in his food, faithful and strong, him the tempter will certainly not overthrow, any more than the wind throws down a rocky mountain.

Though a man recite a hundred poems made up of senseless words, one word of the law is better, which if a man hears, he becomes quiet.

If one man conquer in a battle a thousand times thousand men, and if another conquer himself, he is the greatest of conquerors.

He who holds back rising anger like a rolling chariot, him I call a real driver; other people are but holding the reins.

Let a man overcome anger by love, let him overcome evil by good; let him overcome the greedy by liberality, the liar by truth.

Beware of bodily anger, and control thy body. Leave the sins of the body and with thy body practise virtue.

Beware of the anger of the tongue and control thy tongue. Leave the sins of the tongue and practise virtue with thy tongue.

Beware of the anger of the mind and control thy mind. Leave the sins of the mind, and practise virtue with thy mind.

The wise who control their body, who control their tongue, the wise who control their mind, are indeed well controlled.

There is no fire like passion, there is no shark like hatred, there is no snare like folly, there is no torrent like greed.

The fault of others is easily perceived, but that of one's self is difficult to perceive; a man winnows his neighbor's faults like chaff; but his own faults he hides, as a cheat hides the bad die from the player.

If a man looks after the faults of others and is always inclined to be offended, his own passions will grow and he is far from the destruction of passions.

If anything is to be done, let a man do it, let him attack it vigorously! A careless pilgrim only scatters the dust of his passions more widely.

The thirst of a thoughtless man grows like a creeper.

Whomsoever this fierce poisonous thirst overcomes in this world, his sufferings increase like the abounding Bivana grass.

But from him who overcomes this fierce thirst, difficult to be conquered in this world, sufferings fall off, like water-drops from a lotus leaf.

Dhammapada
(Path of Virtue, or Footstep of the Law)
Trans. Max Müller, *The Sacred Books of the East*

THE CONTROL OF THE MIND
ATTRIBUTED TO BUDDHA
Founder of Buddhism: India, 568?–488? B. C.

All that we are is the result of what we have thought: it is founded on our thoughts, it is made up of our thoughts. If a man speaks or acts with an evil thought, pain follows him, as the wheel follows the foot of the ox that draws the carriage.

All that we are is the result of what we have thought: it is founded on our thoughts, it is made up of our thoughts. If a man speaks or acts with a pure thought, happiness follows him, like a shadow that never leaves him.

As a fletcher makes straight his arrow, a wise man makes straight his trembling and unsteady thought, which is difficult to guard, difficult to hold back.

As a fish taken from his watery home and thrown on the dry ground, our thought trembles all over in order to escape the dominion of the tempter.

It is good to tame the mind, which is difficult to hold in and flighty, rushing wherever it listeth: a tamed mind brings happiness.

Let the wise man guard his thoughts, for they are difficult to perceive, very artful, and they rush wherever they list: thoughts well guarded bring happiness.

Let no man think lightly of evil, saying in his heart, It will not come nigh unto me. Even by the falling of water-drops a water-pot is filled; the fool becomes full of evil, even if he gather it little by little.

Let no man think lightly of good, saying in his heart, It will not come nigh unto me. Even by the falling of water-drops a water-pot is filled; the wise man becomes full of good, even if he gather it little by little.

This mind of mine went formerly wandering

about as it liked, as it listed, as it pleased; but I shall now hold it in thoroughly, as the rider who holds the hook holds in the furious elephant.

Dhammapada
(Path of Virtue, or Footstep of the Law)
Trans. Max Müller, *The Sacred Books of the East*

THE CHARIOTEER
UPANISHADS,
ancient religious literature of India,
probably within 1000 B.C.

Know the self to be sitting in the chariot, the body to be the chariot, the intellect the charioteer, and the mind the reins.

The senses they call the horses, the objects of the senses their roads. When he (the highest self) is in union with the body, the senses, and the mind, then wise people call him the Enjoyer.

He who has no understanding and whose mind is never firmly held, his senses are unmanageable, like vicious horses of a charioteer.

But he who has understanding and whose mind is always firmly held, his senses are under control, like good horses of a charioteer.

He who has no understanding, who is unmindful and always impure, never reaches that place but enters into the round of births. But he who has understanding, who is mindful and always pure, reaches indeed that place from whence he is not born again.

But he who has understanding for his charioteer, and who holds the reins of the mind, he reaches the end of his journey, and that is the highest place of Vishnu.

Katha-Upanishad
Trans. Max Müller, *The Sacred Books of the East*

CHARACTER *
CONFUCIUS
Chinese: his ethical teachings became the foundation of the early national religion of China, which bears his name: 551–478 B. C.

The Master said, A man should say, I am not concerned that I have no place; I am concerned how I may fit myself for one. I am not concerned that I am not known; I seek to be worthy to be known.

The superior man in everything considers righteousness to be essential. He is distressed by his want of ability. He is not distressed by men's not knowing him.

What the superior man seeks is in himself. What the mean man seeks is in others.

The superior man is dignified, but does not wrangle. He is sociable, but not a partisan.

Tsze-kung asked, Is there one word which may serve as a rule of practice for all one's life? The Master said, Is not reciprocity such a word? What you do not want done to yourself, do not do to others.

Sincerity is the way of heaven. The attainment of sincerity is the way of men. He who possesses sincerity is he who without an effort hits what is right, and apprehends without the exercise of thought; he is the sage who naturally and easily embodies the right way. He who attains to sincerity is he who chooses what is good, and firmly holds it fast.

To this attainment there are requisite the extensive study of what is good, accurate inquiry about it, careful reflection on it, the clear discrimination of it, and the earnest practice of it.

Learning without thought is labor lost; thought without learning is perilous.

Analects and *The Doctrine of the Mean*
Trans. James Legge

THINK ON THESE THINGS
The Apostle Paul
Christian, first century

Whatsoever things are true, whatsoever things are honorable, whatsoever things are just, whatsoever things are pure, whatsoever things are lovely, whatsoever things are of good report; if there be any virtue, and if there be any praise, think on these things.

From *The Epistle to the Philippians*
New Testament

CHARACTER OF A HAPPY LIFE
Henry Wotton
English writer and diplomatist, 1568–1639

How happy is he born and taught
That serveth not another's will;
Whose armor is his honest thought,
And simple truth his utmost skill!

Whose passions not his masters are;
Whose soul is still prepared for death,
Untied unto the world by care
Of public fame, or private breath;

Who envies none that chance doth raise,
Nor vice; hath ever understood
How deepest wounds are given by praise;
Nor rules of state, but rules of good;

Who hath his life from rumors freed;
Whose conscience is his strong retreat;
Whose state can neither flatterers feed,
Nor ruin make oppressors great;

Who God doth late and early pray
More of his grace than gifts to lend,
And entertains the harmless day
With a religious book or friend.

This man is freed from servile bands
Of hope to rise, or fear to fall;
Lord of himself, though not of lands,
And having nothing, yet hath all.

LOVE VIRTUE
JOHN MILTON
English Puritan poet, 1608–1674

Love Virtue; she alone is free;
She can teach ye how to climb
Higher than the sphery chime:

Or, if Virtue feeble were,
Heaven itself would stoop to her.

From Comus

SELF-RELIANCE *

RALPH WALDO EMERSON
American philosopher, poet, and essayist; 1803–1882

Whoso would be a man must be a nonconformist. He who would gather immortal palms must not be hindered by the *name* of goodness, but must explore if it *be* goodness. Nothing is at last sacred but the integrity of your own mind. Absolve you to yourself, and you shall have the suffrage of the world.

What I must do is all that concerns me, not what the people think. This rule, equally arduous in actual and in intellectual life, may serve for the whole distinction between greatness and meanness. It is the harder, because you will always find those who think they know what is your duty better than you know it. It is easy in the world to live after the world's opinion; it is easy in solitude to live after our own; but the great man is he who in the midst of the crowd keeps with perfect sweetness the independence of solitude.

A foolish consistency is the hobgoblin of little minds, adored by little statesmen and philosophers and divines. With consistency a great soul has simply nothing to do. He may as well concern himself with his shadow on the wall. Speak what you think now in hard words and to-morrow speak what to-morrow thinks in hard words again, though it contradict everything you said to-day—"Ah, so you shall be sure to be misunderstood."—Is it so bad, then, to be misunderstood? Pythagoras was misunderstood, and Socrates, and Jesus, and Luther, and Copernicus, and Galileo, and Newton, and every pure and wise spirit that ever took flesh. To be great is to be misunderstood.

Self-Reliance

LIBERTY

Abraham Cowley
English poet, 1618–1667

Where honor or where conscience does not bind,
    No other law shall shackle me;
      Slave to myself I will not be;
Nor shall my future actions be confined
      By my own present mind.
Who, by resolves and vows engaged does stand
    For days that yet belong to fate,

Does, like an unthrift, mortgage his estate
    Before it falls into his hand.

                        From *Ode upon Liberty*

THE LAST WORD
MATTHEW ARNOLD
English essayist and poet, 1822–1888

They out-talked thee, hissed thee, tore thee.
Better men fared thus before thee:
Fired their ringing shot and passed,
Hotly charged—and broke at last.
Charge once more, then, and be dumb!
Let the victors, when they come,
When the forts of folly fall,
Find thy body by the wall.

IN MEMORIAM
R. T. HAMILTON BRUCE
WILLIAM E. HENLEY
English poet, 1849–1903

Out of the night that covers me,
    Black as the pit from pole to pole,

I thank whatever gods may be
  For my unconquerable soul.

In the fell clutch of circumstance
  I have not winced nor cried aloud;
Under the bludgeonings of chance
  My head is bloody but unbowed.

Beyond this place of wrath and tears
  Looms but the horror of the shade;
And yet the menace of the years
  Finds, and shall find me, unafraid.

It matters not how strait the gate,
  How charged with punishments the scroll:
I am the master of my fate;
  I am the captain of my soul.

IF—

RUDYARD KIPLING
British author, 1865–1936

If you can keep your head when all about you
Are losing theirs and blaming it on you;
If you can trust yourself when all men doubt
  you,

But make allowance for their doubting too:
If you can wait and not be tired by waiting,
Or being lied about, don't deal in lies,
Or being hated, don't give way to hating,
And yet don't look too good, nor talk too wise;

If you can dream—and not make dreams your
    master;
If you can think—and not make thoughts your
    aim;
If you can meet with Triumph and Disaster
And treat those two impostors just the same:
If you can bear to hear the truth you've spoken
Twisted by knaves to make a trap for fools,
Or watch the things you gave your life to,
    broken,
And stoop and build 'em up with worn-out tools;

If you can make one heap of all your winnings
And risk it on one turn of pitch-and-toss,
And lose, and start again at your beginnings
And never breathe a word about your loss:
If you can force your heart and nerve and
    sinew
To serve your turn long after they are gone,
And so hold on when there is nothing in you
Except the Will which says to them: "Hold
    on!"

If you can talk with crowds and keep your
  virtue,
Or walk with Kings—nor lose the common
  touch;
If neither foes nor loving friends can hurt you,
If all men count with you, but none too much:
If you can fill the unforgiving minute
With sixty seconds' worth of distance run,
Yours is the Earth and everything that's in it,
And—which is more—you'll be a Man, my son!

Rewards and Fairies

Disciplines

TRAINING FOR VICTORY *
EPICTETUS
Greek philosopher, born about 60 A.D.

Difficulties are what show men's character.
Therefore, when a difficult crisis meets you,
remember that you are as the raw youth with
whom God the trainer is wrestling. To what
end? That you may win at Olympia; and that
cannot be done without sweating for it.

Discourses and Manual of Epictetus
Trans. P. E. Matheson

WRESTLING WITH GOD *
Hebrew; this passage, ninth century B.C.

Jacob rose that night and passed over the
ford of Jabbok. Jacob was left alone; and
there wrestled a man with him until the breaking of the day. And when the man saw that he
prevailed not against Jacob, he touched the hol-

low of his thigh; and the hollow of Jacob's thigh was strained, as he wrestled with him.

And he said, "Let me go, for the day breaketh."

And he said, "I will not let thee go, except thou bless me."

And he said unto him, "What is thy name?"

And he said, "Jacob." And the other said, "Thy name shall be called no more Jacob, but Israel; for thou hast striven with God and with men and hast prevailed."

And Jacob asked him, and said, "Tell me, I pray thee, thy name."

And he said, "Wherefore is it that thou dost ask after my name?" And he blessed him there.

And Jacob called the name of the place Peniel; "For," said he, "I have seen God face to face, and my life is preserved."

From *The Book of Genesis*
Old Testament

WORK AND DAYS *

HESIOD

Greek shepherd and poet, probably eighth
century B. C.

Fishes and beasts and winged birds should devour each other, since there is no justice in them. But to men he hath given justice. For if one will speak justice as (one) knoweth, to him Zeus of the far-borne voice giveth weal. But whoso of his will sweareth false witness and lieth, and wrongeth justice and sinneth beyond redemption, his race is dimmer in the afterdays; but the race of him that keepeth his oath is better in time to come. Evil, one may attain easily and in abundance: smooth is the way and it dwelleth very nigh. But in front of virtue have the deathless gods set sweat: long is the way thereto and steep and rough at first. But when one hath reached the top, easy is it thereafter despite its hardness.

Work is no reproach; the reproach is idleness. And whatever be thy lot, work is best.

Wealth is not to be seized violently: god-given wealth is better far. For if a man do seize great wealth by violence of hand, or steal it by craft of tongue, as chanceth oftentimes when greed beguileth the mind of men and shamelessness trampleth upon shame, lightly the gods abase him and make that man's house decay, and weal attendeth him but for a little while.

He who findeth a good neighbor findeth a precious thing.

Plow in spring; but the field that is fallowed

in summer will not belie thee. Sow the fallow field while yet the soil is light. Fallow land is a defender of doom, a comforter of children. For the gods have hidden the livelihood of men.

Hesiod, The Poems and Fragments
Done into English prose by A. W. Mair

SERMONS IN STONES
WILLIAM SHAKESPEARE
English dramatic poet, 1564–1616

Now, my co-mates and brothers in exile,
Hath not old custom made this life more sweet
Than that of painted pomp? Are not these woods
More free from peril than the envious court?
Here feel we but the penalty of Adam,
The seasons' difference; as the icy fang
And churlish chiding of the winter's wind,
Which, when it bites and blows upon my body,
Even till I shrink with cold, I smile, and say
"This is no flattery; these are counselors
That feelingly persuade me what I am."
Sweet are the uses of adversity,
Which, like the toad, ugly and venomous,
Wears yet a precious jewel in his head;
And this our life, exempt from public haunt,

Finds tongues in trees, books in the running
   brooks,
Sermons in stones, and good in every thing.

As You Like It

HABITS

Henri Frédéric Amiel
Swiss scholar and writer, 1821–1881

In the conduct of life, habits count for more
than maxims; because habit is a living maxim,
becomes flesh and instinct. To reform one's
maxims is nothing: it is but to change the title
of the book. To learn new habits is everything,
for it is to reach the substance of life. Life is
but a tissue of habits.

Journal
Trans. Mrs. Humphry Ward

HABIT *

William James
American philosopher and psychologist, 1842–1910

Habit is the enormous fly-wheel of society,
its most precious conservative agent. It alone

is what keeps us all within the bounds of ordinance. It dooms us all to fight out the battle of life upon the lines of our nurture or our early choice, and to make the best of a pursuit that disagrees, because there is no other for which we are fitted, and it is too late to begin again. It is well for the world that in most of us, by the age of thirty, the character has set like plaster, and will never soften again.

The great thing, then, in all education, is to make our nervous system our ally instead of our enemy. It is to fund and capitalize our acquisitions, and live at ease upon the interest of the fund. For this we must make automatic and habitual, as early as possible, as many useful actions as we can, and guard against the growing into ways that are likely to be disadvantageous to us, as one should guard against the plague. The more of the details of our daily life we can hand over to the effortless custody of automatism, the more our higher powers of mind will be set free for their own proper work. There is no more miserable human being than one in whom nothing is habitual but indecision. Full half the time of such a man goes to the deciding, or regretting, of matters which ought to be so ingrained in him as practically not to exist for his consciousness at all.

In the acquisition of a new habit, or the leaving off of an old one, we must take care to launch ourselves with as strong and decided an initiative as possible. Accumulate all the possible circumstances which shall reënforce the right motives; put yourself assiduously in conditions that encourage the new way; make engagements incompatible with the old; take a public pledge, if the case allows; in short, envelop your resolution with every aid you know. This will give your new beginning such a momentum that the temptation to break down will not occur as soon as it otherwise might; and every day during which a breakdown is postponed adds to the chances of its not occurring at all.

Never suffer an exception to occur till the new habit is securely rooted in your life: each lapse is like the letting fall of a ball of string which one is carefully winding up; a single slip undoes more than a great many turns will wind again. Continuity of training is the great means of making the nervous system act infallibly right.

The question of "tapering-off," in abandoning such habits as drink and opium-indulgence, comes in here, and is a question about which experts differ within certain limits and in regard to what may be best for an individual case.

In the main, however, all expert opinion would agree that abrupt acquisition of the new habit is the best way, if there be a real possibility of carrying it out. We must be careful not to give the will so stiff a task as to insure its defeat at the very outset; but, provided one can stand it, a sharp period of suffering, and then a free time, is the best thing to aim at, whether in giving up a habit like that of opium, or in simply changing one's hours of rising or of work.

The Principles of Psychology

THE CONSEQUENCE OF HABIT
George Herbert Betts
American writer, 1868–1934

We owe our children a set of good habits; for habit is to be either their best friend or their worst enemy, not only during childhood, but through all the years. We shall therefore need to repeat every now and then nature's irrevocable law: that back of every habit lies a series of acts; that ahead of every act lies a habit; that habit is nine-tenths of conduct; that conduct is but character in the making; and that character ends in destiny.

Fathers and Mothers

ungraceful; and also because he who has received this true education of the inner being will most shrewdly perceive omissions or faults in art and nature, and, with a true taste, while he praises and rejoices over and receives into his soul the good and becomes noble and good, he will justly blame and hate the bad now in the days of his youth even before he is able to know the reason why; and when reason comes, he will recognize and salute the friend with whom his education has made him long familiar.

The Republic, Book iii
Trans. Benjamin Jowett

GRACIOUS MANNERS *

RALPH WALDO EMERSON

American philosopher, poet, and essayist; 1803–1882

The power of manners is incessant,—an element as unconcealable as fire. The nobility cannot in any country be disguised, and no more in a republic or a democracy than in a kingdom. No man can resist their influence. Manners are very communicable; men catch them from each other.

Manners require time, as nothing is more vulgar than haste. Friendship should be surrounded with ceremonies and respects, and not crushed into corners. Friendship requires more time than poor busy man can usually command.

In persons of character we do not remark manners, because of their instantaneousness. We are surprised by the thing done, out of all power to watch the way of it. Yet nothing is more charming than to recognize the great style which runs through the actions of such.

You cannot rightly train one to an air and manner except by making him the kind of man of whom that manner is the natural expression. Nature forever puts a premium on reality. What is done for effect is seen to be done for effect; what is done for love is felt to be done for love. A man inspires affection and honor because he was not lying in wait for these. The things of a man for which we visit him were done in the dark and cold. A little integrity is better than any career. So deep are the sources of this surface-action that even the size of your companion seems to vary with his freedom of thought. Not only is he larger when at ease and his thoughts generous, but everything around him becomes variable with expression.

In all the superior people I have met I notice directness, truth spoken more truly, as if everything of obstruction, of malformation, had been

trained away. What have they to conceal?
What have they to exhibit? Between simple
and noble persons there is always a quick intelligence; they recognize at sight, and meet on
a better ground than the talents and skills they
may chance to possess, namely, on sincerity
and uprightness.

The highest compact we can make with our
fellows is—"Let there be truth between us two
forevermore."

I have seen manners that make a similar impression with personal beauty: and in memor-
able experiences they are suddenly better than
beauty, and make that superfluous and ugly.
But they must be marked by fine perception,
the acquaintance with real beauty. Then they
must be inspired by the good heart. There is
no beautifier of complexion, or form, or behavior,
like the wish to scatter joy and not pain around
us. It is good to give a stranger a meal, or a
night's lodging. It is better to be hospitable to
his good meaning and thought, and give courage
to a companion. We must be as courteous to a
man as we are to a picture, which we are willing
to give the advantage of a good light.

Behavior

MADE FOR COÖPERATION *

MARCUS AURELIUS
Roman emperor and Stoic philosopher, 121–180

Begin the morning by saying to thyself, I shall meet with the busybody, the ungrateful, arrogant, deceitful, envious, unsocial. All these things happen to them by reason of their ignorance of what is good and evil. But I who have seen the nature of the good, that it is beautiful, and of the bad and that it is ugly, and the nature of him who does wrong, that it is akin to me, not (only) of the same blood but that it participates in (the same) intelligence and (the same) portion of the divinity, I can neither be injured by any of them, nor can I be angry with my kinsman nor hate him. For we are made for coöperation, like feet, like hands. To act against one another, then, is contrary to nature; and it is acting against one another to be vexed and to turn away.

The best way of avenging thyself is not to become like the wrong-doer.

Men exist for the sake of one another. Teach them, then, or bear with them.

The Thoughts of Marcus Aurelius
Trans. George Long

WORLDLY PLACE
Matthew Arnold
English essayist and poet, 1822–1888

Even in a palace life may be led well!
So spake the imperial sage, purest of men,
Marcus Aurelius. But the stifling den
Of common life, where, crowded up, pell-mell,
Our freedom for a little bread we sell,
And drudge under some foolish master's ken,
Who rates us if we peer outside our pen,—
Matched with a palace, is not this a hell?

Even in a palace! On his truth sincere
Who spoke these words, no shadow ever came;
And when my ill-schooled spirit is aflame

Some nobler, ampler stage of life to win,
I'll stop, and say, "There were no succor here!
The aids to noble life are all within."

HAVE YOU LEARNED LESSONS ONLY OF THOSE WHO ADMIRED YOU?

WALT WHITMAN
American poet, 1819–1892

Have you learned lessons only of those who
admired you, and were tender with you,
and stood aside for you?
Have you not learned great lessons from those
who reject you, and brace themselves
against you? or who treat you with
contempt, or dispute the passage
with you?

Stronger Lessons

ENDEAVORS WITHIN OUR ABILITY

EPICTETUS
Greek philosopher, born about 60 A. D.

Of one thing beware, O man; see what is
the price at which you sell your will. If you
do nothing else, do not sell your will cheap.
The great, heroic style, it may be, belongs to
others, to Socrates and men like him.

"If then this is our true nature, why do not
all men, or many, show it?"

What? Do all horses turn out swift; are all dogs good at the scent?

"What am I to do, then? Since I have no natural gifts, am I to make no effort for that reason?"

Heaven forbid. Epictetus is not better than Socrates; if only he is as good as Socrates, I am content. For I shall never be a Milo, yet I do not neglect my body; nor a Croesus, and yet I do not neglect my property; nor, in a word, do we abandon our effort in any field because we despair of the first place.

Discourses and Manual of Epictetus
Trans. P. E. Matheson

PERFECTION IN SMALL THINGS

BEN JONSON
English dramatic poet, 1573?–1637

It is not growing like a tree
    In bulk, doth make man better be;
Or standing long an oak, three hundred year,
To fall a log at last, dry, bald, and sere:
    A lily of a day
    Is fairer far, in May,
Although it fall and die that night;
It was the plant and flower of light.

In small proportions we just beauties see,
And in short measures life may perfect be.

A Pindaric Ode, iii

ART AND LIFE

LEONARDO DA VINCI
Italian painter, sculptor, and scientist; 1452–1519

Thou, O God, dost sell unto us all good things at the price of labor.

In life, beauty perishes; not in art.
The painter contends with, and rivals, nature.

Where there is most power of feeling, there of martyrs is the greatest martyr.

In youth acquire that which may requite you for the deprivations of old age; and if you are mindful that old age has wisdom for its food, you will so exert yourself in youth that your old age will not lack sustenance.

As a well-spent day brings happy sleep, so a life well used brings happy death.

The supreme misfortune is when theory outstrips performance.

Poor is the pupil who does not surpass his master.

Nature never breaks her own law.

Note Books
Trans. Edward McCurdy

I MYSELF AM HEAVEN AND HELL
OMAR KHAYYAM
Persian poet, died about 1123

I sent my soul through the invisible
Some letter of that after-life to spell:
And by and by my soul returned to me,
And answered, "I myself am heaven and hell."

The Rubaiyat
Trans. Edward Fitzgerald

PUNISHMENT
EPICTETUS
Greek philosopher, born about 60 A.D.

What will be the punishment? Perhaps nothing else than, not having done thy duty, thou wilt lose the character of fidelity, modesty, propriety. Do not look for greater penalties than these.

Social Worship
Ed. Stanton Coit

THE DEBT

PAUL LAURENCE DUNBAR
American poet, 1872–1906

This is the debt I pay
Just for one riotous day,—
Years of regret and grief,
Sorrow without relief.

Pay it I will to the end—
Until the grave, my friend,
Gives me a true release,
Gives me the clasp of peace.

Slight was the thing I bought,
Small was the debt, I thought,
Poor was the loan at best—
God! but the interest!

Lyrics of Love and Laughter
Also found in *A Book of American Negro Poetry*

TALES FROM THE PERSIAN
SADI

Persian poet, 1184?–1292

In the annals of Ardsheer Babûkan it is recorded that he asked an Arabian physician what
quantity of food ought to be eaten in the course
of a day. He answered that the weight of one
hundred direms was sufficient. The king asked
what strength could be derived from so small a
quantity. The physician replied, "This quantity is sufficient to support you, and whatever
more you eat, you must carry. We eat to live
and praise God; you believe that you live to
eat."

A man with a disagreeable voice was reading
the Koran aloud, when a holy man passing by
asked what was his monthly stipend. He answered, "Nothing at all." He resumed, "Why
then do you take so much trouble?" He
replied, "I read for the sake of God." The
other rejoined, "For God's sake do not read;
for if you read the Koran in this manner, you
will destroy the splendor of Islamism."

I remember that in the time of childhood I
was very religious: I rose in the night, was

punctual in the performance of my devotions, and abstinent. One night I had been sitting in the presence of my father, not having closed my eyes during the whole time, and with the holy Koran in my embrace, whilst numbers around us were asleep. I said to my father, "Not one of these lifteth up his head to perform his genuflexions: but they are all so fast asleep that you would say they are dead." He replied, "Life of your father, it were better if thou also wert asleep than to be searching out the faults of mankind. The boaster sees nothing but himself, having a veil of conceit before his eyes. If he were endowed with an eye capable of discerning God, he would not discover any person weaker than himself."

The Gulistan (Rose Garden)
Trans. Francis Gladwin

MR. BYENDS[*]

John Bunyan
English preacher and writer, 1628–1688

I saw that quickly after they were got out of the fair (Vanity Fair), they overtook one that was going before them whose name was Byends; so they said to him, "What countryman, sir? and how far go you this way?" He told them he came from the town of Fairspeech and that he was going to the Celestial City; but told them not his name.

"This town of Fairspeech," said Christian, "I have heard of; and as I remember, they say it's a wealthy place."

By. "Yes, I will assure you that it is; and I have very many rich kindred there."

Chr. "Pray, who are your kindred there, if a man may be so bold?"

By. "Almost the whole town; but in particular my Lord Turnabout, my Lord Timeserver, my Lord Fairspeech, from whose ancestors that town first took its name; also Mr. Smoothman, Mr. Facingbothways, Mr. Anything; and the parson of our parish, Mr. Twotongues, was my mother's own brother, and, tell you the truth, I am become a gentleman of good quality; yet my great-grandfather was but a waterman, looking one way and rowing another, and I got most of my estate by the same occupation."

Chr. "Are you a married man?"

By. "Yes, and my wife is a very virtuous woman, the daughter of a virtuous woman; she was my Lady Feigning's daughter; therefore she came of a very honorable family, and is arrived to such a pitch of breeding that she knows how to carry it to all, even to prince and peasant. 'Tis true, we somewhat differ in religion from those of the stricter sort, yet but in two small points: first, we never strive against wind and tide; secondly, we are always most zealous when religion goes in his silver slippers; we love much to walk with him in the street, if the sun shines and the people applaud him."

The Pilgrim's Progress

THE DAY'S WORK

JOHANN WOLFGANG VON GOETHE

German philosopher and dramatic poet, 1749–1832

Use well the moment; what the hour
Brings for thy use is in thy power;
And what thou best canst understand
Is just the thing lies nearest to thy hand.
Art thou little, do that little well, and for thy
comfort know
The biggest man can do his biggest work no
better than just so.
Like the star
That shines afar,
Without haste
And without rest,

Let each man wheel with steady sway
Round the task that rules the day,
    And do his best.

        The Wisdom of Goethe
   Trans. and ed. John Stuart Blackie

ON HIS BLINDNESS

JOHN MILTON

English Puritan poet, 1608–1674

When I consider how my light is spent
Ere half my days, in this dark world and wide,
And that one talent which is death to hide
Lodged with me useless, though my soul more
    bent
To serve therewith my Maker, and present
My true account, lest he returning chide;
"Doth God exact day-labor, light denied?"
I fondly ask. But patience, to prevent
That murmur, soon replies, "God doth not need
Either man's work or his own gifts. Who best
Bear his mild yoke, they serve him best. His
    state
Is kingly: thousands at his bidding speed,
And post o'er land and ocean without rest;
They also serve who only stand and wait."

ART THOU DEJECTED?

Edward Young
English clergyman and author, 1683–1765

Art thou dejected? Is thy mind o'ercast?
Amid her fair ones, thou the fairest choose,
To chase thy gloom.—Go, fix some weighty
    truth;
Chain down some passion; do some generous
    good;
Teach ignorance to see, or grief to smile;
Correct thy friend; befriend thy greatest foe;
Or with warm heart, and confidence divine,
Spring up, and lay strong hold on Him who
    made thee.

Night Thoughts

THE TASK BEFORE US

Robert Louis Stevenson
Scottish novelist, essayist, and poet; 1850–1894

Trying to be kind and honest seems an affair
too simple and too inconsequential for gentlemen of our heroic mould; we had rather set
ourselves to something bold, arduous, and con-
clusive: we had rather found a schism or sup-

press a heresy, cut off a hand or mortify an appetite. But the task before us, which is to coëndure with our existence, is rather one of microscopic fineness, and the heroism required is that of patience. There is no cutting of the Gordian knots of life; each must be smilingly unraveled.

To be honest, to be kind—to earn a little and to spend a little less, to make upon the whole a family happier for his presence, to renounce when that shall be necessary and not be embittered, to keep a few friends, but these without capitulation—above all, on the same grim condition, to keep friends with himself—here is a task for all that a man has of fortitude and delicacy.

A Christmas Sermon

A WAY OF LIFE *

WILLIAM OSLER

British physician, scholar, and author; 1849–1919

Now, for the day itself! What first? Be your own daysman; prepare to lay your own firm hand upon the helm. Get into touch with the finite, and grasp in full enjoyment that sense of capacity in a machine working smoothly.

Join the whole creation of animate things in a deep, heartfelt joy that you are alive, that you see the sun, that you are in this glorious earth which nature has made so beautiful, and which is yours to conquer and enjoy.

What are the morning sensations?—for they control the day. To have a sweet outlook on life you must have a clean body. No dyspeptic can have a sane outlook on life; and a man whose bodily functions are impaired has a lowered moral resistance.

The start is everything, as you well know, and to make a good start, you must feel fit. In the young, sensations of morning slackness come most often from lack of control of the two primal instincts—biological habits—the one concerned with the preservation of the individual, the other with the continuance of the species.

My own rule of life has been to cut out unsparingly any article of diet that had the bad taste to disagree with me, or to indicate in any way that it had abused the temporary hospitality of the lodging which I had provided. To drink, nowadays, but few students become addicted. As moderation is very hard to reach and as it has been abundantly shown that the best of mental and physical work may be done without alcohol in any form, the safest rule for the young man is that which I am sure most of you follow—abstinence.

A bitter enemy to the bright eye and the clear brain of the early morning is tobacco when smoked to excess, as it is now by a large majority of students. Watch it, test it, and if need be, control it. That befogged, woolly sensation reaching from the forehead to the occiput, that haziness of memory, that cold, fishlike eye, that furred tongue and last week's taste in the mouth—too many of you know them—I know them—they often come from too much tobacco.

The other primal instinct is the heavy burden of the flesh which nature puts on all of us to ensure a continuation of the species. To drive Plato's team taxes the energies of the best of us. One of the horses is a raging, untamed devil, who can only be brought into subjection by hard fighting and severe training. This much you all know, as men: once the bit is between his teeth, the black steed, passion, will take the white horse, reason, with you and the chariot, rattling over rocks to perdition.

As the soul is dyed by the thoughts, let no day pass without contact with the best literature of the world. Learn to know your Bible, though not perhaps as your fathers did. In forming character and in shaping conduct, its touch has still its ancient power. You should know its beauties and its strength. Fifteen or twenty minutes day by day will give you fellowship with the great minds of the race, and little by little as the years pass, you extend your friendship with the immortal dead. They will give you faith in your own day. Listen while they speak to you of the fathers. But each age has it own spirit and ideas, just as it has its own manners and pleasures.

While change is the law, certain great ideas flow fresh through the ages, and control us effectually as in the days of Pericles. Mankind, it has been said, is always advancing; man is always the same. The love, hope, fear, and faith that make humanity, and the elemental passions of the human heart, remain unchanged, and the secret of inspiration in any literature is the capacity to touch the chord that vibrates in a sympathy that knows nor time nor place. To whichever of the two great types you belong, whether controlled by emotion or by reason, you will need the leaven of their spirit.

A Way of Life

(An address to students of Yale University)

ODE TO DUTY *

WILLIAM WORDSWORTH
English poet, 1770–1850

Stern Daughter of the Voice of God!
O Duty! if that name thou love
Who art a light to guide, a rod
To check the erring and reprove;
Thou, who art victory and law
When empty terrors overawe,
From vain temptations dost set free,
And calm'st the weary strife of frail humanity!

There are who ask not if thine eye
Be on them, who in love and truth
Where no misgiving is, rely
Upon the genial sense of youth;
Glad hearts! without reproach or blot,
Who do thy work and know it not;
Oh! if through confidence misplaced
They fail, thy saving arms, dread Power,
    around them cast.

I, loving freedom, and untried,
No sport of every random gust,
Yet being to myself a guide,
Too blindly have reposed my trust;

And oft, when in my heart was heard
Thy timely mandate, I deferred
The task, in smoother walks to stray;
But thee I now would serve more strictly, if I
    may.

Stern Lawgiver! yet thou dost wear
The Godhead's most benignant grace;
Nor know we anything so fair
As is the smile upon thy face;
Flowers laugh before thee on their beds
And fragrance in thy footing treads;
Thou dost preserve the stars from wrong;
And the most ancient heavens, through thee,
    are fresh and strong.

To humbler functions, awful Power,
I call thee: I myself commend
Unto thy guidance from this hour;
Oh, let my weakness have an end!
Give unto me, made lowly wise,
The spirit of self-sacrifice;
The confidence of reason give;
And in the light of truth thy bondman let me
    live.

VIRTUES ACQUIRED BY PRACTICE *

ARISTOTLE
Greek philosopher and scientist, 384–322 B.C.

Human excellence is of two kinds, intellectual and moral: now the intellectual springs originally, and is increased subsequently, from teaching (for the most part, that is) and needs therefore experience and time; whereas the moral comes from custom (i. e. ethos, and so the Greek term denoting it is but a slight deflection from the term denoting custom in that language; i. e. ethics—Ed.).

From this fact it is plain that not one of the moral virtues comes to be in us merely by nature: because of such things as exist by nature, none can be changed by custom. A stone, for instance, by nature gravitating downwards, could never by custom be brought to ascend, not even if one were to try to accustom it by throwing it up ten thousand times; nor could fire again be brought to descend, nor in fact could any thing whose nature is in one way be brought by custom to be in another. The virtues then come to be in us neither by nature, nor in despite of nature, but we are furnished by nature with a capacity for receiving them, and are perfected in them through custom. But the virtues we get by doing the acts, which again is the case of other things, as the arts, for instance. Men come to be builders, by building; harp players, by playing on the harp: exactly so, by doing just actions we come to be just; by doing the actions of temperance we come to be temperate; and by doing brave actions, brave.

The Nichomachean Ethics
Ed. J. M. Mitchell

SELF-RECOLLECTION *

HENRI FRÉDÉRIC AMIEL
Swiss scholar and writer, 1821–1881

A capacity for self-recollection—for withdrawal from the outward to the inward—is in fact the condition of all noble and useful activity. If the sailor did not carry with him his own temperature he could not go from the pole to the equator, and remain himself in spite of all. The man who has no refuge in himself, who lives, so to speak, in his front rooms, in the outer whirlwind of things and opinions, is not properly a personality at all. He is one of a crowd, a taxpayer, an elector, an anonymity, but not a man.

He who floats with the current, who does not guide himself according to higher principles, who has no ideal, no convictions—such a man is a mere article of the world's furniture—a thing moved, instead of a living and moving being—an echo, not a voice. The man who has no inner life is the slave of his surroundings, as the barometer is the obedient servant of the air at rest, and the weathercock the humble servant of the air in motion.

Journal
Trans. Mrs. Humphry Ward

INTO THE SILENCE
James Martineau
British: teacher of religion, 1805–1900

Let any true man go into silence: strip himself of all pretence, and selfishness, and sensuality, and sluggishness of soul; lift off thought after thought, passion after passion, till he reaches the inmost depth of all; remember how short a time and he was not at all; how short a time again, and he will not be here; open his window and look upon the night, how still its breath, how solemn its march, how deep its perspective, how ancient its forms of light; and think how little he knows except the perpetuity of God, and the mysteriousness of life:—and it will be strange if he does not feel the Eternal Presence as close upon his soul as the breeze upon his brow; if he does not say, "O Lord, art thou ever near as this, and have I not known thee?"—if the true proportions and the genuine spirit of life do not open on his heart with infinite clearness and show him the littleness of his temptations and the grandeur of his trust. He is ashamed to have found weariness in toil so light, and tears where there was no trial to the brave. He discovers with astonishment how small the dust that has blinded him, and from the height of a quiet and holy love looks down with incredulous sorrow on the jealousies and fears and irritations that have vexed his life. A mighty wind of resolution sets in strong upon him and freshens the whole atmosphere of his soul, sweeping down before it the light flakes of difficulty, till they vanish like snow upon the sea. He is imprisoned no more in a small compartment of time, but belongs to an eternity which is now and here. The isolation of his separate spirit passes away; and with the countless multitude of souls akin to God, he is but as a wave of his unbounded deep. He is at one with Heaven, and hath found the secret place of the Almighty.

> From *Silence and Meditation*
> *Endeavors after the Christian Life*

TASKS IN HOURS OF INSIGHT WILLED

MATTHEW ARNOLD
English essayist and poet, 1822–1888

We cannot kindle when we will
The fire that in the heart resides:
The spirit bloweth and is still;
In mystery our soul abides.
But tasks in hours of insight willed
Can be through hours of gloom fulfilled.

> From *Morality*

MORE STATELY MANSIONS

OLIVER WENDELL HOLMES
American essayist and poet, 1809–1894

Build thee more stately mansions, O my soul,
As the swift seasons roll:—
Leave thy low-vaulted past.

Let each new temple, nobler than the last,
Shut thee from heaven with a dome more vast,
Till thou at length art free,
Leaving thine outgrown shell by life's unresting
sea.

From *The Chambered Nautilus*

THE WAY OF THE WISE
ATTRIBUTED TO BUDDHA
Founder of Buddhism: India, 568?–488? B. C.

Long is the night to him who is awake; long is a mile to him who is tired; long is life to the foolish who do not know the true law.

If a traveler does not meet with one who is his better, or his equal, let him firmly keep to his solitary journey; there is no companionship with a fool.

If a fool be associated with a wise man even all his life, he will perceive the truth as little as a spoon perceives the taste of soup.

If an intelligent man be associated for one minute only with a wise man, he will soon perceive the truth, as the tongue perceives the taste of soup.

Well-makers lead the water (wherever they

like); fletchers bend the arrow; carpenters bend a log of wood; wise people fashion themselves.

As a solid rock is not shaken by the wind, wise people falter not amidst blame and praise.

Wise people, after they have listened to the laws, become serene, like a deep, smooth, and still lake.

Not to blame, not to strike, to live restrained under the law, to be moderate in eating, to sleep and sit alone, and to dwell on the highest thoughts,—this is the teaching of the Awakened (Buddha).

He who walks in the company of fools suffers a long way; company with fools, as with an enemy, is always painful; company with the wise is pleasure, like meeting with kinsfolk.

Therefore, one ought to follow the wise, the intelligent, the learned, the much enduring, the dutiful, the elect; one ought to follow such a good and wise man, as the moon follows the path of the stars.

A man is not just if he carries a matter by violence; no, he who distinguishes both right and wrong, who is learned and guides others, not by violence, but by the same law, being a guardian of the law and intelligent, he is called just.

A man is not an elder because his head is grey; his age may be ripe, but he is called "Old-in-vain."

He in whom there is truth, virtue, pity, restraint, moderation, he who is free from impurity and is wise, he is called an elder.

He who does not rouse himself when it is time to rise, who, though young and strong, is full of sloth, whose will and thought are weak, that lazy and idle man never finds the way to knowledge.

Watching his speech, well restrained in mind, let a man never commit any wrong with his body! Let a man but keep these three roads of action clear, and he will achieve the way which is taught by the wise.

If by leaving a small pleasure one sees a great pleasure, let a wise man leave the small pleasure and look to the great.

Good people shine from afar, like the snowy mountains; bad people are not seen, like arrows shot by night.

If a man find a prudent companion who walks with him, is wise, and lives soberly, he may walk with him, overcoming all dangers, happy, but considerate.

If a man find no prudent companion who walks with him, is wise and lives soberly, let him walk alone, like a king who has left his conquered country behind,—like an elephant in the forest.

Dhammapada
(Path of Virtue, or Footstep of the Law)
Trans. Max Müller, *The Sacred Books of the East*

A MORAL CODE *
Babylonian, 2100–1100 B. C.

Has he estranged son from father?

Has he estranged father from son?

Has he estranged mother from daughter?

Has he estranged daughter from mother?

Has he estranged mother-in-law from daughter-in-law?

Has he estranged daughter-in-law from mother-in-law?

Has he estranged brother from brother?

Has he estranged friend from friend?

Has he estranged companion from companion?

Has he not released a prisoner, has he not loosened the bound one?

Has he not permitted the prisoner to see the
    light?
Has he, in the case of the captive, commanded,
    "Take hold of him," in the case of one
    bound said, "Bind him"?

Is it a sin against a god, a transgression against
    a goddess?
Has he offended a god, neglected a goddess?
Has he neglected father or mother, insulted the
    elder sister?
Given too little, refused the larger amount?
For "no" said "yes," for "yes" said "no"?
Has he used false weights?
Has he taken the wrong sum, not taken the
    correct amount?
Has he drawn a false boundary, not drawn the
    right boundary?
Has he removed the limit, mark, or boundary?
Has he possessed himself of his neighbor's
    house?

Has he shed his neighbor's blood?
Has he stolen his neighbor's garment?
Has he divided a family once united?
Has he set himself up against a superior?
Was his mouth frank, but his heart false?
Was it "yes" with his mouth, but "no" with his
    heart?

Has he taught what was impure, instructed in
what was not proper?

Did he follow the path of evil?

Did he overstep the bounds of what was just?

Trans. Morris Jastrow
The Sacred Books and Early Literature of the East
Ed. Chas. F. Horne

THE TEN COMMANDMENTS *
Hebrew; the first portion, in present form, from
fifth century B. C.

In the third month after the children of
Israel were gone forth out of the land of Egypt,
the same day came they into the wilderness
of Sinai.

And Moses went up unto God, and the Lord
called unto him out of the mountain.

And the Lord said unto Moses, "Go unto thy
people, and sanctify them to-day and to-
morrow, and let them wash their garments, and
be ready against the third day; for the third
day the Lord will come down in the sight of all
the people of Mount Sinai. And thou shalt
set bounds unto the people round about, saying,
'Take heed to yourselves that ye go not up into
the mount, or touch the border of it: whosoever

toucheth the mount shall be surely put to death.' "

And Moses went down from the mount unto the people, and sanctified the people; and they washed their garments. And he said unto the people, "Be ready against the third day."

And it came to pass on the third day when it was morning that there were thunders and lightnings and a thick cloud upon the mount, and the voice of a trumpet exceeding loud; and all the people that were in the camp trembled. And Moses brought forth the people out of the camp to meet God; and they stood at the nether part of the mount. And Mount Sinai, the whole of it, smoked, because the Lord descended upon it in fire; and the smoke thereof ascended as the smoke of a furnace, and the whole mount quaked greatly. And when the voice of the trumpet waxed louder and louder, Moses spake, and God answered him by a voice.

This portion, seventh century B. C.

And God spake all these words, saying, "I am the Lord thy God, who brought thee out of the land of Egypt, out of the house of bondage.

Thou shalt have no other gods before me.

Thou shalt not make unto thee a graven image.

Thou shalt not take the name of the Lord thy God in vain.

Remember the Sabbath day, to keep it holy.

Honor thy father and thy mother.

Thou shalt not kill.

Thou shalt not commit adultery.

Thou shalt not steal.

Thou shalt not bear false witness.

Thou shalt not covet."

And all the people perceived the thunderings and the lightnings, and the voice of the trumpet, and the mountain smoking; and when the people saw it, they trembled, and stood afar off.

And they said unto Moses, "Speak thou with us, lest we die."

And Moses said unto the people, "Fear not: for God is come to prove you, and that his fear may be before you, that ye sin not."

And the people stood afar off, and Moses drew near unto the thick darkness where God was.

From *The Book of the Exodus, Old Testament*

WISDOM OF THE SERBIANS *
Nicholai Velimirovic
Contemporary Serbian clergyman

Be humble, for the worst thing in the world is of the same stuff as you; be confident, for the stars are of the same stuff as you.

Our life is obscure, and our death is obscure. God is the only light of both.

God is not hidden, but our eyes are too small to see him.

When two blind men sit quarreling about what is light, they are like two men quarreling about what is God.

Different languages but the same prayer; different prayers, but the same God—

Never in prayer try to teach God what he should do for you, but rather ask him what you should do for him.

God may be either accompanying or pursuing you. It depends upon you.

To forgive the sins of men means for us nothing more than to confess our own sins. To forgive the sins of men means for God nothing less than to let events be without consequences, which contradicts either human experience or science. (Rephrased—Ed.)

There is no harvest without seed. We see after a harvest of evil the seed which time has concealed.

By using our hands we become strong; by using our brains, wise; but by using our hearts, merciful.

What is it to be a gentleman? To be the first to thank, and the last to complain.

When you pass the tomb of a man who died for cross and freedom, you should bow your head low; and when you pass the palace of a man who lives for wealth and pleasure, only turn your head the other way.

It is better that your good deed should be forgotten than that your evil deed should make you famous.

A lake at the foot of a mountain is a mirror for the mountain; just so is the past a mirror for mankind.

Men with little wisdom have much passion; men with much wisdom have great compassion and little passion.

A good custom hallows life and keeps men in brotherly unity.

Our bodies are only bridges over which our souls communicate with one another.

If a man casts clay at the sun, it falls back

on his face; if he casts stones against God, they fall on his head.

Lift up your hearts to heaven. The foulest water is purified when it is lifted to the clouds of heaven.

All men that God created can live on the earth. God gave space and air enough for all, if men would only give good will.

Freedom is an atmosphere which makes the sun brighter, and the air clearer, and the honey sweeter.

To die for the cross and freedom means two lives and no death.

A wolf never can so badly enslave a fellow-wolf as a man can enslave a fellow-man.

It is not easier to live in freedom than to fight for freedom. One must fight for freedom like an archangel, but one must live in freedom as a saint.

When you fight for freedom you are helping every slave of the world, not only yourself.

When men are quarreling about the land, God is standing among them and whispering, "I am the Proprietor!"

Serbia in Light and Darkness

REFLECTIONS AND MAXIMS*
WILLIAM PENN
Friend (Quaker): founder of
the State of Pennsylvania; 1644–1718

Discipline—If thou wouldst be happy and easy in thy family, above all things observe discipline.

Every one in it should know his duty; and there should be a time and place for everything; and whatever else is done or omitted, be sure to begin and end with God.

Neither urge another to that thou wouldst be unwilling to do thyself; nor do thyself what looks to thee unseemly and intemperate in another.

Right Marriage—Never marry but for love; but see that thou lovest what is lovely.

If love be not thy chiefest motive, thou wilt soon grow weary of a married state and stray from thy promise to search out thy pleasures in forbidden places.

They that marry for money cannot have the true satisfaction of marriage, the requisite means being wanting.

The satisfaction of our senses is low, short, and transient; but the mind gives a more raised and extended pleasure, and is capable of a happiness founded upon reason, not bounded and limited by the circumstances that bodies are confined to.

Between a man and his wife nothing ought to rule but love. Authority is for children and servants; yet not without sweetness.

As love ought to bring them together, so it is the best way to keep them well together.

A husband and wife that love and value one another show their children and servants that they should do so too. Others visibly lose their authority in their families by their contempt of one another, and teach their children to be unnatural by their own examples.

Silence is wisdom where speaking is folly, and always safe.

If thou thinkest twice before thou speakest once, thou wilt speak twice the better for it.

In all debates let truth be thy aim, not victory or an unjust interest, and endeavor to gain, rather than to expose, thy antagonist.

Men are too apt to be concerned for their credit more than for the cause.

Temper—Nothing does reason more right than the coolness of those that offer it. For truth often suffers more by the heat of its

defenders than from the arguments of its op-
posers.

Complete Virtue—If thou hast not conquered
thyself in that which is thy own particular
weakness, thou hast no title to virtue though
thou art free of other men's.

If thou wouldst conquer thy weakness, thou
must never gratify it.

It is no sin to be tempted, but to be overcome.

What man in his right mind would conspire
his own hurt? Men are beside themselves when
they transgress their convictions.

Thou wouldst take much pains to save thy
body. Take some, prithee, to save thy soul.

Religion—Public worship is very commend-
able if well performed. We owe it to God and
good example. But we must know that God is
not tied to time or place, who is everywhere at
the same time. And this we shall know as far
as we are capable, if, wherever we are, our
desires are to be with him.

Let us choose, therefore, to commune where
there is the warmest sense of religion; where
devotion exceeds formality, and practice most
corresponds with profession, and where there

is at least as much charity as zeal. For where this society is to be found, there shall we find the Church of God.

God is better served in resisting a temptation to evil than in many formal prayers.

We are too ready to retaliate rather than forgive, or gain by love and information.

And yet we could hurt no man that we believe loves us.

Let us then try what love will do. For if men do once see we love them, we should soon find they would not harm us.

Force may subdue, but love gains; and he that forgives first wins the laurel.

If I am even with my enemy, the debt is paid; but if I forgive it, I oblige him for ever.

He that lives in love lives in God, says the beloved disciple. And, to be sure, a man can live nowhere better.

Jealousy—The jealous are troublesome to others, but a torment to themselves.

Jealousy is a kind of civil war in the soul, where judgment and imagination are at perpetual jars.

This civil dissension in the mind, like that of the body politic, commits great disorders and lays all waste.

Nothing stands safe in its way: nature, interest, religion must yield to its fury.

It violates contracts, dissolves society, breaks wedlock, betrays friends and neighbors.

Friendship—There can be no friendship where there is no freedom. Friendship loves a free air, and will not be penned up in straight and narrow enclosures. It will speak freely and act so too, and take nothing ill where no ill is meant; nay, where it is, it will easily forgive and forget too upon small acknowledgments.

A true friend unbosoms freely, advises justly, assists readily, adventures boldly, takes all patiently, defends courageously, and continues a friend unchangeably. These being the qualities of a friend, we are to find them before we choose one.

The covetous, the angry, the proud, the jealous, the talkative cannot but make ill friends as well as false.

In short, choose a friend as thou dost a wife, till death separate you.

Some Fruits of Solitude

THE FRUITS OF FRIENDSHIP *
Edward Young
English clergyman and author, 1683-1765

Know'st thou, Lorenzo, what a friend contains?
As bees mixed nectar draw from fragrant
    flowers,
So men from friendship, wisdom and delight;
Twins tied by nature, if they part they die.
Hast thou no friend to set thy mind abroach?
Good sense will stagnate; thoughts shut up want
    air
And spoil, like bales unopened to the sun.
Had thought been all, sweet speech had been
    denied;
Speech, thought's canal. Speech, thought's
    criterion too!
Thought in the mine may come forth gold or
    dross;
When coined in words, we know its real worth.
If sterling, store it for thy future use:
'Twill buy thee benefit, perhaps renown.
Thought, too, delivered is the more possessed;
Teaching, we learn; and giving, we retain
The births of intellect; when dumb, forgot.
Speech ventilates our intellectual fire;
Speech burnishes our mental magazine;
Brightens, for ornament; and whets, for use.

Nature, in zeal for human amity,
Denies or damps an undivided joy.
Joy is an import; joy is an exchange;
Joy flies monopolists: it calls for two.

Night Thoughts

TO KEEP A TRUE LENT
ROBERT HERRICK
English poet, 1591–1674

Is this a fast—to keep
    The larder lean,
      And clean
From fat of veals and sheep?

Is it to quit the dish
    Of flesh, yet still
      To fill
The platter high with fish?

Is it to fast an hour
    Or ragged to go,
      Or show
A downcast look and sour?

No! 'Tis a fast to dole
    Thy sheaf of wheat,
      And meat,
Unto the hungry soul;

It is to fast from strife,
    From old debate
        And hate;
To circumcise thy life;

To show a heart grief-rent;
    To starve thy sin,
        Not bin—
And that's to keep thy Lent.
                                        Hesperides

WORK MAY YET BE DONE
Alfred Tennyson
English poet, 1809-1892

There lies the port, the vessel puffs her sail;
There gloom the dark, broad seas. My
        mariners,
Souls that have toiled, and wrought, and thought
        with me,—
That ever with a frolic welcome took
The thunder and the sunshine, and opposed
Free hearts, free foreheads—you and I are old;
Old age hath yet his honor and his toil.
Death closes all; but something ere the end,
Some work of noble note, may yet be done,
Not unbecoming men that strove with gods.

The lights begin to twinkle from the rocks;

The long day wanes; the slow moon climbs; the deep

Moans round with many voices. Come, my friends,

'Tis not too late to seek a newer world.

Push off, and sitting well in order, smite

The sounding furrows; for my purpose holds

To sail beyond the sunset and the baths

Of all the western stars until I die.

It may be that the gulfs will wash us down;

It may be we shall touch the Happy Isles,

And see the great Achilles, whom we knew.

Though much is taken, much abides; and though

We are not now that strength which in old days

Moved earth and heaven, that which we are, we are,—

One equal temper of heroic hearts,

Made weak by time and fate, but strong in will

To strive, to seek, to find, and not to yield.

From Ulysses

DISCIPLIANS
303

The lights begin to twinkle from the rocks;
The long day wanes; the slow moon climbs; the
deep
Moans round with many voices. Come, my
friends,
'Tis not too late to seek a newer world.
Push off, and
To strive, to seek, to find,

Exemplars

HERO WORSHIP *
Thomas Carlyle
Scottish essayist and historian, 1795–1881

Great men, taken up in any way, are profitable company. We cannot look, however imperfectly, upon a great man without gaining something by him. He is the living light-fountain, which it is good and pleasant to be near. The light which enlightens, which has enlightened the darkness of the world; and this not as a kindled lamp only, but rather as a natural luminary shining by the gift of heaven; a flowing light-fountain, as I say, of native original insight, of manhood and heroic nobleness,—in whose radiance all souls feel that it is well with them——

To me it is very cheering to consider that no skeptical logic, or general triviality, insincerity, and aridity of any time and its influences can destroy this noble inborn loyalty and worship that is in man. In times of unbelief, which soon

have to become times of revolution, much down
rushing, sorrowful decay and ruin is visible to
everybody. For myself in these days, I seem
to see in this indestructibility of hero-worship
the everlasting adamant lower than which the
confused wreck of revolutionary things cannot
fall. The confused wreck of things crumbling
and even crashing and tumbling all round us in
these revolutionary ages will get down so far,
no farther. It is an eternal cornerstone, from
which they can begin to build themselves up
again.

Heroes and Hero Worship

THE SOLE TITLE TO NOBILITY *
JUVENAL
Latin poet and reformer of morals
by satire; about 60–140

What is the use of pedigrees? What boots
it, Poticus, to be accounted of an ancient line,
and to display the painted faces of your ancestors, and the Æmiliani standing in their
cars? What profit is it to vaunt in your ca-
pacious genealogy of Corvinus, and in many a
collateral line to trace dictators and masters
of the horse begrimed with smoke, if before the

very faces of the Lepidi you lead an evil life? To what purpose are the images of so many warriors, if the dice-box rattles all night long in the presence of the Numantini, if you retire to rest at the rising of that star at whose dawning those generals set their standards and camps in motion?

Though your long line of ancient statues adorn your ample halls on every side, the sole and only real nobility is virtue. Be a Paulus, or Cossus, or Drusus in moral character. Set that before the images of your ancestors. Let that, when you are consul, take precedence of the fasces themselves. What I claim from you first is the noble qualities of the mind. If you deserve indeed to be accounted a man of blameless integrity and staunch love of justice, both in word and deed, then I recognize the real nobleman. All hail, Gætulicus, or thou, Silanus, or from whatever other blood descended —a rare and illustrious citizen, thou fallest to the lot of thy rejoicing country!

For who would call him noble that is unworthy of his race, and distinguished only for his illustrious name?

Who considers dumb animals highly bred, unless strong and courageous? Surely it is on this score we praise the fleet horse, to grace whose speed full many a palm glows, and Victory, in the circus hoarse with shouting, stands exulting by. He is the steed of fame, from whatever pasture he comes, whose speed is brilliantly before the others, and whose dust is first on the plain. But the brood of Corytha and Hirpinus' stock are put up for sale if victory sit but seldom on their yoke. In their case no regard is had to their pedigree,—their dead sires win them no favor. Therefore that we may admire you, and not yours, first achieve some noble act that I may inscribe on your statue's base besides those honors that we pay, and ever shall pay, to those to whom you are indebted for all.

Prove yourself a good soldier, a faithful guardian, an incorruptible judge. If ever you shall be summoned as a witness in a doubtful and uncertain cause, though Phalaris himself command you to turn liar and dictate the perjuries with his bull placed before your eyes, deem it to be the summit of impiety to prefer existence to honor, and for the sake of life to sacrifice life's only end.

The Satires of Juvenal, viii
Trans. Lewis Evans

FOR A' THAT AND A' THAT *

ROBERT BURNS

Scottish lyric poet, 1759–1796

Is there, for honest poverty,
    That hangs his head, and a' that?
The coward-slave, we pass him by,
    We dare be poor for a' that!
      For a' that, and a' that,
      Our toils obscure, and a' that;
The rank is but the guinea stamp;
    The man's the gowd for a' that.

What tho' on hamely fare we dine,
    Wear hodden-grey, and a' that;
Gie fools their silks, and knaves their wine,
    A man's a man for a' that.
      For a' that, and a' that,
      Their tinsel show, and a' that;
The honest man, tho' e'er sae poor,
    Is king o' men for a' that.

Then let us pray that come it may,
    As come it will for a' that,
That sense and worth, o'er a' the earth,
    May bear the gree, and a' that

> For a' that, and a' that,
> It's coming yet, for a' that,
> That man to man, the warld o'er,
> Shall brothers be, for a' that.

A MESSAGE TO GARCIA *

Elbert Hubbard
American writer, 1859–1915

When war broke out between Spain and the United States, it was very necessary to communicate quickly with the leader of the Insurgents. Garcia was somewhere in the mountain fastnesses of Cuba—no one knew where. No mail nor telegraph message could reach him. The President must secure his coöperation, and quickly.

Some one said to the President, "There is a fellow by the name of Rowan who will find Garcia for you, if anybody can."

Rowan was sent for and given a letter to be delivered to Garcia. How "the fellow by the name of Rowan" took the letter, sealed it up in an oilskin pouch, strapped it over his heart, in four days landed by night off the coast of Cuba from an open boat, disappeared into the jungle, and in three weeks came out on the other side of the Island, having traversed a hostile country on foot and delivered his letter to Garcia are things I have no special desire now to tell in detail.

The point I wish to make is this: McKinley gave Rowan a letter to be delivered to Garcia; Rowan took the letter and did not ask, "Where is he?"

General Garcia is dead now, but there are other Garcias.

No man who has endeavored to carry out an enterprise where many hands were needed but has been well-nigh appalled at times by the inability or unwillingness to concentrate on a thing and do it.

My heart goes out to the man who does his work when the "boss" is away as well as when he is at home.

Civilization is one long, anxious search for just such individuals. He is wanted in every city, town, and village—in every office, shop, store, and factory. The world cries out for such; he is needed, and needed badly—the man who can carry a message to Garcia.

A Message to Garcia

THE CHARACTER OF THE HAPPY WARRIOR *

WILLIAM WORDSWORTH
English poet, 1770–1850

Who is the happy warrior? Who is he
That every man in arms should wish to be?
It is the generous spirit, who, when brought
Among the tasks of real life, hath wrought
Upon the plan that pleased his boyish thought;
Whose high endeavors are an inward light
That makes the path before him always bright;
Who doomed to go in company with pain,
And fear, and bloodshed, miserable train!
Turns his necessity to glorious gain,
In face of these doth exercise a power
Which is our human nature's highest dower.
'Tis he whose law is reason, who depends
Upon that law as on the best of friends;
Whose powers shed round him in the common
    strife,
Or mild concerns of ordinary life,
A constant influence, a peculiar grace;
But who, if he be called upon to face
Some awful moment to which heaven has joined
Great issues, good or bad for human kind,
Is happy as a lover, and attired
With sudden brightness, like a man inspired;

And, through the heat of conflict, keeps the law
In calmness made, and sees what he foresaw;
Or if an unexpected call succeed,
Come when it will, is equal to the need;
He who, though thus endued as with a sense
And faculty for storm and turbulence,
Is yet a soul whose master-bias leans
To homefelt pleasures and to gentle scenes,
Sweet images! which, wheresoe'er he be,
Are at his heart; and such fidelity
It is his darling passion to approve;
More brave for this, that he hath much to
    love.
'Tis, finally, the man who lifted high,
Conspicuous object in a nation's eye,
Or left unthought-of in obscurity,
Who, with a toward or untoward lot,
Prosperous or adverse, to his wish or not,
Plays in the many games of life that one
Where what he most doth value must be won;
Whom neither shape of danger can dismay,
Nor thought of tender happiness betray;
Who, whether praise of him must walk the
    earth
Forever and to noble deeds give birth,
Or he must fall, to sleep without his fame
And leave a dead, unprofitable name,
Finds comfort in himself and in his cause;

And while the mortal mist is gathering, draws
His breath in confidence of heaven's applause:
This is the happy warrior; this is he
That every man in arms should wish to be.

MASTERS OF DESTINY *

EPICTETUS
Greek philosopher, born about 60 A.D.

What must a man have ready to help him, in
emergencies? Surely this: he must ask himself, "What is mine, and what is not mine?
What may I do, what may I not do?" I must
be imprisoned. But must I whine as well? I
must suffer exile. Can any one there hinder
me from going with a smile, and a good courage, and at peace?

"But I will chain you."

What say you, fellow? Chain me? My leg
you will chain—yes; but my will—no: not even
Zeus can conquer that.

"I will imprison you."

My bit of a body you mean.

It was in this spirit that Agrippinus used to
say—do you know what? "I will not stand in
my own way!" News was brought to him,

"Your trial is on in the Senate!" "Good luck to it, but the fifth hour is come"—this was the hour when he used to take his exercise and have a cold bath,—"Let us go and take exercise." When he had taken his exercise, they came and told him, "You are condemned." "Exile or death?" he asked. "Exile." "And my property?" "It is not confiscated." "Well, then, let us go to Aricia and dine."

Here you see the result of training as training should be, of the will to get and will to avoid, so disciplined that nothing can hinder or frustrate them.

I must die, must I?—And die how?—As befits one who gives back what is not his own.

(Man's) true work is to study to remove from his life mourning and lamentation, the "ah, me" and "alas, for my misery"; the talk of "bad fortune" and "misfortune"; and to learn what is death, what is exile, what is imprisonment, what is the cup of hemlock;—that he may be able to say in prison, "My dear Crito, if it pleases the gods, so be it"; and not such words as "Miserable old man that I am, is it for this I kept my grey hairs?"

Cleanse your own heart, cast out from your mind pain, fear, desire, envy, ill-will, avarice, cowardice, passion uncontrolled. These things you cannot cast out unless you look to God alone; on him alone set your thoughts, and consecrate yourself to his commands. If you wish for anything else, with groaning and sorrow you will follow what is stronger than you, ever seeking peace outside you, and never able to be at peace; for you seek it where it is not, and refuse to seek it where it is.

What is the first business of the philosopher? Will nothing but what God wills. Then who shall hinder you, who compel you? You will be as free as Zeus himself.

Discourses and Manual of Epictetus
Trans. P. E. Matheson

FAITH *
Christian, first century

Faith is the assurance of things hoped for, the proving of things not seen. For therein the elders had witness borne to them. By faith we understand that the worlds have been framed by the word of God, so that what is seen hath not been made out of things which do appear.

By faith Abraham, when he was called, obeyed to go out unto a place which he was to receive for an inheritance; and he went out, not knowing whither he went. By faith he became a sojourner in the land of promise, as in a land not his own, dwelling in tents, with Isaac and Jacob, the heirs with him of the same promise; for he looked for the city which hath the foundations, whose builder and maker is God.

By faith Moses, when he was grown up, refused to be called the son of Pharaoh's daughter, choosing rather to be evil entreated with the people of God than to enjoy the pleasures of sin for a season, accounting the reproach of Christ greater riches than the treasures of Egypt; for he looked unto the recompense of reward.

And what shall I more say? for the time will fail me if I tell of Gideon, Barak, Samson, Jephthah; of David and Samuel and the prophets: who through faith subdued kingdoms, wrought righteousness, obtained promises, stopped the mouths of lions, quenched the power of fire, escaped the edge of the sword, from weakness were made strong, waxed mighty in war, turned to flight armies of aliens. Women received their dead by a resurrection; and others were tortured, not accepting their deliverance, that they might obtain a better resurrection; and others had trial of mockings and scourgings, yea, moreover, of bonds and imprisonment; they were stoned, they were sawn asunder, they were tempted, they were slain with the sword; they went about in sheepskins, in goatskins, being destitute, afflicted, evil entreated (of whom the world was not worthy), wandering in deserts and mountains and caves, and the holes of the earth. And these all, having had witness borne to them through their faith, received not the promise, God having provided some better thing concerning us, that apart from us they should not be made perfect.

Therefore let us also, seeing we are compassed about with so great a cloud of witnesses, lay aside every weight, and the sin which doth so easily beset us, and let us run with patience the race that is set before us, looking unto Jesus, the author and perfecter of our faith, who for the joy that was set before him endured the cross, despising shame, and hath sat down at the right hand of the throne of God.

From *The Epistle to the Hebrews*
New Testament

ALL PROGRESS IS THE WORK OF FAITH

JAMES FREEMAN CLARKE
American preacher, 1810–1888

All human action, all good endeavor, all the progress of civilization, is the work of faith. In the eleventh chapter of the Epistle to the Hebrews the writer says that "by faith" Abraham, Isaac, Jacob, and all the great heroes of Israel accomplished their noble deeds. So it has been ever since. By faith the Apostle Paul crossed the Ægean Sea, and went from Asia to Europe to convert a new world to Christ. By faith the missionaries of the gospel went among the savage Goths and Vandals with the same divine purpose, and saved Roman civilization from ruin. By faith, in later days, the Jesuits went among the North American Indians, and Livingstone among the African barbarians, not counting their lives dear, so that they might finish their course with joy. By faith Coster invented the printing-press; by faith Watt discovered the steam-engine, Stephenson the locomotive, Daguerre the sunportraits. By faith Howard reformed the prisons; Wesley gave spiritual life to the lowest classes in England; Clarkson and Wilberforce abolished the slave trade; Garrison and Abraham Lincoln put an end to slavery in the United States. By faith Dr. Howe penetrated into the darkness of Laura Bridgman's mind and carried knowledge there. By faith Channing, Bushnell, and Theodore Parker shook the pillars of irrational belief. By faith Robertson and Stanley gave a larger life to the Church of England.

Thus we see that faith abides,—faith in truths as yet unseen, in laws not yet discovered, in great realities outside of our present vision. All human knowledge, human endeavor, earthly progress depends on faith that beyond what we know there is a great world of truth and good still to be discovered.

And this is, in reality, faith in God. For God is the eternal Truth, the omniscient Good. He is behind all things, before all things, and above all things. We do not see him, but faith leads directly and inevitably to him.

Every Day Religion

REVEALERS OF THE TRUTH[*]
EPICTETUS
Greek philosopher, born about 60 A. D.

O great good fortune! O great benefactor,
who shows us the way! And yet—though all
men have raised temples and altars to Triptol-
emus for teaching us the cultivation of the crops,
what man of you ever set up an altar in honor
of him who found the truth and brought it to
light and published it among all men—not the
truth of mere living, but the truth that leads
to right living? Who ever dedicated a shrine
or an image for this gift, or worships God for
it? I say, shall we, who offer sacrifices because the gods gave us wheat or the vine, never
give thanks to God that they produced this manner of fruit in the mind of men, whereby they
were to show us the true way of happiness?

Discourses and Manual of Epictetus
Trans. P. E. Matheson

BEING TRUE TO ONE'S CONVICTIONS *

Thomas H. Huxley

English biologist, 1825–1895

14 Waverley Place, Sept. 23, 1860.

My dear Kingsley:

My convictions, positive and negative, on all the matters of which you speak are of long and slow growth and are firmly rooted. I have searched over the grounds of my belief, and if wife and child and name and fame were all to be lost to me one after the other as the penalty, still I will not lie.

To begin with the great doctrine you discuss. I neither deny nor affirm the immortality of man. I see no reason for believing in it, but, on the other hand, I have no means of disproving it.

Pray understand that I have no *a priori* objections to the doctrine. No man who has to deal daily and hourly with nature can trouble himself about *a priori* difficulties. Give me such evidence as would justify me in believing anything else, and I will believe that. Why should I not? It is not half so wonderful as the conservation of force, or the indestructibility of matter. Whoso clearly appreciates all that is implied in the falling of a stone can have no difficulty about any doctrine simply on account of its marvelousness. But the longer I live, the more obvious it is to me that the most sacred act of a man's life is to say and to feel, "I believe such and such to be true." All the greatest rewards and all the heaviest penalties of existence cling about that act.

I cannot conceive of my personality as a thing apart from the phenomena of my life. Nor does it help me to tell me that the aspirations of mankind—that my own highest aspirations even—lead me towards the doctrine of immortality. I doubt the fact, to begin with; but if it be so, even, what is this but in grand words asking me to believe a thing because I like it? Science has taught to me the opposite lesson. My business is to teach my aspirations to conform themselves to fact, not to try and make facts harmonize with my aspirations.

Science seems to me to teach in the highest and strongest manner the great truth which is embodied in the Christian conception of entire surrender to the will of God. Sit down before fact as a little child, be prepared to give up every preconceived notion, follow humbly wherever and to whatever abysses nature leads, or you shall learn nothing. I have only begun to learn content and peace of mind since I have resolved at all risks to do this.

Kicked into the world a boy without guide or training, or with worse than none, I confess to my shame that few men have drunk deeper of all kinds of sin than I. Happily, my course was arrested in time—before I had earned absolute destruction—and for long years I have been slowly and painfully climbing, with many a fall, towards better things. And when I look back, what do I find to have been the agents of my redemption: the hope of immortality or of future reward? I can honestly say that for these fourteen years such a consideration has not entered my head. No, I can tell you exactly what has been at work. *Sartor Resartus* led me to know that a deep sense of religion was compatible with the entire absence of theology. Secondly, science and her methods gave me a resting-place independent of authority and tradition. Thirdly, love opened up to me a view of the sanctity of human nature, and impressed me with a deep sense of responsibility. I have spoken more openly and distinctly to you than I ever have to any human being except my wife.

If you can show me that I err in premises or conclusion, I am ready to give up these as I would any other theories. But at any rate you will do me the justice to believe that I have not reached my conclusions without the care befitting the momentous nature of the problems involved.

Ever yours very faithfully,

T. H. HUXLEY

(From a letter written by Thomas H. Huxley, after the death of a son, to Charles Kingsley.)

Life and Letters of Thomas H. Huxley
By his son, Leonard Huxley

THE LIFE OF THE INTELLECT

JOHN TYNDALL
British physicist, 1820–1893

It is perfectly possible for you and me to purchase intellectual peace at the price of intellectual death. The world is not without refuges of this description; nor is it wanting in persons who seek their shelter, and try to persuade others to do the same. The unstable and the weak have yielded and will yield to this persuasion, and they to whom repose is sweeter than the truth. But I would exhort you to refuse the offered shelter, and to scorn the base repose; to accept, if the choice be forced upon

you, commotion before stagnation, the leap of
the torrent before the stillness of the swamp.

From The Belfast Address

TRUTH

GEOFFREY CHAUCER

English poet, who established the use of the English
language in the writing of poetry; 1340?–1400

Flee   fro   the   prees,[1]   and   dwelle   with
    sothfastnesse,
Suffice unto thy thyng, though hit be smal;
For hord [2] hath hate, and clymbyng tikelnesse,
Prees hath envye, and wele blent overal; [3]
Savour no more than thee bihove [4] shal;
Werk wel thy-self, that other folk canst rede; [5]
And trouthe shal delivere, it is no drede.[6]

Tempest [7] thee noght [8] al croked [9] to redresse,
In trust of hir that turneth as a bal:
Gret reste stant [10] in litel besynesse;
An eek [11] be war [12] to sporne [13] ageyn an al; [14]
Stryve noght, as doth the crokke [15] with the wal.
Daunte [16] thyself, that dauntest otheres dede; [17]
And trouthe shal delivere, it is no drede.

That thee is sent, receyve in buxumnesse; [18]
The wrastling for this worlde axeth [19] a fal.
Her nis non hoom, [20] her nis but wildernesse;
Forth, pilgrim, forth! Forth, beste, out of thy
    stal!
Know thy contree, look up, thank God of al;
Hold the hye wey, [21] and lat thy gost [22] thee
    lede, [23]
And trouthe shal delivere, it is no drede.

---

1. crowd
2. plenty
3. well-being blinds everything
4. profit
5. counsel
6. doubt
7. violently distress thyself
8. not
9. crooked
10. stands
11. also
12. wary
13. kick
14. awl
15. crock
16. subdue
17. deed
18. obedience
19. requests
20. Here is not home
21. high way
22. spirit
23. lead

From *Truth*
The Chaucerian text as edited by
Alfred W. Pollard and others.

THE PURE LIGHT *
Christian, first century

The lamp of the body is the eye; if therefore
thine eye be single, thy whole body shall be full

of light. But if thine eye be evil, thy whole body shall be full of darkness. If therefore the light that is in thee be darkness, how great is the darkness!

Why beholdest thou the mote that is in thy brother's eye, but considerest not the beam that is in thine own eye? Or how wilt thou say to thy brother, Let me cast out the mote out of thine eye; and lo, the beam is in thine own eye? Thou hypocrite, cast out first the beam out of thine own eye; and then shalt thou see clearly to cast out the mote out of thy brother's eye.

Ye are the light of the world. A city set on a hill cannot be hid. Neither do men light a lamp and put it under the bushel, but on the stand; and it shineth unto all that are in the house. Let your light shine before men, that they may see your good works, and glorify your Father which is in heaven.

From *The Gospel According to Matthew*
New Testament

THE BEATITUDES
Christian, first century

Blessed are the poor in spirit:
  For theirs is the kingdom of heaven.

Blessed are they that mourn:
For they shall be comforted.
Blessed are the meek:
For they shall inherit the earth.
Blessed are they that hunger and thirst after
righteousness:
For they shall be filled.

Blessed are the merciful:
For they shall obtain mercy.
Blessed are the pure in heart:
For they shall see God.
Blessed are the peacemakers:
For they shall be called sons of God.

Blessed are they that have been persecuted for
righteousness' sake:
For theirs is the kingdom of heaven.

Blessed are ye when men shall reproach you,
and persecute you, and say all manner of evil
against you falsely, for my sake. Rejoice, and
be exceeding glad, for great is your reward in
heaven; for so persecuted they the prophets
which were before you.

From *The Gospel According to Matthew*
New Testament

TURNING GRIEF INTO THE GIVING
OF SUCCOR
John Bright
English statesman, 1811–1889

I was in the depths of grief, I might almost say of despair, for the light and sunshine of my house had been extinguished. All that was left on earth of my young wife, except the memory of a sainted life and a too brief happiness, was lying still and cold in the chamber above us. Mr. Cobden called upon me as his friend, and addressed me, as you might suppose, with words of condolence. After a time he looked up and said, "There are thousands of houses in England at this moment where wives, mothers, and children are dying of hunger. Now," he said, "when the first paroxysm of your grief is past, I would advise you to come with me, and we will never rest till the Corn Law is repealed."

I accepted his invitation. I knew that the description he had given of the homes of thousands was not an exaggerated description. I felt in my conscience that there was a work which somebody must do, and therefore I accepted his invitation, and from that time we never ceased to labor hard on behalf of the resolution which we had made.

Now, do you suppose that I wish you to imagine that he and I, when I say "we," were the only persons engaged in this great question? We were not even the first, though afterwards, perhaps, we became the foremost before the public. But there were others before us; and we were joined, not by scores, but by hundreds, and afterwards by thousands, and afterwards by countless multitudes; and afterwards famine itself, against which we had warred, joined us; and a great minister was converted, and minorities became majorities, and finally the barrier was entirely thrown down. And since then though there has been suffering, and much suffering, in many homes in England, yet no wife and no mother and no little child has been starved to death as the result of a famine made by law.

Life of John Bright
G. M. Trevelyan

CLEMENT ANTONINUS *
MARCUS AURELIUS
Roman emperor and Stoic philosopher, 121–180

A LETTER WRITTEN BY LUCIUS VERUS TO MARCUS AURELIUS

(Lucius Verus was an adopted brother, whom Marcus named as coëmperor. Avidius Cassius was military governor of Syria. Ed.)

Dear Marcus:

Avidius Cassius is avid to be Emperor, at least he seems so to me; and long ago in my grandfather's time, your father's time, he showed himself so. I wish you would see that he is kept under observation. He is dissatisfied with everything we do, he is collecting great resources, and he laughs at our letters. He calls you a philosophical old woman and me a prodigal fool. Please consider what should be done. I don't dislike the man; but, if you keep in the camp a man whom the soldiers like to hear and like to see, look out lest you mismanage your own interests and your children's.

LUCIUS VERUS.

THE REPLY OF MARCUS AURELIUS

Dear Lucius:

I have read your letter; it is rather more anxious-minded than becomes an Emperor, and does not accord with present-day usage. For if Heaven has destined Cassius to receive the Empire, we could not kill him even if we wished. You remember your great-grandfather's saying: "No man can kill his successor." And if not, without any act of severity on our part, he will of himself fall into the trap of fate. Besides we cannot make him out a traitor; nobody has come forward to accuse him, and as you yourself say, the soldiers love him. And also, it is in the nature of trials for high treason that people think that even those whose guilt is proved are the victims of power. So let him go his own gait, especially as he is a good general, strict and brave; indeed the State cannot do without him. As to your suggestion that I should safeguard the welfare of my children by putting him to death, oh, no; if Avidius deserves more than my children to be loved, and if it is better for the Empire that Cassius live rather than they, let them perish.

MARCUS.

(Ten years later, believing that Marcus was dead, Cassius launched the rebellion. The following is part of the speech read by Marcus to his soldiers. Ed.)

Fellow soldiers: I do not come before you to express indignation nor to complain. Is it right to be angry with the divine will, in whose power all things are? But perhaps one may pity those who meet misfortune without their fault; and that is now my case. Is it not very hard for us to pass on from war to war? Is it not horrible to be at war with our own people? But to find there is no loyalty in men outdoes such hardship and outdoes such horror. My very best friend has plotted against me and forced me, against my will, to take the field, though I have committed no act of injustice, nor done what I ought not to have done. What virtue or friendship can be counted on as sure after this experience of mine? Has not faith suffered wreck, has not good hope suffered wreck? If I alone were in danger, I should have made light of the affair, for I was not born immortal; but as there has been public secession, or rather rebellion, and the war affects us all, I cannot. I should have liked, had it been possible, to summon Cassius to come into court and argue the matter out with him, either before you or before the Senate; and I would gladly have resigned my throne in his favor without a struggle if that had seemed for the good of the State. For it is for the sake of the State that I undergo hardship and danger, and have spent so much time here away from

Italy, although I am now an old man, without much strength, and cannot take food without distress, nor sleep without worry. But since Cassius would never be willing to agree to such a meeting,—for how could he put faith in me after he has been so faithless to me?—you must be of good courage.

There is but one thing that I am afraid of, fellow soldiers, for I shall speak the whole truth to you, and that is lest he kill himself, to avoid the shame of coming into our presence, or that someone else, knowing that I am on the way to take the field against him, may do the deed. Then I shall be robbed of the great prize of victorious war, such as no man ever had. What is that prize? To forgive the man who has done me wrong, to remain a friend to him who has violated my friendship, and to remain faithful to him after he has broken faith with me. Perhaps you find this hard to understand, but you ought not to disbelieve it. For all good things have not utterly perished from the earth; there is in us still a remnant of our antique virtue. And if anyone does disbelieve it, that makes me wish so much the more for him to behold what he would not believe could be done. I should at least derive some profit from the present evils, if I were able to settle

the matter with honor, and show to all the world
that it is possible to deal righteously even with
civil war.

(Cassius was killed; the rebellion failed. Marcus wrote as follows to the Roman Senate. Ed.)

With respect to Cassius's rebellion, I beg and
beseech you, Conscript Fathers, to put aside
thoughts of punishment and have regard for my
notions, or rather yours, of duty and of mercy:
let not the Senate condemn a single man to
death. Let no Senator be punished, no nobleman's blood be spilt, let the banished come home,
let the proscribed take back their property.
Would that I could call back from the dead those
who have already suffered the penalty! The
punishments inflicted by an emperor for wrongs
done him are never in favor; the more just he is,
the crueler he will be thought. So you will
please pardon the children of Avidius Cassius,
his son-in-law, and wife. But why should I
say "pardon"? For they have done nothing.
Let them live in safety, and know that they
live under Marcus. Let them live on the patri-
mony alloted to them, let them enjoy their gold,
their silver, and their clothes; let them be rich,
unmolested, and free to go about at will; let
them take about everywhere, in all countries,

this example of your and my conception of what is right. Nor is the exemption of children and wives from proscription, Conscript Fathers, a great act of clemency. Indeed, I ask of you to deliver all of the Senatorial and Equestrian orders who were privy to the rebellion from death, proscription, fear, disgrace, or odium, and in short from every evil consequence, and confer this upon my reign, that public opinion shall approve the death of every man who in time of rebellion has lost his life for treason.

(The Senate, which in time of alarm had proclaimed Cassius a public enemy and confiscated his property, hailed this act of clemency with tumultuous approval. Ed.)

Pious Antoninus, may the gods keep you! Clement Antoninus, may the gods keep you! You have willed what was right, we have done our duty. No violence has power to hurt a good government. We ask that you stay in Rome. In the name of your philosophy, your patience, your learning, your nobility, your goodness— You conquer your enemies and overcome them that hate you, for the gods protect you.

Marcus Aurelius
Henry Dwight Sedgwick

DR. JESSE W. LAZEAR

WALTER REED

American military surgeon and bacteriologist; discoverer of the cause of yellow fever infection as the bite of a certain species of mosquito; 1851–1902

It is fitting that I should pay brief tribute to the memory of a former member of this Faculty, the late Dr. Jesse W. Lazear, United States Army. I can hardly trust myself to speak of my late colleague, since the mention of his name brings back such scenes of anxiety and depression as one recalls only with pain. Along with these sad memories, however, come other recollections of a manly and fearless devotion to duty such as I have never seen equaled. In this discharge of the latter, Dr. Lazear seemed absolutely tireless and quite oblivious of self. Filled with an earnest enthusiasm for the advancement of his profession and for the cause of science, he let no opportunity pass unimproved. Although the evening might find him discouraged over the difficulties at hand, with the morning's return he again took up the task full of eagerness and hope. During a service of less than a year in Cuba he won the good will and respect of his brother officers and the affection of his immediate associates. Almost at the beginning of what promised to be a life full of usefulness and good works he was suddenly stricken, and, dying, added one more name to that imperishable roll of honor in which none others belong than martyrs to the cause of humanity. It is my own earnest wish that, whatever credit may hereafter be given to the work of the American Commission in Cuba during the past year, the name of my late colleague, Dr. Lazear, may be always associated therewith.

(From an address before the Medical and Chirurgical Faculty of Maryland, 1901.)

Member of the Yellow Fever Commission in 1900 with the rank of Acting Assistant Surgeon. He died of yellow fever at Quemados, Cuba, 28 of September, 1900. With more than the courage and devotion of the soldier, he risked and lost his life to show how a fearful pestilence is communicated and how ravages may be prevented.

(From the inscription, written by Charles W. Eliot, on a memorial tablet erected by the friends of Dr. Lazear at the Johns Hopkins Hospital.)

> *Walter Reed and Yellow Fever*
> Howard A. Kelly

THE LAST WORDS OF
CAPTAIN SCOTT *

Robert F. Scott

English explorer, who reached the South Pole one
month after Amundsen, the discoverer; 1868–1912

[The principal aim of (Capt. R. F. Scott) was
the advancement of knowledge. Readers of his
journal will be deeply impressed with the beauty
of his character. The chief traits which shone forth
through his life were conspicuous in the hour of his
death. There was no thought of himself, only the
earnest desire to give comfort and consolation to
others in their sorrow. His very last lines were
written lest he who induced him to enter upon
Antarctic work should now feel regret for what
he had done: "If I cannot write to Sir Clements,
tell him I thought much of him, and never re-
gretted his putting me in command of the *Discovery.*"

Sir Clements R. Markham.]

Extracts from two of the twelve letters Capt.
Scott wrote during the last few days of his expedition to the South Pole:

(To Mrs. Bowers)

My dear Mrs. Bowers,

I am afraid this will reach you after one of
the heaviest blows of your life.

I write when we are very near the end of
our journey, and I am finishing it in company

with two gallant, noble gentlemen. One of these is your son. He had come to be one of my closest and soundest friends, and I appreciate his wonderful upright nature, his ability and energy. As the troubles have thickened, his dauntless spirit ever shone brighter and he has remained cheerful, hopeful, and indomitable to the end.

My whole heart goes out in pity for you.

Yours,

R. SCOTT

To the end he has talked of you and his sisters. One sees what a happy home he must have had and perhaps it is well to look back on nothing but happiness.

He remains unselfish, self-reliant, and splendidly hopeful to the end, believing in God's mercy to you.

(To SIR J. M. BARRIE)

My dear Barrie,

We are pegging out in a very comfortless spot. Hoping this letter may be found and sent to you, I write a word of farewell. We are showing that Englishmen can still die with a bold spirit, fighting it out to the end. It will be known that we have accomplished our object in reaching the Pole, and that we have done everything possible, even to sacrificing ourselves in

order to save sick companions. Goodbye. I
am not at all afraid of the end, but sad to miss
many a humble pleasure which I had planned
for the future on our long marches. I may not
have proved a great explorer, but we have done
the greatest march ever made and come very
near to great success. Goodbye, my dear
friend,

Yours ever,

R. SCOTT

Later (*in the same note*)—We are very near
the end, but have not and will not lose our good
cheer. We have had four days of storm in our
tent, and nowhere's food or fuel. We did in-
tend to finish ourselves when things proved like
this, but we have decided to die naturally in the
track.

Scott's Last Expedition
Ed. Leonard Huxley

SOCRATES' SPEECH AT THE TRIAL[*]

PLATO

Greek philosopher: disciple of
Socrates, and teacher of Aristotle; 427–347 B. C.

The truth is this. I am more than seventy
years old, and this is the first time I have ever

come before a court of law. I have to defend myself, Athenians, against the charges of my accusers.

I have made many enemies and people say that I am "a wise man." For the bystanders always think that I am wise myself in any matter wherein I convict another man of ignorance. But, my friends, I believe that only God is really wise. And the young men follow me about, (and) try their hands at cross-examining other people, and I imagine they find a great abundance of men who think that they know a great deal when in fact they know little or nothing. And then the persons who are cross-examined get angry with me instead of with themselves and say that Socrates is an abominable fellow who corrupts young men.

Perhaps some one will say: "Are you not ashamed, Socrates, of following pursuits which are very likely now to cause your death?" I should answer him with justice, and say, "My friend, if you think that a man of any worth at all ought to reckon the hours of life and death when he acts, or that he ought to think of anything but whether he is acting rightly or wrongly, and as a good or a bad man would act, you are grievously mistaken." For this, Athenians, I believe to be the truth: wherever ⸲

man's post is, whether he has chosen it of his own will or whether he has been placed at it by his commander, there it is his duty to remain and face the danger, without thinking of death, or of any other thing except dishonor.

When the generals whom you chose to command me, Athenians, placed me at my post at Potidæa, and at Amphipolis, and at Delium, I remained where they placed me and ran the risk of death, like other men; and it would be very strange conduct on my part if I were to desert my post now from fear of death or of any other thing when God has commanded me, as I am persuaded that he has done, to spend my life in searching for wisdom, and in examining myself and others. For to fear death, my friends, is only to think ourselves wise without being wise: for it is to think that we know what we do not know. For anything that men can tell, death may be the greatest good that can happen to them; but they fear it as if they knew quite well that it is the greatest of evils.

If you were to say to me, "Socrates, this time we will let you go, but on this condition, that you cease from carrying on this search of yours, and from philosophy; if you are found following those pursuits again, you shall die": I say, if you offered to let me go on these terms, I should reply, "Athenians, I hold you in the highest regard and love, but I will obey God rather than you; and as long as I have breath and strength I will not cease from philosophy, and from exhorting you, and declaring the truth to every one of you whom I meet, saying, as I am wont, 'You are a citizen of Athens, a city which is very great and very famous for wisdom and power of mind. Are you not ashamed of caring so much for the making of money, and for reputation? Will you not think or care about wisdom, and truth, and the perfection of your soul?'" And therefore, Athenians, either acquit me, or do not acquit me; but be sure that I shall not alter my way of life; no, not if I have to die for it many times.

(He is found guilty, by 281 to 220 votes, and is condemned to death)

Perhaps, my friends, you think that I have been defeated because I was wanting in the arguments by which I could have persuaded you to acquit me. There are some things which neither I nor any other man may do in order to escape from death. There are many ways of avoiding death in every danger, if a man will not scruple to say and to do anything. But, my friends, I think that it is a much harder thing to escape from wickedness than from death; for wickedness is swifter than death. And now I, who am old and slow, have been overtaken by the slower pursuer; and my accusers, who are clever and swift, have been overtaken by the swifter pursuer, which is wickedness. And now I shall go hence, sentenced by you to death; and they will go hence, sentenced by truth to receive the penalty of wickedness and evil. Perhaps it was right for these things to be so; and I think that they are fairly measured.

If we reflect we shall see that we may well hope that death is a good. For the state of death is one of two things: either the dead man wholly ceases to be, and loses all sensation; or, according to the common belief, it is a change and a migration of the soul into another place. And if death is the absence of all sensation, and like the sleep of one whose slumbers are unbroken by any dreams, it will be a wonderful gain. If that is the nature of death, I for one count it a gain. For then it appears that eternity is nothing more than a single night.

But if death is a journey to another place, and the common belief be true, that there are all who have died, what good could be greater than this, my judges? What would you not give to converse with Orpheus and Hesiod and Homer?

I am willing to die many times, if this be true.

And you, too, judges, must face death with a good courage, and believe this as a truth, that no evil can happen to a good man, either in life or after death.

The Apology
Trans. F. J. Church

THE BETTER PART
MATTHEW ARNOLD
English essayist and poet, 1822–1888

Long fed on boundless hopes, O race of man,
How angrily thou spurn'st all simpler fare!
"Christ," someone says, "was human as we are;
No judge eyes us from Heaven, our sin to scan;

We live no more, when we have done our span."
"Well, then, for Christ," thou answerest, "who
    can care?
From sin, which Heaven records not, why
    forbear?
Live we like brutes, our life without a plan!"

So answerest thou; but why not rather say:
"Hath man no second life?—*Pitch this one*
    high!
Sits there no judge in Heaven, our sin to see?

More strictly, then, the inward judge obey!
Was Christ a man like us? *Ah! let us try*
If we then, too, can be such men as he!"

THE IMITATION OF CHRIST*
Thomas à Kempis
German mystic, 1380–1471

The more a man is at one within himself and
becometh single in heart, so much the more and
higher things doth he without labor understand;
for that he receiveth the light of the understanding from above. A pure, sincere, and
stable spirit is not distracted in a multitude of
works; for that it worketh all to the honor of
God, and inwardly striveth to be at rest from
all self-seeking.

Truly, when the day of judgment cometh, we
shall not be examined as to what we have read,
but what we have done; not how well we have
spoken, but how religiously we have lived. And
he is truly very learned that doeth the will of
God, and forsaketh his own will.

Fire proveth iron, and temptation a just man.
We know not oftentimes what we are able to do,
but temptation sheweth us what we are.

Yet we must be watchful, especially in the beginning of the temptation; for the enemy is then more easily overcome, if he be not suffered in any wise to enter the door of our hearts, but be resisted without the gate at his first knock.

Without charity the outward work profiteth nothing; but whatsoever is done of charity, be it never so little and contemptible in the sight of the world, it becometh wholly fruitful. For God weigheth more the love out of which a man worketh than the work which he doeth.

Endeavor to be patient in bearing with the defects and infirmities of others, of what sort soever they be; for that thyself also hast many failings which must be borne with by others. If thou canst not make thyself such an one as thou wouldest, how wilt thou be able to have another in all things to thy liking?

We would willingly have others perfect, and yet we amend not our own faults. We will have others severely corrected, and will not be corrected ourselves. The large liberty of others displeaseth us, and yet we will not have our own desires denied us. We will have others bound down by ordinances, and in no sort do we ourselves endure further restraint.

And thus it appeareth how seldom we weigh

our neighbor in the same balance with ourselves.

Oftentimes, too, we perceive not our own inward blindness how great it is. Oftentimes we do evil, and excuse it worse. We are sometimes moved with passion, and we think it zeal. We reprehend small things in others, and pass over our own greater matters. Quickly enough we feel and weigh what we suffer at the hands of others; but we mind not how much others suffer from us. He that well and rightly considereth his own works will find little cause to judge hardly of another.

Count not of great importance who is for thee, or against thee; but let this be thy aim and care, that God be with thee in everything thou doest.

Great tranquillity of heart hath he that careth neither for the praises nor the fault-finding of men. He will easily be content and pacified whose conscience is pure. Thou art not the more holy, if thou art praised; nor the more worthless, if thou art found fault with. What thou art, that thou art; neither by words canst thou be made greater than what thou art in the sight of God.

If thou consider what thou art within thee, thou wilt not care what men talk of thee.

Man looketh on the countenance, but God on
the heart.   Man considereth the deeds, but God
weigheth the intentions.

Of the Imitation of Christ

THE HUMAN CHRIST
Charles F. Dole
American preacher and writer, 1845–1927

I carry a beautiful picture enshrined in my
mind.   It is the image of the perfect man.
Strength, justice, courage, truth, grace, faithfulness are in every line of the face.   Kindness,
sympathy, hope, gladness, enthusiasm, constant
good-will shine out of the eyes.

Unknown cost of effort, peril, pain, sorrow,
and sympathy has gone into this face.   But it
is not worn or sad.   The look of victory is there
—of good overcoming evil.   There is firm rebuke in the face of the picture, at meanness,
oppression, cruelty, selfishness, and pride.
But infinite humanity also is there, as of one
who believes in me to the last, expects the best
of me, is determined to win me to his radiant
faith in the right.   The face is not too serious;
it casts on me many a smile of genial good humor.   There is no companionship in the world

quite equal to it. In its presence I am refreshed, strengthened, and heartened for every enterprise.

No one has ever seen in bodily form the ideal face of my picture. It belongs to no single nation, or color, or race, or religion. It is not man alone; it has womanly tenderness along with its strength. It is as pure of evil thought as it is fearless of danger. It is a universal man, the son and heir of the universe. It is the image of God; it is doubtless my best self —the man I would choose to become.

The man in the shrine of my heart is like a wonderful composite photograph. All illustrious human persons and values have gone into making it. Whatever faults and foibles good men have ever had fall away. All the good are in my picture, but it is greater than any one of them all. The prophet of Nazareth, who blessed little children, is with me, and many a dim figure of great prophets before him. The Buddha is with me, with his vast pity for suffering humanity. Socrates, drinking the hemlock and scorning to save his life by running away from his duty, has entered into the soul of my picture. The brave English King Alfred is there, and many a true-hearted statesman and patriot: our own Washington at Valley Forge.

and Abraham Lincoln writing the Proclamation of Emancipation, or visiting his wounded soldiers in the hospitals. The men and women who have made and moulded the lives of each of us are in the picture, loving fathers and mothers, high-minded teachers, honest merchants, faithful workmen, good physicians. Even the heroes of story are with us—the noble bishop in *Les Misérables, Romola,* and *Adam Bede.* Contributions fresh from human life go daily into making my picture. It is never complete, because it is infinite, like the life of God. Yet nothing that I possess is so real.

I too help in making the picture. Every good thought, every kind act or word, every utterance of good-will develops and deepens the picture. To know the real man in my heart, to love him, to keep company with him; most of all, to do his bidding and not to dare or wish to move against his will—this is to be at one with myself; this is to love all true men everywhere; this is the essence of worship and communion with God.

JESUS

Theodore Parker
American preacher and reformer, 1810–1860

O thou great friend to all the sons of men,
Who once appeared in humblest guise below,
Sin to rebuke and break the captive's chain,
To call thy brethren forth from want and woe,—
Thee would I sing. Thy truth is still the light
Which guides the nations—groping on their way,
Stumbling and falling in disastrous night,
Yet hoping ever for the perfect day:
Yes, thou art still the Life, thou art the Way
The holiest know,—Light, Life, and Way of
 Heaven!
And they who dearest hope and deepest pray
Toil by the Light, Life, Way which thou hast
 given.
And by thy truth aspiring mortals trust
To uplift their bleeding brothers from the dust.

Autobiography, Poems, and Prayers

The Home

JESUS AND THE CHILDREN
Christian, first century

In that hour came the disciples unto Jesus, saying, "Who is then greatest in the kingdom of heaven?" And he called to him a little child, and set him in the midst of them, and said: "Verily I say unto you, except ye turn, and become as little children, ye shall in no wise enter into the kingdom of heaven. Whosoever therefore shall humble himself as this little child, the same is the greatest in the kingdom of heaven. And whoso shall receive one such little child in my name receiveth me; but whoso shall cause one of these little ones which believe on me to stumble, it is profitable for him that a great millstone should be hanged about his neck, and that he should be sunk in the depth of the sea."

Then were there brought unto him little children, that he should lay his hands on them, and pray; and the disciples rebuked them. But

Jesus said, "Suffer little children, and forbid them not, to come unto me: for of such is the kingdom of heaven."

From *The Gospel According to Matthew*
New Testament

CHILDREN

ALGERNON CHARLES SWINBURNE
English poet, 1837–1909

Of such is the kingdom of heaven.
   No glory that ever was shed
From the crowning star of the seven
   That crown the north world's head;

No word that ever was spoken
   Of human or godlike tongue
Gave ever such godlike token
   Since human harps were strung.

No sign that ever was given
   To faithful or faithless eyes
Showed ever beyond clouds riven
   So clear a Paradise.

Earth's creeds may be seventy times **seven**
   And blood have defiled each creed,
If of such be the kingdom of heaven,
   It must be heaven indeed.

Appearing as *xxii* in *A Dark Month*

FIRST FOOTSTEPS

ALGERNON CHARLES SWINBURNE
English poet, 1837–1909

A little way, more soft and sweet
　　Than field aflower with May,
A babe's feet, venturing, scarce complete
　　　　A little way.

Eyes full of dawning day
　　Look up for mother's eyes to meet,
Too blithe for song to-day.

Glad as the golden spring to greet
　　Its first live leaflet's play,
Love, laughing, leads the little feet
　　　　A little way.

THE BEGINNING

RABINDRANATH TAGORE
Philosopher and poet of India, 1861–1941

"Where have I come from, where did you
pick me up?" the baby asked its mother.

She, half crying, half laughing, and clasping
the baby to her breast,—

"You were hidden in my heart as its desire, my darling.

You were in the dolls of my childhood's games; and when with clay I made the image of my god every morning, I made and unmade you then.

You were enshrined with our household deity, in his worship I worshiped you.

In all my hopes and my loves, in my life, in the life of my mother, you have lived.

In the lap of the deathless Spirit who rules our home you have been nursed for ages.

When in girlhood my heart was opening its petals, you hovered as a fragrance about it.

Your tender softness bloomed in my youthful limbs, like a glow in the sky before the sunrise.

Heaven's first darling, twin-born with the morning light, you have floated down the stream of the world's life, and at last you have stranded on my heart.

As I gaze on your face, mystery overwhelms me: you who belong to all have become mine.

For fear of losing you I hold you tight to my breast. What magic has snared the world's treasure in these slender arms of mine?"

The Crescent Moon

MY LITTLE CHILD

RABINDRANATH TAGORE

Philosopher and poet of India, 1861–1941

Say of him what you please, but I know my child's failings.

I do not love him because he is good, but because he is my little child.

How should you know how dear he can be when you try to weigh his merits against his faults?

When I must punish him, he becomes all the more a part of my being.

When I cause his tears to come, my heart weeps with him.

I alone have a right to blame and punish, for he only may chastise who loves.

The Crescent Moon

THE AMERICAN BOY

THEODORE ROOSEVELT

President of the United States, 1858–1919

Of course, what we have a right to expect of the American boy is that he shall turn out to be a good American man. Now, the chances are strong that he won't be much of a man unless he is a good deal of a boy. He must not be a coward or a weakling, a bully, a shirk, or a prig. He must work hard and play hard. He must be clean-minded and clean-lived, and able to hold his own under all circumstances and against all comers. It is only on these conditions that he will grow into the kind of American man of whom America can be really proud.

The Roosevelt Book

TAURI'S SONG *
Laguna Indian (Pueblo)

Tauri (young Eagle) was at work far from his native village. When asked for a song, he said, "I will sing you my own song that I sing to my wife."

"But how can you sing to her when she is at home in Laguna and you are here?"

"I sing to her though I am far away, and she, too, sings to me. The meaning of my song is this: I am here, working for you. All the while I work, I think of you. Take care of yourself, and take care of the horses, and the sheep, and the fields."

"But your song has no words."

"No, but this is what it means. So, when I am far away, we sing to each other."

The Indian Book
Comp. Natalie Curtis

LOVE AND RELIGION
Henri Frédéric Amiel
Swiss scholar and writer, 1821-1881

Love at its highest point—love sublime, unique, invincible—leads us straight to the brink of the great abyss, for it speaks to us directly of the infinite and of eternity. It is eminently religious; it may even become religion. When all around a man is wavering and changing, when everything is growing dark and featureless to him in the far distance of an unknown future, when the world seems but a fiction or a fairy tale, and the universe a chimera, when the whole edifice of ideas vanishes in smoke, and all realities are penetrated with doubt, what is the fixed point which may still be his? The faithful heart of a woman! There he may rest his head; there he will find strength to live, strength to believe, and, if need be, strength to die in peace with a benediction on his lips. Who knows if love and its beatitude,

clear manifestation as it is of the universal
harmony of things, is not the best demonstration of a fatherly and understanding God, just
as it is the shortest road by which to reach
him? Love is a faith, and one faith leads to
another.

Journal
Trans. Mrs. Humphry Ward

THE DEAR TOGETHERNESS
WILLIAM CHANNING GANNETT
American preacher and hymn writer, 1840–1923

I dreamed of paradise,—and still,
Though sun lay soft on vale and hill
And trees were green and rivers bright,
The one dear thing that made delight,
By sun or stars or Eden weather,
Was just that we two were together.

I dreamed of heaven,—with God so near!
The angels trod the shining sphere,
And each was beautiful; the days
Were choral work, were choral praise:
And yet in heaven's far-shining weather
The best was, still,—we were together!

I woke,—and lo, my dream was true,
The happy dream of me and you!
For Eden, heaven, no need to roam,—
The foretaste of it all is home,
Where you and I through this world's weather
Still work and praise and thank together.

Together weave from love a nest
For all that's good and sweet and blest
To brood in, till it come a face,
A voice, a soul, a child's embrace,—
And then what peace of Bethlehem weather,
What songs as we go on together!

Together greet life's solemn real,
Together own one glad ideal,
Together laugh, together ache,
And think one thought, "each other's sake,"
And hope one hope,—in new world weather
To still go on, and go together!

The Thought of God

THE PEASANT WOMAN *

CATHERINE BRESHKOVSKY

Russian: "The Little Grandmother of the Russian Revolution"; for thirty-two years in prison, or in exile in Siberia; 1844–1934

Nothing is so wonderfully majestic as a good sample of a peasant woman. She is robust, benevolent, and condescending. Conscious of her vivid strength, she works and surveys like an energetic queen, fearing nothing, and acting for ten persons at once. All her dozen children do not embarrass her. Every one gets his place, his occupation, and she rules the house just by words and smiles. Such women are the benefit of every people, and the blessing of the world.

Our Russian women are not only brave but endowed with a delicious tenderness of heart; and both these qualities make them unselfish, ready to help, and to take upon their shoulders every hard work.

The Little Grandmother of the Russian Revolution

Ed. Alice Stone Blackwell

A PIONEER MOTHER [*]
Hamlin Garland
American novelist and poet, 1860–1940

She was neither witty, nor learned in books, nor wise in the ways of the world, but I contend that her life was noble. There was something in her unconscious heroism which transcends wisdom and the deeds of those who dwell in the rose-golden light of romance. Now that her life is rounded into the silence whence it came, its significance appears.

To me she was never young, for I am her son, and as I first remember her she was a large, handsome, smiling woman—deft and powerful of movement, sweet and cheery of smile and voice. She played the violin then, and I recall how she used to lull me to sleep at night with simple tunes like "Money Musk" and "Dan Tucker." She sang, too, and I remember her clear soprano rising out of the singing of the Sunday congregation at the schoolhouse with thrilling sweetness and charm. Her hair was dark, her eyes brown, her skin fair and her lips rested in lines of laughter.

My father's return from the war brought solace and happiness, but increased her labors, for he set to work with new zeal to widen his acres of plow-land.

I have the sweetest recollections of my mother's desire to make us happy each Christmas-time, and to this end she planned jokes for herself and little surprises for us. We were desperately poor in those days, for my father was breaking the tough sod of the natural meadows and grubbing away trees from the hillside, "opening a farm," as he called it, and there was hardly enough extra money to fill three stockings with presents. So it came about that mother's stocking often held more rags and potatoes than silks or silverware. But she always laughed and we considered it all very good fun then. Its pathos makes my heart ache now.

I don't know what her feelings were about these constant removals to the border, but I suspect now that each new migration was a greater hardship than those which preceded it. With the blindness of youth and the spirit of seeking which I inherited I saw no tear on my mother's face. I inferred that she, too, was eager and exalted at the thought of "going West." I now see that she must have suffered each time the bitter pangs of doubt and unrest which strike through the woman's heart when called upon to leave her snug, safe fire for a ruder cabin in strange lands.

Our new house was a small one with but three rooms below and two above, but it had a little lean-to which served as a summer kitchen. It was a bare home, with no touch of grace other than that given by my mother's cheery presence. Her own room was small and crowded, but as she never found time to occupy it save to sleep I hope it did not trouble her as it does me now as I look back to it.

Each year, as our tilled acres grew, churning and washing and cooking became harder, until at last it was borne in upon my boyish mind that my mother was condemned to never-remitting labor. She was up in the morning before the light, cooking breakfast for us all, and she seldom went to bed before my father. She was not always well and yet the work had to be done. We all worked in those days, even my little sister ran on errands; and perhaps this was the reason why we did not realize more fully the grinding weight of drudgery which fell on this pioneer's wife.

Churning and milking we boys did for her, and the old up and down churn was a dreaded beast to us as it was to all the boys of the countryside; and yet I knew mother ought not to do such work, and I went to the dasher regularly but with a wry face. Father was not niggardly of labor-saving implements, and a clothes-wringer and washer and a barrel churn came along and they helped a little, but work never "lets up" on a farm. There are always three meals to get and the dishes to wash, and each day is like another so far as duties are concerned. Sunday brings little rest for housewives even in winter.

But into those monotonous days some pleasure came. The neighbors dropped in of a summer evening, and each Sunday we drove away to church. In winter we attended all the "lyceums" and church "sociables," and took part in occasional "surprise parties." In all these neighborhood jollities my mother had a generous hand. Her coming always added to the fun. "Here comes Mrs. Garland!" some one would say, and every face shone brighter because of her smile.

At last a great change came to us all. My parents and my sister and brother journeyed westward into South Dakota and settled in the little town of Ordway, on a treeless plain, while I turned eastward, intent on further education.

I mention this going especially because, when

it became certain that my people were leaving never to return, the neighbors thronged about the house one August day to say good-by, and with appropriate speeches presented mother with some silver and glassware. These were the first nice dishes she had ever owned and she was too deeply touched to speak a word of thanks. But the givers did not take so much virtue to themselves. Some of them were women who had known the touch of my mother's hand in sickness and travail. Others had seen her close the eyes of their dead—for she had come to be a mother to every one who suffered. Those who brought the richest gifts considered them a poor return for her own unstinting helpfulness.

I did not see her again for nearly four years, and my heart contracted with a sudden pain at sight of her. She was growing old. Her hair was gray, and as she spoke, her voice was weak and tremulous. She was again on the farm and working as of old—like one on a treadmill. My father, too, was old. He had not prospered. A drought had swept over the fair valley and men on all sides were dropping away into despair.

Old as she was, and suffering constantly from

pain in her feet and ankles, she was still mother
to every one who suffered. Even while I was
there she got up on two demands in the middle
of the night and rode away across the plain in
answer to some suffering woman's call for help.
She knew death intimately. She had closed the
eyes of many a world-weary wife or suffering
child, and more than once a poor outcast woman
of the town, sick and alone, felt the pitying
touch of her lips.

I saw with greater clearness than ever before
the lack of beauty in her life. She had a few
new things, but they were all cheap and poor.
She now had one silk dress—which her son had
sent her. All else was calico. But worse than
all was the bleak, burning, wind-swept plain—
treeless, scorched, and silent save for the song
of the prairie lark. I felt the monotony of
her surroundings with greater keenness than
ever before.

Our parting at this time was the most painful moment of my life. I had my work to do in
Boston. I could earn nothing out on the plain,
so I must go, but I promised it would not be for
long. In my heart I determined that the remainder of her life should be freer from care
and fuller of joy. I resolved to make a home

for her in some more hospitable land, but the cling of her arms to my neck remained with me many days.

I have a purpose in this frank disclosure of my mother's life. It is not from any self-complacency, God knows, for I did so little and it came so late—I write in the hope of making some other work-weary mother happy. There is nothing more appealing to me than neglected age. To see an old father or mother sitting in loneliness and poverty dreaming of an absent son who never comes, of a daughter who never writes, is to me more moving than Hamlet or Othello. If we are false to those who gave us birth we are false indeed.

Most of us in America are the children of working people, and the toil-worn hands of our parents should be heaped to overflowing with whatever good things success brings to us. They bent to the plow and the washboard when we were helpless. They clothed us when clothing was bought with blood, and we should be glad to return this warmth, this protection, an hundredfold. Fill their rooms with sunshine and the odor of flowers—you sons and daughters of the pioneers of America. Gather them around you, let them share in your success, and

when some one looks askance at them, stand
beside them and say: "These gray old heads,
these gnarled limbs, sheltered me in days when
I was weak and life was stern."

Then will the debt be lessened—for in such
coin alone can the wistful hearts be paid.

A Pioneer Mother

THE MOTHER AND THE CHILD *
Maria Montessori
Italian educator, 1870—

We deceive ourselves in thinking that we give
all to the child when we give him air and food.
Food and air are not enough for man's body:
all the physiological functions depend on the
well-being, and that is the only key to the whole
of life. So also the child's body lives by the
freedom of the soul.

A new hour is about to strike for the relations between mother and child. The modern
mother, who is prepared to care perfectly for
the physical life, and who for such a mission
has only yesterday opened her mind to new
studies and new ideas and has accepted new responsibilities, is about to take a step forward.
Like care, dictated by science, will be demanded
of her tomorrow for the intellectual hygiene of

the child and for the health of his inner life.

No longer will medicine alone furnish her the necessary teachings, but also a renewed pedagogy based on the positive facts of science. The girls who yesterday in order to be better mothers took hospital training will tomorrow go to children's schools to learn the art of protecting the new lives which are about to be intrusted to them by nature. Then the maternal mission will become complete, and woman will turn her step toward motherhood with open eyes and with the dignity of one who is no longer only a creator, but also a protector, of posterity, one who guards and saves the body and mind of the new humanity.

The Mother and the Child

THE RIGHT OF THE CHILD *
FRIEDERICH FROEBEL
German philosopher and educator, founder of the kindergarten; 1782–1852

All that does not grow out of one's inner being, all that is not one's own original feeling and thought, or that at least does not awaken that, oppresses and defaces the individuality of man instead of calling it forth, and nature becomes thereby a caricature. Shall we never cease to stamp human nature, even in childhood, like coins; to overlay it with foreign images and foreign superscriptions, instead of letting it develop itself and grow into form according to the law of life planted in it by God the Father, so that it may be able to bear the stamp of the divine, and become an image of God?

This theory of love is to serve as the highest goal and pole-star of human education, and must be attended to in the germ of humanity, the child, and truly in his very first impulses. The conquest of self-seeking egoism is the most important task of education; for selfishness isolates the individual from all communion, and kills the life-giving principle of love. Therefore the first object of education is to teach to love, to break up the egoism of the individual, and to lead him from the first stage of communion in the family through all the following stages of social life to the love of humanity, or to the highest self-conquest by which man rises to divine unity.

To learn to comprehend nature in the child, —is not that to comprehend one's own nature and the nature of mankind? And in this comprehension is there not involved a certain degree of comprehension of all things else? It should therefore at least be the beginning; and the love of childhood should be awakened in the mind (and in a wider sense, this is the love of humanity), so that a new, free generation of men can grow up by right care.

Reminiscences of Friederich Froebel, Vol. x
Baroness von Bülow

THE FATHER AND THE MOTHER *
Henri Frédéric Amiel
Swiss scholar and writer, 1821–1881

Self-government with tenderness—here you have the condition of all authority over children. The child must discover in us no passion, no weakness of which he can make use; he must feel himself powerless to deceive or to trouble us; then he will recognize in us his natural superiors, and he will attach a special value to our kindness, because he will respect it. The child who can rouse in us anger, or impatience, or excitement, feels himself stronger than we, and a child only respects strength. The mother should consider herself as her child's sun, a changeless and ever radiant world, whither the small restless creature, quick at tears and laughter, light, fickle, passionate, full of storms, may come for fresh stores of light, warmth, and electricity, of calm and of courage. The mother represents goodness, providence, law; that is to say, the divinity, under that form of it which is accessible to childhood. The religion of a child depends on what its mother and its father are, and not on what they say. The inner and unconscious ideal which guides their life is precisely what touches the child; their words, their remonstrances, their punishments, their bursts of feeling even, are for him merely thunder and comedy; what they worship, this it is which his instinct divines and reflects.

The child sees what we are, behind what we wish to be. He is a magnifying mirror. This is why the first principle of education is: train yourself; and the first rule to follow if you wish to possess yourself of a child's will is: master your own.

Journal
Trans. Mrs. Humphry Ward

SONG OF THE HOUSE

Sung by the *old man of the songs*, or
shaman, at the dedication of a house
Navajo Indian

Rising Sun! when you shall shine,
    Make this house happy,

Beautify it with your beams;
    Make this house happy.

God of Dawn! your white blessings spread;
    Make this house happy.

Guard the doorway from all evil;
    Make this house happy.

White Corn! Abide herein;
    Make this house happy.

Soft Wealth! May this hut cover much;
    Make this house happy.

Heavy Rain! Your virtues send;
    Make this house happy.

Corn Pollen! Bestow content;
    Make this house happy.

May peace around this family dwell;
    Make this house happy.

      The American Anthropologist, Vol. vi.

BOOK III

THE COMMONWEALTH

The Common Lot

OUR OBLIGATION TO THE RACE *
Edwin Grant Conklin
American biologist, 1863—

I think that notable human improvement can take place only upon two conditions. (1) The physical and intellectual improvement of the individual through environment and training must not interfere with his racial and ethical obligations. Individual freedom must be subordinated to racial welfare. (2) The promotion of human evolution must be undertaken by society as its greatest work. Not only has society greater freedom and greater power than the individual, but it persists while men come and go. Our hereditary lines are so interwoven with those of other races and will be so entangled with other lines in the future that any selfish or narrow policy of improving our family or class can have little permanent value. We shall rise only as our race rises. The individual is not really a separate and independent being, but a minor unit in the great organism of hu-

379

manity and his greatest duty is to transmit unimpaired and undefiled a noble heritage to generations yet unborn.

Heredity and Environment in the
Development of Man

HUMANITY AND THE INDIVIDUAL
Auguste Sabatier
French clergyman, 1839–1901

Humanity does not exist outside of the individual man, nor without him; the individual man does not exist outside of humanity and without it. The individual and society are the object one of the other. Their apparently contradictory rights are, in reality, mutual duties. The moral dignity of a society is measured by what it does to educate and form the personality of its members; the moral dignity of an individual, by what he does for his brothers and for the social body to which he belongs. The well-being of one necessarily depends on that of the other. Where individuality is weak, without initiative or energy, the social body, whatever its extent in space, is neither strong nor really great.

That society which, to maintain itself, op-

presses individual souls and sacrifices their
rights and their culture to its own tranquillity
is like a mother who should devour her children.
The individual who by his own selfishness ex-
ploits or destroys the social bond is the perverse or heedless child who to warm himself
sets fire to the house of his fathers. Social
authority and individual autonomy are not
more hostile, and can no more legitimately be
opposed to one another, than the final destiny
of man from that of humanity.

Religions of Authority and the
Religion of the Spirit
Trans. Louise Seymour Houghton

THE COMMON LIFE *

Marcus Aurelius
Roman emperor and Stoic philosopher, 121–180

As thou thyself art a component part of a
social system, so let every act of thine be a component part of social life. Whatever act of
thine then has no reference either immediately
or remotely to a social end is of the nature of
a mutiny, just as when in a popular assembly
a man acting by himself stands apart from the
general agreement.

Whether the universe is (a concourse of) atoms, or nature (is a system), let this first be established, that I am a part of the whole which is governed by nature; next, I am in a manner intimately related to the parts which are of the same kind with myself. For, remembering this, inasmuch as I am a part, I shall be discontented with none of the things which are assigned to me out of the whole; for nothing is injurious to the part if it is for the advantage of the whole. For the whole contains nothing which is not for its advantage; and all natures indeed have this common principle; but the nature of the universe has this principle besides, that it cannot be compelled even by any external cause to generate anything harmful to itself. And inasmuch as I am in a manner intimately related to the parts which are of the same kind with myself, I shall do nothing unsocial, but I shall rather direct myself to the things which are of the same kind with myself, and I shall turn all my efforts to the common interest, and divert them from the contrary.

Have I done something for the general interest? Well, then, I have had my reward.

The Thoughts of Marcus Aurelius
Trans. George Long

THE CALLING OF A CITIZEN *

EPICTETUS

Greek philosopher, born about 60 A.D.

Consider who you are;—first, a man: that is, one who has nothing more sovereign than will, but all else subject to this, and will itself free from slavery or subjection. Consider then from what you are parted by reason. You are parted from wild beasts, you are parted from sheep.

On these terms you are a citizen of the universe and a part of it; not one of those marked for service, but of those fitted for command; for you have the faculty to understand the divine governance of the universe and to reason on its sequence. What then is the calling of a citizen? To have no personal interest, never to think about anything as though he were detached, but to be like the hand or the foot, which, if they had the power of reason and understood the order of nature, would direct every impulse and every process of the will by reference to the whole. That is why it is well said by philosophers that if the good man knew coming events beforehand he would help on nature, for he would realize that, by the

ordering of the universe, this task is allotted
him.

Discourses and Manual of Epictetus
Trans. P. E. Matheson

ONE AND INSEPARABLE *
Giuseppe Mazzini
Italian patriot, and defender of
republicanism, 1805–1872

We improve with the improvement of humanity; nor without the improvement of the whole
can you hope that your own moral and material
conditions will improve. Generally speaking,
you cannot, even if you would, separate your life
from that of humanity; you live in it, by it, for
it. I charge you then, O my brothers, by your
duty and by your own interest not to forget
that your first duties—duties without fulfilling
which you cannot hope to fulfil those owed to
family and country—are to humanity. You
are all brothers. Ask yourselves whenever you
do an action in the sphere of your country,
or your family, If what I am doing were done
by all and for all, would it advantage or injure
humanity? and if your conscience answers, It
would injure humanity, desist; desist, even if

it seem to you that an immediate advantage for your country or your family would ensue from your action. Be apostles of this faith, apostles of the brotherhood of nations, and of the unity of the human race—a principle admitted today in theory, but denied in practice. Be such apostles wherever and in whatever way you are able. Neither God nor man can demand more of you.

The Duties of Man and Other Essays

CHANT COMMUNAL

Horace Traubel
American poet and editor, 1858–1919

What can I do? I can talk out when others are silent. I can say man when others say money. I can stay up when others are asleep. I can keep on working when others have stopped to play. I can give life big meanings when others give life little meanings. I can say love when others say hate. I can say every man when others say one man. I can try events by a hard test when others try it by an easy test.

What can I do? I can give myself to life when other men refuse themselves to life.

Chants Communal

THE RELIGION OF CREATIVE EFFORT

Stanton Coit
English writer and lecturer, 1857 – 1944

Ours is the religion of unfaltering hope and trust for all mankind. The material universe is more and more yielding up her subtlest and most elusive forces into our hands for the healing of disease and for the unifying of the nations into one community, so that all may think together like one mind, and work to the same end in the spirit of love. Likewise, through the application of the methods of science to the facts of mind and of society, the hitherto unexplored depths of man's inner nature are revealing undreamed-of powers of self-development.

Ours thus becomes the religion of creative energy, of salvation, spiritual and material, through personal and civic effort.

Social Worship
Ed. Stanton Coit

THE DEMOCRATIC IDEAL
GILBERT MURRAY
British classical scholar, 1866—

The essential doctrine of democracy is that each man, as a free human soul, lives of his free will in the service of the whole people. This ideal is no doubt hard to attain, but it is not hard to aim at. It is the only ideal permanently possible for any society that has emerged from the rule of mere custom or the divine right of kings.

In certain ancient Greek cities a man, before casting a vote, swore in the presence of the gods that he was voting to the best of his judgment for the good of the whole city. And that is still the spirit in which every good citizen ought to vote, and as a rule does vote.

The externals of democracy as a form of government can be attained easily enough: parliamentary institutions, universal suffrage, abolition of privileges and the like. But democracy as a spirit is not attained until the average citizen feels the same instinctive loyalty toward the whole people that an old-fashioned royalist felt toward his king.

It is that spirit which is first needed in order

to build up the organization for preventing war.

The League of Nations and the Democratic Idea

THE COMMON LOT *

JANE ADDAMS

American: head resident of Hull House, Chicago; writer on social reforms, 1860–1935

It is well to remind ourselves, from time to time, that "ethics" is but another word for "righteousness," that for which many men and women of every generation have hungered and thirsted, and without which life becomes meaningless.

To attain individual morality in an age demanding social morality, to pride one's self on the results of personal effort when the time demands social adjustment, is utterly to fail to apprehend the situation.

All about us are men and women who have become unhappy in regard to their attitude toward the social order itself; toward the dreary round of uninteresting work, the pleasures narrowed down to those of appetite, the declining consciousness of brain power, and the lack of mental food which characterizes the lot of the large proportion of their fellow-citizens.

The test which they would apply to their conduct is a social test. They fail to be content with fulfillment of their family and personal obligations, and find themselves striving to respond to a new demand involving a social obligation.

We are learning that a standard of social ethics is not attained by traveling a sequestered byway, but by mixing on the thronged and common road where all must turn out for one another, and at least see the size of one another's burdens. To follow the path of social morality results perforce in the temper if not the practice of the democratic spirit, for it implies that diversified human experience and resultant sympathy which are the foundation and guarantee of democracy.

There are many indications that this conception of democracy is growing among us. We have come to have an enormous interest in human life as such, accompanied by confidence in its essential soundness. Partly through this wide reading of human life, we find in ourselves a new affinity for all men, which probably never existed in the world before. Evil itself does not shock us as it once did, and we count only that man merciful in whom we recognize an understanding of the criminal. We have learned as common knowledge that much of the insensibility and hardness of the world is due to the lack of imagination which prevents a realization of the experiences of other people. Already there is a conviction that we are under a moral obligation in choosing our experiences, since the result of those experiences must ultimately determine our understanding of life. We know instinctively that if we grow contemptuous of our fellows, and consciously limit our intercourse to certain kinds of people whom we have previously decided to respect, we not only tremendously circumscribe our range of life, but limit the scope of our ethics.

The identification with the common lot, which is the essential idea of democracy, becomes the source and expression of social ethics. It is as though we thirsted to drink at the great wells of human experience because we knew that a daintier or less potent draught would not carry us to the end of the journey, going forward as we must in the heat and jostle of the crowd.

Democracy and Social Ethics

INBROTHERED
Edwin Markham
American writer, 1852–1940

There is a destiny that makes us brothers:
   None goes his way alone;
All that we send into the lives of others
   Comes back into our own.

A Creed
Lincoln and Other Poems

AND WHAT SHALL YOU SAY?
Joseph S. Cotter, Jr.
American writer, 1895–1919

Brother, come!
And let us go unto our God.
And when we stand before him
I shall say—
"Lord, I do not hate;
I am hated.
I scourge no one;
I am scourged.
I covet no lands;
My lands are coveted.
I mock no peoples;

My peoples are mocked."
And, brother, what shall you say?

Band of Gideon
Also found in *A Book of American Negro Poetry*

THE JEW TO JESUS
FLORENCE KIPER FRANK
American writer, 1886—

O man of mine own people, I alone
Among these alien ones can know thy face,
I who have felt the kinship of our race
Burn in me as I sit where they intone
Thy praises,—those who, striving to make
    known
A God for sacrifice, have missed the grace
Of thy sweet human meaning in its place,
Thou who art of our blood-bond and our own.

Are we not sharers of thy Passion? Yea,
In spirit-anguish closely by thy side
We have drained the bitter cup, and, tortured,
    felt

With thee the bruising of each heavy welt.
In every land is our Gethsemane.
A thousand times have we been crucified.

The Jew to Jesus and Other Poems

MANY PARTS, ONE BODY

THE APOSTLE PAUL
Christian, first century

Just as the body is one and yet has many
parts, and all the parts of the body, many as
they are, form one body, so it is with Christ.
For we have all—Jews or Greeks, slaves or
free men—been baptized in one spirit to form
one body, and we have all been saturated with
one Spirit. For the body does not consist of
one part but of many. If the foot says, "As
I am not a hand, I am not a part of the body,"
that does not make it any less a part of the
body. And if the ear says, "As I am not an
eye, I am not a part of the body," that does not
make it any less a part of the body. If all
the body were eye, how would we hear? If it
were all ear, how could we have a sense of
smell? As it is, God has arranged the parts,

every one of them in a body as he wished them
to be. If they were all one part, where would
the body be? As it is, there are many parts,
but one body. The eye cannot say to the
hand, "I do not need you," or the head to
the feet, "I do not need you." On the contrary, the parts of the body that are considered
most delicate are indispensable, and the parts
of it that we think common, we dress with
especial care, and our unpresentable parts receive especial attention which our presentable
parts do not need. God has so adjusted the
body and given such especial distinction to
its inferior parts that there is no clash in the
body, but its parts all alike care for one another.
If one part suffers, all the parts share its sufferings. If a part has honor done it, all the
parts enjoy it too. Now you are Christ's body,
and individually parts of it.

From *The First Epistle to the Corinthians*
The New Testament
An American translation by Edgar J. Goodspeed

MUTUAL AID A FACTOR IN EVOLUTION

PETER ALEXEIVICH KROPOTKIN
Russian geographer, author, and
political reformer, 1842–1921

As soon as we study animals—not in laboratories and museums only, but in the forest and prairie, in the steppe and in the mountains —we at once perceive that though there is an immense amount of warfare and extermination going on amidst various species, and especially amidst various classes of animals, there is, at the same time, as much, or perhaps even more, of mutual support, mutual aid, and mutual defence amidst animals belonging to the same species or, at least, to the same society. Sociability is as much a law of nature as mutual struggle. Of course it would be extremely difficult to estimate, however roughly, the relative numerical importance of both these series of facts. But if we resort to an indirect test, and ask Nature: "Who are the fittest: those who are continually at war with each other, or those who support one another?" we at once see that those animals which acquire habits of mutual aid are undoubtedly the fittest. They have more chances to survive, and they attain, in their respective classes, the highest development and bodily organization. If the numberless facts which can be brought forward to support this view are taken into account, we may safely say that mutual aid is as much a law of animal life as mutual struggle; but that as a factor of evolution, it most probably has a far greater importance, inasmuch as it favors the development of such habits and characters as insure the maintenance and further development of the species, together with the greatest amount of welfare and enjoyment of life for the individual, with the least waste of energy.

Mutual Aid a Factor in Evolution

THE MORAL SENSE IN MAN *

JUVENAL
Latin poet and reformer of morals
by satire, about 60–140

We alone, endued with that venerable distinction of reason and a capacity for divine things, with an aptitude for the practice as well as the reception of all arts and sciences, have received, transmitted to us from heaven's high citadel, a moral sense, which brutes prone and stooping towards earth are lacking in. In the beginning of the world, the common Creator of all vouchsafed to them only the principle of vitality; to us he gave souls also, that an instinct of affection reciprocally shared might urge us to seek for and to give assistance; to unite in one people those before widely scattered; to emerge from the ancient wood, and abandon the forests where our fathers dwelt; to build houses, to join another's dwelling to our own homes that the confidence mutually engendered by a neighbor's threshold might add security to our slumbers; to cover with our arms a fellow-citizen when fallen or staggering from a wound; to sound the battle-signal from a common clarion; to be defended by the same ramparts, and closed in by the key of a common portal.

But now the unanimity of serpents is greater than ours. The wild beast of similar genus spares his kindred spots. When did ever lion, though stronger, deprive his fellow-lion of life? In what wood did ever boar perish by the tusks of a boar larger than himself? The tigress of India maintains unbroken harmony with each tigress that ravens. Bears, savage to others, are yet at peace among themselves.

The Satires of Juvenal, viii, x, xv
Trans. Louis Evans

THE CREED OF THE REPUBLIC *
Giuseppe Mazzini
Italian patriot, and defender of
republicanism, 1805–1872

We believe for each people and its component individuals the same that we believe for humanity and its component peoples. We believe in association between the individuals who compose each nation as the sole means of their progress, the principle destined to govern all their institutions, and the pledge of concord in their labors. We believe in liberty and equality among the men of each country, in the inviolability of ego, which is the conscience of individuals, and assigns to them their office in the nation.

We believe for every state in the people, the sole master, the sole sovereign, the sole interpreter of the law of humanity which rules the mission of each nation: in the people one and indivisible, that knows neither caste nor privilege save that of genius and of virtue, neither proletariat nor aristocracy of land or money, but only faculties and active forces consecrated, for the good of all, to the administration of the surface of the globe, our common heritage:—in the people free and independent, with an organization that shall harmonize individual faculties and social thought; the people living by its own labor and the fruits thereof, pursuing in concord the greatest possible good of all, yet respecting the rights of the individual:—in the people made one family, with one faith, one tradition, one thought of love, and advancing to the ever fuller accomplishment of its mission, reverent to the message of the generations, but resolved to use the present as a bridge betwixt past and future.

The Duties of Man and Other Essays

Vocations

THE ARTISANS [*]
Hebrew, about 180 B. C.

The wisdom of the scribe cometh by opportunity of leisure; and he that hath little business shall become wise. How shall he become wise that holdeth the plow? He will set his heart upon turning his furrows; and his wakefulness is to give his heifers their fodder. So is every artificer and workmaster that passeth his time by night as by day; they that cut gravings of signets, and his diligence is to make great variety; he will set his heart to preserve likeness in his portraiture and he will be wakeful to finish his work. So is the smith sitting by the anvil and considering the unwrought iron; the vapor of the fire will waste his flesh, and in the heat of the furnace will he wrestle with his work; the noise of the hammer will be ever in his ear, and his eyes are upon the pattern of the vessel; he will set his heart upon perfecting his works, and he will be wakeful to adorn them perfectly. So is the potter sitting at his work and turning the wheel about with his feet, who is alway anxiously set at his work, and all his handiwork is by number; he will fashion the clay with his arm, and will bend its strength in front of his feet; he will apply his heart to finish the glazing, and he will be wakeful to make clean the furnace. All these put their trust in their hands; and each becometh wise in his own work. Without these shall not a city be inhabited, and men shall not sojourn and walk up and down therein. They shall not be sought for in the council of the people, and in the assembly they shall not mount on high; they shall not sit on the seat of the judge, and they shall not understand the covenant of judgment; neither shall they declare instruction and judgment, and where parables are they shall not be found. But they will maintain the fabric of the world; and in the handiwork of their craft is their prayer.

From *The Book of Ecclesiasticus*
Old Testament Apocrypha

TOOLS AND THE MAN *
Thomas Carlyle
Scottish essayist and historian, 1795–1881

The latest gospel in this world is, Know thy work and do it. Know what thou canst work at; and work at it like a Hercules! That will be the better plan.

Blessed is he who has found his work; let him ask no other blessedness. He has a work, a life-purpose; he has found it, and will follow it! Labor is life: from the inmost heart of the worker rises his God-given force, the sacred, celestial life-essence breathed into him by Almighty God.

Hast thou valued patience, courage, perseverance, openness to light; readiness to own thyself mistaken, to do better next time? All these, all virtues, in wrestling with the dim brute powers of fact, in ordering of thy fellows in such wrestle there, and elsewhere not at all, thou wilt continually learn.

And who art thou that braggest of thy life of idleness; complacently showest thy bright gilt equipages, sumptuous cushions, appliances of folding of the hands to more sleep? Thou art an original figure in this creation. One monster there is in the world: the idle man.

My brother, the brave man has to give his life away. Give it, I advise thee:—thou dost not expect to sell thy life in an adequate manner? What price, for example, would content thee? Why, God's entire creation to thyself, the whole universe of space, the whole eternity of time, and what they hold: that is the price which would content thee. Thou wilt never sell thy life, or any part of thy life, in a satisfactory manner. Give it, like a royal heart; let the price be nothing: thou hast then, in a certain sense, got all for it!

The proper epic of this world is not now "Arms and the Man"; it is "Tools and the Man." All true work is religion. Admirable was that of the old monks, "Laborare est orare." "Work is worship." Older than all preached gospels was this unpreached, inarticulate, but ineradicable, forever-enduring gospel: work, and therein have well-being. Man, son of earth and of heaven, lies there not, in the innermost heart of thee, a spirit of active method, a force for work?

All true work is sacred; in all true work, were it but true hand-labor, there is something of divineness. No man has worked, or can work, except religiously; not even the poor day laborer, the weaver of your coat, the sewer of your shoes. All men, if they work not as in a great taskmaster's eye, will work wrong, work unhappily for themselves and you. Labor, wide as the earth, has its summit in heaven. Sweat of the brow; and up from that to sweat of the brain, sweat of the heart, which includes all Kepler calculations, Newton meditations, all sciences, all spoken epics, all acted heroisms, martyrdoms,—up to that "agony of bloody sweat," which all men have called divine! O brother, if this is not "worship," then I say, the more pity for worship; for this is the noblest thing yet discovered under God's sky. Who art thou that complainest of thy life of toil? Complain not. Look up, my wearied brother; see thy fellow workmen there, in God's eternity; sacred band of the immortals, celestial body-guard of the empire of mankind. Laborare est orare—in a thousand senses— true work is worship.

Past and Present

Two men I honor, and no third. First, the toil-worn craftsman that with earth-made implement laboriously conquers the earth, and makes her man's. Venerable to me is the hard hand, crooked, coarse; wherein notwithstanding lies a cunning virtue, indefeasibly royal, as of the sceptre of the planet. Venerable too is the rugged face, all weather tanned, besoiled, with its rude intelligence; for it is the face of a man living manlike. Oh, but the more venerable for thy rudeness, and even because we must pity as well as love thee! Hardly entreated brother! For us was thy back so bent, for us were thy straight limbs and fingers so deformed; thou wert our conscript, on whom the lot fell, and fighting our battles wert so marred. For in thee too lay a God-created form, but it was not to be unfolded; encrusted must it stand with the thick adhesions and defacements of labor; and thy body, like thy soul, was not to know freedom. Yet toil on, toil on; thou art in thy duty, be out of it who may; thou toilest for the altogether indispensable, for daily bread.

A second man I honor, and still more highly: him who is seen toiling for the spiritually indispensable; not daily bread, but the bread of life. Is not he too in his duty; endeavoring toward inward harmony; revealing this by act or by word, through all his outward endeavors, be they high or low? Highest of all, when his outward and his inward endeavor are one; when we can name him artist, not earthly craftsman only, but inspired thinker, who with heaven-made implement conquers heaven for us! If the poor and humble toil that we have food, must not the high and glorious toil for him in return, that he have light, have guidance, freedom, immortality?—these two in all their degrees, I honor; all else is chaff and dust, which let the wind blow whither it listeth.

Unspeakably touching is it, however, when I find both dignities united, and he that must toil outwardly for the lowest of man's wants is also toiling inwardly for the highest. Sublimer in this world know I nothing than a peasant saint, could such now anywhere be met with. Such a one will take thee back to Nazareth itself; thou wilt see the splendor of heaven spring forth from the humblest depths of earth, like a light shining in great darkness.

Sartor Resartus

EDUCATION *

GOTTHOLD EPHRAIM LESSING
German philosopher and dramatist, 1729–1781

Education is revelation coming to the individual man; and revelation is education which has come, and is yet coming, to the human race.

Education has its goal in the race, no less than in the individual. That which is educated is educated for something.

The flattering prospects which are opened to the pupil, the honor and well-being which are painted to him, what are they more than means of educating him to become a man, who, when these prospects of honor and well-being have vanished, shall be able to do his duty?

This is the aim of human education, and should not the divine education extend as far? Is that which is successful in the way of art with the individual not to be successful in the way of nature with the whole? Blasphemy! Blasphemy!

No! It will come, it will assuredly come, the time of the perfecting, when man, the more convinced his understanding feels itself of an ever better future, will nevertheless not be necessitated to borrow motives of action from this future, for he will do the right because it is right, not because arbitrary rewards are annexed thereto, which formerly were intended simply to fix and strengthen his unsteady gaze in recognizing the inner, better rewards of well-doing.

It will assuredly come, the time of a new eternal gospel, which is promised us in the primer of the New Testament itself.

The Education of the Human Race
Trans. F. W. Robertson

THE IDEAL OF THE SCIENTIST *
Louis Pasteur
French: founder of the science
of bacteriology, 1822–1895

Ever since I can remember my life as a man, I do not think I have ever spoken for the first time with a student without saying to him, Work perseveringly. Work can be made into a pleasure, and alone is profitable to man, to his city, to his country. It is even more natural that I should thus speak to you. The common soul (if I may so speak) of an assembly of young men is wholly formed of the most generous feelings. You have just given proof of this assurance, and I have felt moved to the heart in hearing you applaud, as you have just been doing, such men as de Lesseps, Helmholtz, and Virchow. Your language has borrowed from ours the beautiful word enthusiasm, bequeathed to us by the Greeks (en theos) an inward God. It was almost with a divine feeling that you just now cheered those great men.

One of our writers said, addressing young men in the preface of one of his works, "Whatever career you may embrace, look up to an exalted goal; worship great men and great things." But, if work should be the very life of your life, if the cult for great men and great things should be associated with your every thought, that is still not enough. Try to bring into everything you undertake the spirit of scientific method, founded on the immortal works of Galileo, Descartes, and Newton.

The Life of Pasteur
René Vallery-Radot
Trans. Mrs. R. L. Devonshire

THE TEACHER

LESLIE PINCKNEY HILL
Contemporary American Teacher

Lord, who am I to teach the way
To little children day by day,
So prone myself to go astray?

I teach them knowledge, but I know
How faint they flicker and how low
The candles of my knowledge glow.

I teach them power to will and do,
But only now to learn anew
My own great weakness through and
    through.

I teach them love for all mankind
And all God's creatures; but I find
My love comes lagging far behind.

Lord, if their guide I still must be,
Oh, let the little children see
The teacher leaning hard on thee!

Wings of Oppression
Also found in *A Book of American Negro Poetry*

THE TORCH BEARERS *
ALFRED NOYES
English poet, 1880—

COPERNICUS

                    I speak
Not for myself, but for the age unborn.
I caught the fire from those who went before,
The bearers of the torch who could not see

The goal to which they strained. I caught
    their fire,
And carried it, only a little way beyond;
But there are those that wait for it, I know,
Those who will carry it on to victory.
I dare not fail them. Looking back, I see
Those others,—fallen, with their arms out-
    stretched,
Dead, pointing to the future.

TYCHO BRAHE

They thought him a magician, Tycho Brahe,
The astrologer, who wore the mask of gold.
Perhaps he was. There's magic in the truth;
And only those who find and follow its laws
Can work its miracles.

                There's one way,
And only one, to knowledge of the law
Whereby the stars are steered, and so to read
The future, even perhaps the destinies
Of men and nations,—only one sure way,
And that's to watch them, watch them, and
    record
The truth we know, and not the lies we dream.

Dear, while I watch them, though the hills and
    sea
Divide us, every night our eyes can meet

Among those constant glories. Every night
Your eyes and mine, upraisèd to that bright
    realm,
Can, in one moment, speak across the world.

WOTTON TO KEPLER

How sure the soul is that if truth destroy
The temple, in three days the truth will build
A nobler temple; and that order reigns
In all things. Even your atheist builds his
    doubt
On that strange faith; destroys his heaven and
    God
In absolute faith that his own thought is true
To law, God's lanthorn to our stumbling feet;
And so, despite himself, he worships God,
For where true souls are, there are God and
    heaven.

CELESTE AND GALILEO

    "Think, father, through all ages now
No one can ever watch that starry sky
Without remembering you. Your fame . . ."
"Celeste, beware of that. Say truth, not fame.
If there be any happiness on earth,
It springs from truth alone, the truth we live
In act and thought.   I have looked up there and
    seen

Too many worlds to talk of fame on earth.
Fame, on this grain of dust among the stars,
The trumpet of a gnat that thinks to halt
The great sun-clusters moving on their way
In   silence!   Yes,   that's   fame;   but   truth,
    Celeste,
Truth and its laws are constant, even up there;
That's where one man may face and fight the
    world.
His weakness turns to strength. He is made
    one
With universal forces, and he holds
The password to eternity.
Gate after gate swings back through all the
    heavens.
No sentry halts him, and no flaming sword.
Say truth, Celeste, not fame."

                        "No, for I'll say
A better word," I told him. "I'll say love."
He took my face between his hands and said—
His face all dark between me and the stars—
"What's love, Celeste, but this dear face of
    truth
Upturned to heaven?"

                He left me, and I heard,
Some twelve hours later, that this man whose
    soul
Was dedicate to Truth was threatened now

With torture, if his lips did not deny
The truth he loved.

NEWTON

Fools have said
That knowledge drives out wonder from the
world;
They'll say it still, though all the dust's ablaze
With miracles at their feet; while Newton's
laws
Foretell that knowledge one day shall be song,
And those whom Truth has taken to her heart
Find that it beats in music.
"I know not how my work may seem to
others—"
So wrote our mightiest mind—"but to myself
I seem a child that wandering all day long
Upon the sea-shore gathers here a shell,
And there a pebble, colored by the wave,
While the great ocean of truth, from sky to
sky
Stretches before him, boundless, unexplored."

HERSCHEL

Who that once has seen
How truth leads on to truth, shall ever dare
To set a bound to knowledge?

> The records grow
> Unceasingly, and each new grain of truth
> Is packed, like radium, with whole worlds of
> light.

Watchers of the Sky

ART THE GIVER OF VISION *
JOSEPH CONRAD
English novelist, 1857–1924

Art may be defined as a single minded attempt to render the highest kind of justice to the visible universe, by bringing to light the truth, manifold and one, underlying its every aspect. It is an attempt to find in its forms, in its colors, in its light, in its shadows, in the aspects of matter and in the facts of life what of each is fundamental, what is enduring and essential— their one illuminating and convincing quality— the very truth of their existence. The artist, then, like the thinker or scientist, seeks the truth and makes his appeal.

The artist descends within himself, and in that lonely region of stress and strife, if he be deserving and fortunate, he finds the terms of his appeal.

He speaks to our capacity for delight and wonder, to the sense of mystery surrounding our lives; to our sense of pity, and beauty, and pain; to the latent feeling of fellowship with all creation and to the subtle, but invincible, conviction of solidarity that knits together the loneliness of innumerable hearts to the solidarity in dreams, in joy, in sorrow, in aspirations, in illusions, in hope, in fear, which binds men to each other, which binds together all humanity—the dead to the living and the living to the unborn. All art, therefore, appeals primarily to the senses, and the artistic aim when expressing itself in written words must also make its appeal through the senses, if its high desire is to reach the secret spring of responsive emotions. It must strenuously aspire to the plasticity of sculpture, the color of painting, and to the magic suggestiveness of music—which is the art of arts. And it is only through complete, unswerving devotion to the perfect blending of form and substance; it is only through an unremitting, never-discouraged care for the shape and ring of sentences that an approach can be made to plasticity, to color; and the light of magic suggestiveness may be brought to play for an evanescent instant over the common-place surface of words: of the old, old words, worn thin, defaced by ages of careless usage.

My task which I am trying to achieve is, by the power of the written word, to make you hear, to make you feel—it is, before all, to make you *see*. That and no more, and it is every-thing. If I succeed, you shall find there ac-cording to your deserts encouragement, consola-tion, fear, charm—all you demand, and perhaps also that glimpse of truth for which you have forgotten to ask.

From the preface to *The Nigger of the Narcissus*

MUSIC
ROBERT BROWNING
English poet, 1812–1889

But here is the finger of God, a flash of the will
    that can,
  Existent behind all laws, that made them and
    lo, they are!
And I know not if save in this such gift be
    allowed to man,
  That out of three sounds he frame, not a
    fourth sound, but a star.

Consider it well: each tone of our scale in itself
    is naught;
It is everywhere in the world,—loud, soft,
    and all is said.
Give it to me to use! I mix it with two in my
    thought;
And there! Ye have heard and seen; con-
    sider, and bow the head.

                      From *Abt Vogler*

THE HEROIC MUSICIAN *
Romain Rolland
French writer, 1866 – 1944

Beloved Beethoven! He is the most heroic
soul in modern art. He is the grandest and
best friend of those who suffer and struggle.
When we are saddened by worldly miseries, it
is he who comes near to us, as he used to go and
play to a mother in grief, and, without uttering
a word, thus console her by the song of his own
plaintive resignation. And when we are utterly exhausted in the eternal battle uselessly
waged against mediocrity, vice, and virtue, it is
an unspeakable boon to find fresh strength in
this great ocean-torrent of strong will and

faith. An atmosphere of courage emanates from his personality, a love of battle, the exultation of a conscious feeling of the God within. It seems that in his constant communion with nature he had ended by assimilating its deep and mighty powers. Grillparzer, who admired Beethoven with a kind of awe, said of him, "He penetrated into regions where art melts away and unites with the wild and capricious elements." Schumann wrote similarly of his *Symphony in C Minor:* "Every time it is performed it exercises an unvarying power on us, like natural phenomena which fill us with awe and amazement every time they occur." And Schindler, his confidential friend, says, "He possessed the spirit of nature." It is true, "Beethoven is a force of nature; and this battle of elemental power against the rest of nature is a spectacle of truly Homeric grandeur."

His whole life is like a stormy day. At the beginning—a fresh, clear morning, perhaps a languid breeze, scarcely a breath of air. But there is already in the still air a secret menace, a dark foreboding. Large shadows loom and pass; tragic rumblings; murmuring awesome silences; the furious gusts of the winds of the *Eroica* and the *C Minor.* However, the freshness of the day is not yet gone. Joy remains joy; the brightness of the sky is not overcast; sadness is never without a ray of hope.

But after 1810 the poise of the soul is disturbed. A strange light glows. Mists obscured his deepest thoughts; some of the clearer thoughts appear as vapor rising; they disappear, are dispelled, yet form anew; they obscure the heart with their melancholy and capricious gloom; often the musical idea seems to vanish entirely, to be submerged, but only to reappear again at the end of a piece in a veritable storm of melody. Even joy has assumed a rough and riotous character. A bitter feeling becomes mingled in all his sentiments. Storms gather as evening comes on. Heavy clouds are big with tempests. Lightning flashes o'er the black of night. The climax of the hurricane is approaching. Suddenly, at the height of the tempest, the darkness is dispersed. Night is driven away and the clear, tranquil atmosphere is restored by a sheer act of will power. What a conquest was this! What Napoleonic battle can be likened to it? What was Austerlitz glory to the radiance of this superhuman effort, this victory, the most brilliant that has ever been won by an infirm and lonely spirit? Sorrow personified, to whom the world refused joy, created joy himself to give to the world. He forged it from his own misery, as he proudly said in reviewing his life. And indeed it was the motto of his whole heroic soul: Joy through suffering.

(Ludwig van Beethoven, 1770–1827, German: composer of instrumental music.)

The Heroic Musician
Trans. B. Constance Hull

THE VILLAGE PREACHER *
OLIVER GOLDSMITH
Irish poet, dramatist, and novelist, 1728–1774

Near yonder copse, where once the garden
    smiled,
And still where many a garden-flower grows
    wild;
There, where a few torn shrubs the place dis-
    close,
The village preacher's modest mansion rose.
A man he was to all the country dear,
And passing rich with forty pounds a year;
Remote from towns he ran his godly race,
Nor e'er had changed, nor wished to change,
    his place;

Unpractised he to fawn, or seek for power,
By doctrines fashioned to the varying hour;
Far other aims his heart had learned to prize,
More skilled to raise the wretched than to rise.
His house was known to all the vagrant train;
He chid their wanderings, but relieved their
    pain:
The long-remembered beggar was his guest,
Whose beard descending swept his aged breast;
The ruined spendthrift, now no longer proud,
Claimed kindred there, and had his claims
    allowed;
The broken soldier, kindly bade to stay,
Sat by his fire, and talked the night away,
Wept o'er his wounds, or, tales of sorrow done,
Shouldered his crutch and showed how fields
    were won.
Pleased with his guests, the good man learned
    to glow,
And quite forgot their vices in their woe;
Careless their merits or their faults to scan,
His pity gave ere charity began.

Thus to relieve the wretched was his pride.
And e'en his failings leaned to virtue's side;
But in his duty prompt at every call,
He watched and wept, he prayed and felt for
    all;

And, as a bird each fond endearment tries
To tempt its new-fledged offspring to the skies,
He tried each art, reproved each dull delay,
Allured to brighter worlds, and led the way.
At church, with meek and unaffected grace,
His looks adorned the venerable place:
Truth from his lips prevailed with double sway,
And fools who came to scoff remained to pray.
The service past, around the pious man,
With steady zeal, each honest rustic ran;
Even children followed with endearing wile,
And plucked his gown to share the good man's
    smile.
His ready smile a parent's warmth expressed;
Their welfare pleased him, and their cares dis-
    tressed:
To them his heart, his love, his griefs were
    given,
But all his serious thoughts had rest in heaven.
As some tall cliff that lifts its awful form
Swells from the vale and midway leaves the
    storm,
Though round its breast the rolling clouds are
    spread,
Eternal sunshine settles on its head.

From *The Deserted Village*

THE PARSON *

GEOFFREY CHAUCER

English poet, who established the use of the English
language in the writing of poetry; 1340?–1400.

A good man was ther of religioun,
A good man there was, of religion,

And was a Povre Persoun of a Toun;
Who was a poor parson of a town;

But riche he was of holy thoght and werk;
But rich he was in holy thought and work;

He was also a lerned man, a clerk.
He was also a learned man, a clerk,

That Christes Gospel trewely wolde he preche;
That Christ's gospel would truly preach.

His parisshens devoutly wolde he teche.
His parishioners devoutly would he teach.

Benygne he was, and wonder diligent,
Benign he was, and wondrous diligent,

And in adversitee ful pacient;
And in adversity full patient;

And swich he was y-preved ofte sithes.
And such he provéd was, oft times.

Ful looth were hym to cursen for his tithes,
Full loath was he to punish for his tithes,

But rather wolde he yeven, out of doute,
But rather would he give, without a doubt,

Unto his poure parisshens aboute,
Unto his poor parishioners about,

Of his offryng and eek of his substaunce:
Of his offering and also his substance;

He koude in litel thing have suffisaunce.
He could in little find sufficient.

Wyd was his parisshe, and houses fer asonder;
Wide was his parish, the houses far apart;

But he ne lafte nat, for reyn ne thonder,
But he failed not, for rain or thunder,

In siknesse nor in meschief, to visite
In sickness or in mischief, to visit

The ferreste in his parisshe, muche and lite,
The farthest in his parish, rich and poor,

Upon his feet, and in his hand a staf.
Upon his feet, and in his hand a staff.

This noble ensample to his sheep he gaf,
This noble example to his sheep he gave

That first he wroghte, and afterward he
    taughte.
That first he wrought, and afterward he taught.

And though he hooly were, and vertuous,
And, though he holy was and virtuous,

He was to synful man nat despitous,
He was not merciless to sinful man,

Ne of his speche daungerous ne digne,
Nor in his speech formidable nor proud,

But in his techyng descreet and benygne.
But in his teaching discreet and benign.

To drawen folk to hevene by fairnesse,
*To draw folk unto heaven by the beauty of a
    life,*

By good ensample, was his bisynesse.
By good example—this was his business.

He waited after no pomp and reverence,
He waited not for pomp and reverence,

Ne maked him a spicéd conscience;
Nor made sophisticated his conscience;

But Cristes loore, and his apostles twelve,
But the love of Christ and his apostles twelve,

He taughte, and first he folwed it him selve.
He taught, and first he followed it himself.

From *The Prologue,*
The *Canterbury Tales,* line 477 ff.
The Chaucerian text as edited by
Alfred W. Pollard and others

THE PLOUGHERS *
HUGH LATIMER (1485–1555)
English clergyman: one of the chief promoters
in England of the Reformation; 1485?–1555.

I told you in my firſt ſermon, honorable audi-
I told you in my first sermon, honorable audi-

ence, that I purpoſed to declare unto you. ii
ence, that I purposed to declare unto you two

thinges. The one what fede fhuld be fowen in
things. The one, what seed should be sown in

Gods field, in Goddes plough land. And the
God's field, in God's plough land. And the

other who fhould be the fowers. Gods worde
other, who should be the sowers. God's word

is a feede to be fowen in Goddes fielde, that is
is a seed to be sown in God's field; that is,

the faithful congregation, and the preacher
the faithful congregation, and the preacher

is the fower.
is the sower.

No man yat putteth his hand to the plough
No man that putteth his hand to the plough

and loketh backe is apte for the kingdom of
and looketh back is fit for the kingdom of

god. That is to fay, let no preacher be neg-
God. That is to say, let no preacher be neg-

ligente in doinge his office. Ye may not be
ligent in   his office. You may not be

offended wyth my fimilitude: in that I com-
offended with my similitude, in that I com-

pare preachynge to the laboure and worke of
pare preaching to the labor   and work of

ploughinge, and the preacher to a ploughman.
ploughing, and the preacher to a ploughman.

Ye maye not be offended wyth thys my fimili-
You may not be offended   at   this   simili-

tude,   for I haue ben fchlaundered of
tude of mine.   I have been condemned by

fome perfonnes for fuch thynges. But as
some persons for such things. But as

preachers muft be ware and circumfpect yat
preachers must be watchful and circumspect that

they geue not any iuft occafion to be fchlaun-
they do not give just occasion for condemna-

dered and yll fpoken of by the hearers, fo
tion and ill speech by their hearers, so

muft not the auditours be offended without
must not the auditors be offended without

caufe. For heauen is in the gofpel likened
cause. For, in the gospel, heaven is likened

to a mufterde feede. It is compared alfo to
to a mustard seed. It is compared, also, to

a piece of leauen. What derogation is thys
a piece of leaven. In what is this figure

to heauen? Ye maye not then, I
derogatory to heaven? You may not, then, I

fay, be offended with my fimilitude, for be-
say, be offended with my similitude be-

caufe I lyken preachyng to a ploughmans la-
cause I liken preaching to a ploughman's la-

boure and a prelate to a ploughman. But now
bor and a prelate to a ploughman. But now

you wyll afke me whom I cal a prelate. A
you will ask me whom I call a prelate. A

prelate is that man, what foeuer he be, yat hath
prelate is that man, whosoever he be, that has

a flocke to be taughte of hym, who foeuer
a flock to teach,   whoever

hath any fpirituall charge in the fayethfull
has   spiritual charge in the faithful

congregation, and who fo euer he be that
congregation, and whosoever he be whose

hath cure of foule.   And wel may
task is the cure of the soul. And well may

the preacher and the ploughman be lykened to-
the preacher be likened to the plough-

gether. Fyrfte for their labour of all ceafons
man: first, in their labor at all seasons

of the yere. For there is no tyme of the yere,
of the year, for there is no time of the year

in whiche the ploughman hath not fome fpeciall
in which the ploughman has not some special

worke to do, as in my countrey in Lecestre
work to do, as in my country in Leicester-

Shire, the ploughe man hath a tyme to fet furth
shire—the ploughman has a time to set forth

and to affaie hys plough, and other tymes for
and to try his plough, and other times for

other neceffari workes to be done. And then
other necessary work.

they alfo maye be likenede together for the
They also may be likened   in the

diuerfitie of workes and varietie of offices yat
diversity of work they have to do and the va-

they haue to do.   For as the ploughman
riety of their offices. For as the ploughman

firft fetteth furth hys plough and then tilleth
first sets forth his plough and then tills

hys lande and breaketh it in furroughes and
his land, and breaks it into furrows, and

fometime ridgeth it vp agayne. And at an
sometimes ridges it   again, and at an-

other tyme harroweth it, and clotteth it, and
other time harrows it, and clots   it, and

fometyme doungeth it, and hedgeth it, diggeth
sometimes fertilizes it, and hedges it, digs

it, and weedeth it, pourgeth and maketh it
it, and weeds it, purges and makes it

cleane. So the prelate, the preacher hath mani
clean; so the prelate, the preacher, has

diuers offices to do. He hath a bufie worke
divers offices to perform. He has a busy work

to bringe his flocke to a ryght fayth and
to bring his flock to a right faith and

then to confirme them in the fame fayeth,
then to confirm them in that faith,

Nowe ridgyinge them vp agayne, with the
now ridging them up again with the

gofpel, Nowe weedinge them by mak-
gospel, now weeding them by mak-

ynge them forfake fynne. Nowe clottinge
ing them forsake sin; now clotting

them, by breakynge their ftonie hertes, and by
them, by breaking their stony hearts, and by

making them fupple herted, and makyng them
making their hearts supple, and making them

to haue hertes of flefhe, that is foft hertes.
to have hearts of flesh, that is, soft hearts,

Nowe teachinge to knowe God ryghtly, and to
now teaching them to know God rightly, and to

knowe theyr duetie to God and to theyre neygh-
know their duty to God and to their neigh-

boures. Nowe exhorting them when they knowe
bors; now exhorting them when they know

theyr duety, that they do it and be diligente in
their duty to do it diligently:

it: fo that they haue a continuall worke to do.
so they have work to do continually.

They haue great laboures, and therefore
They have great labors, and therefore

they ought to haue good liuinges, that they maye
they ought to have good livings, that they may

comodioufly feade theyr flocke, for the preach-
commodiously feed their flock, for the preach-

ynge of the word of God vnto the people is
ing of the word of God unto the people is

called meate. Not ftrauberies, that come
called meat—not strawberries, that come

but once a yeare and tary not longe, but are
but once a year and tarry not long, and are

fone gone. It is no deynties. The people
soon gone. It is not dainties. The people

mufte haue meate that mufte be familier and
must have meat that   is   familiar and

continuall, and dayly geuen vnto them to fede
constant, and daily given   them to feed

vpon. By thys then it appeareth that a prelate
upon. By this then it appears that a prelate,

or anye that hath cure of foule muft diligentlie
or any whose care it is to cure souls, must labor

and subftancially worke and laboure.
diligently.

Sermon on the Ploughers
English Reprints
Ed. Edward Arber

THE PHYSICIAN *
HIPPOCRATES
Greek physician, about 460–377 B.C.

I swear by Apollo Physician, by Asclepius,
by Health, by Panacea, and by all the gods

and goddesses, making them my witnesses, that
I will carry out, according to my ability and
judgment, this oath and this indenture. To
hold my teacher in this art equal to my own
parents; to make him partner in my livelihood;
when he is in need of money to share mine with
him; to consider his family as my own brothers,
and to teach them this art, if they want to learn
it, without fee or indenture. I will use treatment to help the sick according to my ability and
judgment, but never with a view to injury and
wrong doing. I will keep pure and holy both
my life and my art. Into whatsoever houses I
enter, I will enter to help the sick, and I will
abstain from all intentional wrong-doing and
harm. And whatsoever I shall see or hear in
the course of my profession, as well as outside
my profession in my intercourse with men, if it
be what should not be published abroad, I will
never divulge, holding such things to be holy
secrets. Now if I carry out this oath, and
break it not, may I gain forever reputation
among all men for my life and for my art;
but if I transgress it and forswear myself,
may the opposite befall me.

The Oath

I urge you not to be too unkind, but to consider carefully your patient's superabundance

or means. Sometimes give your services for
nothing, calling to mind a previous benefaction
or present satisfaction. And if there be an
opportunity of serving one who is a stranger in
financial straits, give full assistance to all such.
For where there is love of man, there is also
love of the art. For some patients, though conscious that their condition is perilous, recover
their health simply through their contentment
with the goodness of the physician. And it is
well to superintend the sick to make them well,
to care for the healthy to keep them well, but
also to care for one's own self, so as to observe
what is seemly.

Precepts
Trans. W. H. S. Jones

AN HONEST LAWYER

Abraham Lincoln

President of the United States during the Civil
War; preserver of the Union, and emancipator of the
slaves, 1809–1865

There is a vague popular belief that lawyers
are necessarily dishonest. I say vague, because
when we consider to what extent confidence

and honors are reposed in and conferred upon lawyers by the people, it appears improbable that this impression of dishonesty is very distinct and vivid. Yet the impression is common, almost universal. Let no young man choosing the law for a calling for a moment yield to the popular belief. Resolve to be honest at all events; and if in your own judgment you cannot be an honest lawyer, resolve to be honest without being a lawyer. Choose some other occupation rather than one in the choosing of which you do, in advance, consent to be a knave.

(From notes prepared by Lincoln for a lecture in law, 1850.)

Abraham Lincoln as a Man of Letters
By Luther Emerson Robinson

ADVICE TO A CLIENT
ABRAHAM LINCOLN
President of the United States during the Civil War; preserver of the Union, and emancipator of the slaves; 1809–1865

Yes, we can doubtless gain your case for you; we can set a whole neighborhood at loggerheads; we can distress a widowed mother and her six fatherless children, and thereby get for you six hundred dollars to which you seem to have a legal claim, but which rightfully belongs, it appears to me, as much to the woman and her children as it does to you. You must remember, however, that some things legally right are not morally right. We shall not take your case, but we will give you a little advice for which we will charge you nothing. You seem to be a sprightly, energetic man. We would advise you to try your hand at making six hundred dollars in some other way.

(As reported by William H. Herndon, Lincoln's junior law partner.)

Lincoln the Lawyer
By Frederick Trevor Hill

THE LAWYER *

WILFRED T. GRENFELL

English: Christian physician and teacher to the fishermen of Labrador, 1865–1940

Surely, the true lawyer's ideal is not a crime, a retribution, a fee, though he too is tempted to keep so close to the mill which grinds out dollars that he may lose the full vision of his potentiality. Christ as a lawyer would, exactly

as if a doctor, be working for big and worthy
ends—to produce conditions that would abolish
crime—and so unselfishly working for the
elimination of his own profession. To me it
seems just as certain that if the true physician
must treat the whole man, if he is to cure physical ailments, so normal obliquities demand the
same treatment of the true lawyer. That disease leads to sin and crime is quite as true as
that sin and crime lead to disease. A man in
the full flush of health and in good surroundings
is less likely to become a criminal than a weakling in a bad environment.

The Adventure of Life

A GOOD MAN OF BUSINESS *
Charles Dickens
English novelist, 1812–1870

"Oh, captive, bound," cried the phantom;
"not to know that ages of incessant labor by
immortal creatures for this earth must pass into
eternity before the good of which it is suscep-
tible is all developed! Not to know that any
Christian spirit working kindly in its little
sphere, whatever it may be, will find its mor-

tal life too short for its vast means of usefulness! Not to know that no space of regret can make amends for one life's opportunities misused! Yet such was I!"

"But you were always a good man of business, Jacob," faltered Scrooge, who now began to apply this to himself.

"Business!" cried the Ghost, wringing its hands again. "Mankind was my business. The common welfare was my business; charity, mercy, forbearance, and benevolence, were all my business. The dealings of my trade were but a drop of water in the comprehensive ocean of my business!"

A Christmas Carol

The Gift and the Giver

THE ONLY REAL HEATHEN
WILFRED T. GRENFELL
English: Christian physician and teacher to
the fishermen of Labrador, 1865–1940

The only real heathen and heretics are the
purely selfish. It is for our own sakes as well
as theirs that we desire their conversion.
For while they are losing all life has to give,
we are losing the share they might contribute.

The Adventure of Life

NOT WHAT WE GIVE
JAMES RUSSELL LOWELL
American poet and essayist, 1819–1891

Not what we give, but what we share,
   For the gift without the giver is bare:

Who gives himself with his alms feeds three,
　Himself, his hungering neighbor, and Me.
　　　　　　　From *The Vision of Sir Launfal*

WHO IS MY NEIGHBOR?

Christian, first century

A certain lawyer stood up and tempted (Jesus) saying, "Master, what shall I do to inherit eternal life?"

And he said unto him, "What is written in the law? how readest thou?"

And he answering said, "Thou shalt love the Lord thy God with all thy heart, and with all thy soul, and with all thy strength, and with all thy mind; and thy neighbor as thyself."

And he said unto him, "Thou hast answered right: this do, and thou shalt live."

But he, desiring to justify himself, said unto Jesus, "And who is my neighbor?"

Jesus made answer and said: "A certain man was going down from Jerusalem to Jericho; and he fell among robbers, which both stripped him and beat him, and departed, leaving him half dead. And by chance a certain priest

was going down that way: and when he saw
him, he passed by on the other side. And in
like manner a Levite also, when he came to
the place, and saw him, passed by on the other
side. But a certain Samaritan, as he journeyed,
came where he was: and when he saw him he
was moved with compassion, and came to him,
and bound up his wounds, pouring on them
oil and wine; and he set him on his own beast,
and brought him to an inn, and took care of
him. And on the morrow he took out two
pence, and gave them to the host, and said,
'Take care of him; and whatsoever thou spend-
est more, I, when I come back again, will repay
thee.' Which of these three, thinkest thou,
proved neighbor unto him that fell among the
robbers?"

And he said, "He that shewed mercy on him."

And Jesus said unto him, "Go, and do thou
likewise."

From *The Gospel According to Luke*
New Testament

THE DOCTOR'S BIG FEE *

Wilfred T. Grenfell

English: Christian physician and teacher to
the fishermen of Labrador, 1865-1940

Do you see that steep, rocky cape over
there? It is the most northerly you can dis-
tinguish. There is a little village just behind
that head. It is hidden away in a rift in the
mountain which forms a tiny cove for a safe an-
chorage. I had as big a fee there only two days
ago as ever I received when I was practising
in London.

Deep-Water "Crik," we call it. About half
a dozen fishermen's families live there. Three
days ago a boat came over at daylight to see
if they could get a doctor, and I was debating
as to the advisability of leaving the hospital,
when an old skipper from a schooner in the
harbor came ashore to tell me: "It's t' old
Englishman; Uncle Solomon they calls him."

It was nearly midday before we started for
the cape. As soon as we landed, a black-
bearded, bright-faced man of about fifty gave
us a hearty greeting, and such evident happiness
lit up his peculiarly piercing eyes that it made
us feel a little more cheerful, even before he had
taken us into his house. There we found a cup

of steaming hot tea prepared. That tea did not seem a whit less sweet because "there be ne'er a drop o' milk in t' harbor, Doctor, and molasses be scarce, too, till t' fish be dry."

Everything was clean. The pots and pans and tin cooking-utensils shone so brightly from the walls that the flame of the tiny kerosene lamp suggested ten hundredfold the candle-power it possessed.

Three children were playing on the hearth with a younger man, evidently their father. "No, Doctor, they aren't ours exactly," replied our host, in answer to my question, "but us took Sam as our own when he was born, and his mother lay dead. and he've been with us ever since. Those be his little ones. You remember Kate, his wife?"

I remembered her very well, and the struggle we had had in trying to save her.

"Skipper John," I said, as soon as the tea was over, "let's get out and see the old Englishman. He'll be tired waiting."

"Youse needn't go out, Doctor. He be upstairs in bed."

"Upstairs" was a triangular space. At each end was a tiny window, and the whole, windows included, had been divided longitudinally by a single thickness of hand-sawn lumber, up to the tiny cross-beams. There was no lofting, and both windows were open: a cool breeze was blowing right through. Cheerfulness was given by a bright white paper which had been pasted on over everything. Home-made rag mats covered the planed boards.

"Uncle Solomon, it's the Doctor," I called. A trembling old hand came out to meet mine.

"Not so well, Uncle Solomon? No pain, I hope?"

"No pain, Doctor, thank t' good Lord—and Skipper John," he added. "He took us in, Doctor, when t' old lady and I were starving."

When the interview was over I found my host's hand on my shoulder. "You'll be wanting a good hot cup o' tea, I knows, Doctor. And t' wife's made you a bit o' toast, and a taste o' hot berry jam. We are so grateful you comed, Doctor. But thanks aren't dollars."

"No, Skipper," was all I said. "We doctors, anyhow, find them quite as scarce."

"Well, Doctor," he added, "please God if I gets a skin t' winter I'll try and pay you for your visit anyhow. But I hasn't a cent in the world just now. The old couple has taken the little us had put by."

"Skipper John, what relation are those people to you?"

"Well, Doctor, no relation 'zactly."

"Do they pay nothing at all?"

"Them has nothing," he replied.

"Why did you take them in?"

"They was homeless, Doctor, and the old lady was already blind."

"How long have they been with you?"

"Just twelve months come Saturday."

"Thanks, Skipper," was all I could say; but I found myself standing with my hat off in the presence of this man. I thought then, and still think, I had received one of my largest fees.

Labrador Days

THE WIDOW'S MITES
Christian, first century

He looked up and saw the rich men that were casting their gifts into the treasury. And he saw a certain poor widow casting in thither two mites. And he said, "Of a truth I say unto you this poor widow cast in more than they all: for all these did of their superfluity cast in unto the gifts; but she of her want did cast in all the living that she had."

From *The Gospel According to Luke*
New Testament

THE MEASURE OF RESPONSIBILITY
XENOPHON
Greek military commander and
historian, about 434–355 B.C.

(Written in appreciation of Socrates)

Though his sacrifices were humble, according to his means, he thought himself not a whit inferior to those who made frequent and magnificent sacrifices out of great possessions. The gods (he said) could not well delight more in great offerings than in small—for in that case must the gifts of the wicked often have found more favor in their sight than the gifts of the upright—and man would not find life worth having, if the gifts of the wicked were received with more favor by the gods than the gifts of the upright. No, the greater the piety of the giver, the greater (he thought) was the delight of the gods in the gift. He would quote with approval the line:

"According to thy power render sacrifice

to the immortal gods;" and he would add that in our treatment of friends and strangers, and in all our behavior, it is a noble principle to *render according to our power.*

Memorabilia, i
Trans. E. C. Marchant

ABOU BEN ADHEM
Leigh Hunt
English poet and essayist, 1784–1859

Abou Ben Adhem (may his tribe increase)
Awoke one night from a deep dream of peace
And saw within the moonlight in the room,
Making it rich and like a lily in bloom,
An angel writing in a book of gold:—
Exceeding peace had made Ben Adhem bold
And to the presence in the room he said,
"What writest thou?"—The vision raised its
        head
And, with a look made of all sweet accord,
Answered, "The names of those who love the
        Lord."
"And is mine one?" said Abou. "Nay, not so,"
Replied the angel. Abou spoke more low
But cheerly still, and said, "I pray thee, then,
Write me as one that loves his fellow-men."

The angel wrote, and vanished. The next night
It came again with a great, wakening light
And showed the names whom love of God had
blessed,
And lo! Ben Adhem's name led all the rest.

THE SPARROW *
Ivan Sergiewich Turgenev
Russian novelist, 1818–1883

I was returning from hunting and walking
along an avenue of the garden, my dog running
in front of me.

Suddenly he took shorter steps, and began
to steal along as though tracking game.

I looked along the avenue and saw a young
sparrow, with yellow about its beak and down
on its head. It had fallen out of the nest
(the wind was violently shaking the birch
trees in the avenue) and sat unable to move,
helplessly flapping its half-grown wings.

My dog was slowly approaching it, when,
suddenly darting down from a tree close by,
an old dark-throated sparrow fell like a stone
right before his nose, and all ruffled up, terrified,
with despairing and pitiful cheeps, it flung itself

twice towards the open jaws of shining teeth.

It sprang to save; it cast itself before its nestling, but all its tiny body was shaking with terror; its note was harsh and strange. Swooning with fear, it offered itself up!

What a huge monster must the dog have seemed to it! And yet it could not stay on its high branch out of danger. A force stronger than its will flung it down.

My Trésor stood still, drew back. Clearly he too recognized this force.

I hastened to call off the disconcerted dog, and went away, full of reverence.

Love, I thought, is stronger than death or the fear of death. Only by it, by love, life holds together and advances.

Dream Tales and Prose Poems
Trans. Constance Garnett

THE SPIRIT OF YOUTH *
JANE ADDAMS
American: head resident of Hull House, Chicago;
writer on social reforms, 1860–1935

Even as we pass by the joy and beauty of youth on the streets without dreaming it is there, so we may hurry past the very presence of august things without recognition. We may easily fail to sense those spiritual realities, which in every age have haunted youth and called to him without ceasing. It may relieve the mind to break forth in moments of irritation against "the folly of the coming generation," but whoso pauses on his plodding way to call even his youngest and rashest brother a fool ruins thereby the joy of his journey,—for youth is so vivid an element in life that unless it is cherished all the rest is spoiled. The most praiseworthy journey grows dull and leaden unless companioned by youth's iridescent dreams. The mature of each generation run a grave risk of putting their efforts in a futile direction, in a blind alley as it were, unless they can keep in touch with the youth of their own day and know at least the trend in which eager dreams are driving them. These young people have the advantage of "morning in their hearts"; they have such power of direct action, such ability to stand free from fear, to break through life's trammelings, that in spite of ourselves we become convinced that

"They to the disappointed earth shall give
The lives we meant to live."

All of us forget how very early we are in the

experiment of founding self-government in this trying climate of America, and that we are making the experiment in the most materialistic period of all history, having as our court of last appeal against that materialism only the wonderful and inexplicable instinct for justice which resides in the hearts of men,—which is never so irresistible as when the heart is young. We may cultivate this most precious possession, or we may disregard it. We may listen to the young voices rising clear above the roar of industrialism and the prudent councils of commerce, or we may become hypnotized by the sudden new emphasis placed upon wealth and power and forget the supremacy of spiritual forces in men's affairs. It is as if we ignored a wistful, over-confident creature who walked through our city streets calling out, "I am the spirit of Youth! With me, all things are possible!"

Each generation of moralists and educators find themselves facing an inevitable dilemma; first, to keep the young committed to their charge "unspotted from the world," and, second, to connect the young with the ruthless and materialistic world all about them in such wise that they may make it the arena for their spiritual endeavor. This, of course, has ever been the task of religion, to make the sense of obligation personal, to touch morality with enthusiasm, to bathe the world in affection—and on all sides we are challenging the teachers of religion to perform this task for the youth of the city.

For thousands of years definite religious instruction has been given by authorized agents to the youth of all nations, emphasized through tribal ceremonials, the assumption of the Roman toga, the Barmitzvah of the Jews, the First Communion of thousands of children in Catholic Europe, the Sunday Schools of even the least formal of evangelical sects. It is as if men had always felt that this expanding period of human life must be seized upon for spiritual ends, that the tender issue and newly awakened emotions must be made the repository for the historic ideals and dogmas, which are, after all, the most precious possessions of the race. How has it come about that so many of the city youth are not given their share in our common inheritance of life's best goods? Why are their tender feet so often ensnared even when they are going about youth's legitimate business?

The Spirit of Youth

THE GREATEST OF THESE IS LOVE
THE APOSTLE PAUL
Christian, first century

If I speak with the tongues of men and of angels, but have not love, I am become sounding brass, or a clanging cymbal. And if I have the gift of prophecy, and know all mysteries and all knowledge; and if I have all faith, so as to remove mountains, but have not love, I am nothing. And if I bestow all my goods to feed the poor, and if I give my body to be burned, but have not love, it profiteth me nothing.

Love suffereth long, and is kind; love envieth not; love vaunteth not itself, is not puffed up, doth not behave itself unseemly, seeketh not its own, is not provoked, taketh not account of evil; rejoiceth not in unrighteousness, but rejoiceth with the truth; beareth all things, believeth all things, hopeth all things, endureth all things. Love never faileth: but whether there be prophecies, they shall be done away; whether there be tongues, they shall cease; whether there be knowledge, it shall be done away. For we know in part, and we prophesy in part; but when that which is perfect is come, that which is in part shall be done away.

When I was a child, I spake as a child, I felt as a child, I thought as a child: now that I am become a man, I have put away childish things. For now we see in a mirror, darkly; but then face to face: now I know in part; but then shall I know even as also I have been known.

But now abideth faith, hope, love, *these* three; and the greatest of these is love.

From *The First Epistle to the Corinthians*
New Testament

LOVE YOUR ENEMIES
Christian, first century

Ye have heard that it was said, An eye for an eye, and a tooth for a tooth: but I say unto you, Resist not him that is evil; but whosoever smiteth thee on thy right cheek, turn to him the other also. And if any man would go to law with thee, and take away thy coat, let him have thy cloak also. And whosoever shall compel thee to go one mile, go with him twain. Give to him that asketh thee, and from him that would borrow of thee turn not thou away.

Ye have heard that it was said, Thou shalt love thy neighbor, and hate thine enemy: but I say unto you, Love your enemies, and pray for them that persecute you; that ye may be the sons of your Father which is in heaven: for he maketh his sun to rise on the evil and the good, and sendeth rain on the just and the unjust. For if ye love them that love you, what reward have ye? do not even the publicans the same? And if ye salute your brethren only, what do ye more than others? do not even the Gentiles the same? Ye therefore shall be perfect, as your heavenly Father is perfect.

From *The Gospel According to Matthew*
New Testament

A LIVING SACRIFICE
THE APOSTLE PAUL
Christian, first century

I appeal to you, therefore, brothers, by this mercy of God, to offer your bodies in a living sacrifice that will be holy and acceptable to God; that is your rational worship. You must not adopt the customs of this world, but by your new attitude of mind be transformed so that you can find out what God's will is—what is good, pleasing, and perfect.

By the favor that God has shown me, I would tell every one of you not to think too highly of himself, but to think reasonably, judging himself by the degree of faith God has allowed him. For just as there are many parts united in our human bodies, and the parts do not all have the same function, so, many as we are, we form one body through union with Christ, and we are individually parts of one another. We have gifts that differ with the favor that God has shown us, whether it is that of preaching, differing with the measure of our faith, or of practical work, differing in the field of service, or the teacher who exercises his gift in teaching, the speaker, in his exhortation, the giver of charity, with generosity, the office-holder, with devotion, the one who does acts of mercy, with cheerfulness. Your love must be genuine. You must hate what is wrong, and hold to what is right. Be affectionate in your love for the brotherhood, eager to show one another honor, not wanting in devotion, but on fire with the Spirit. Serve the Lord. Be happy in your hope, steadfast in time of trouble, persistent in prayer. Supply the needs of God's people, be unfailing in hospitality. Bless your persecutors; bless them; do not curse them. Rejoice with those who rejoice, weep with those who weep. Live in harmony with one another. Do not be too ambitious, but accept humble tasks. Do not be conceited. Do not pay anyone back with evil for evil. See that you are above reproach in the eyes of everyone. If possible, for your part, live peaceably with everyone. Do not take your revenge, dear friends, but leave room for God's anger, for the Scripture says, "Vengeance belongs to me; I will pay them back, says the Lord." No! if your enemy is hungry, feed him! If he is thirsty, give him something to drink! For if you do, you will heap burning coals upon his head! Do not be conquered by evil, but conquer evil with good.

From *The Epistle to the Romans*
New Testament
An American translation by Edgar J. Goodspeed

DUTIES AND RIGHTS

GIUSEPPE MAZZINI
Italian patriot, and defender of
republicanism, 1805–1872

I want to speak to you of your duties. I want to speak to you as my heart dictates to

me of the most sacred things which we know—
of God, of humanity, of the fatherland, of the
family.

Why do I speak to you of your duties before speaking to you of your rights? Why do
I speak to you of self-sacrifice and not of conquest; of virtue, moral improvement, education,
and not of material well-being?

Certainly rights exist; but where the rights
of an individual come into conflict with those
of another, how can we hope to reconcile and
harmonize them without appealing to something
superior to all rights? And where the rights
of an individual, or of many individuals, clash
with the rights of the country, to what tribunal
are we to appeal? With the theory of happiness, of well-being, as the primary aim of
existence we shall only form egoistic men, worshipers of the material, who will carry the
old passions into the new order of things and
corrupt it in a few months. We have therefore
to find a principle of education superior to any
such theory, which shall guide men to better
things, teach them constancy in self-sacrifice
and link them with their fellow men.

Material improvement is essential, and we
shall strive to win it for ourselves; but not because the one thing necessary for man is to be

well fed and housed, but rather because you cannot have a sense of your own dignity or any
moral development while you are engaged, as
at the present day, in a continual duel with
want. You need, then, a change in your
material conditions to enable you to develop
morally; you need to work less so as to have
some hours of your day to devote to the improvement of your minds. You must strive,
then, for this change, and you will obtain it,
but you must strive for it as a means, not as
an end; strive for it from a sense of duty, not
only as a right; strive for it in order to make
yourselves better, not only to make yourselves
materially happy. To make yourselves better—
this must be the aim of your life.

We believe in the holy, inexorable, dominating
idea of duty, the sole standard of life: duty
that embraces family, fatherland, humanity;
duty that bids us promote the progress of
others that our own may be effected, and of
ourselves that it may profit that of others;
duty, without which no right exists. that creates
the virtue of self-sacrifice, in truth the only
pure virtue, holy and mighty in power, the
noblest jewel that crowns and hallows the human
soul.

The Duties of Man and Other Essays

WHAT HAVE I DONE?

Louis Pasteur
French: founder of the science
of bacteriology, 1822–1895

Young men, have confidence in those powerful and safe methods, of which we do not yet know all the secrets. And, whatever your career may be, do not let yourselves become tainted by a deprecating and barren skepticism, do not let yourselves be discouraged by the sadness of certain hours which pass over nations. Live in the serene peace of laboratories and libraries. Say to yourselves first, "What have I done for my instruction?" and as you gradually advance, "What have I done for my country?" until the time comes when you may have the immense happiness of thinking that you have contributed in some way to the progress and to the good of humanity. But whether our efforts are, or not, favored by life, let us be able to say, when we come near the great goal, "I have done what I could."

The Life of Pasteur
René Vallery-Radot
Trans. Mrs. R. L. Devonshire

EVERLASTING MONUMENTS[*]

PERICLES

Athenian statesman and patron of art, 490–429 B. C.

I have dwelt upon the greatness of Athens because I want to show you that we are contending for a higher prize than those who enjoy none of these privileges, and to establish by manifest proof the merit of these men whom I am now commemorating. Their loftiest praise has already been spoken. For in magnifying the city I have magnified them, and men like them whose virtues made her glorious. And of how few Hellenes can it be said as of them, that their deeds when weighed in the balance have been found equal to their fame! None of these men was enervated by wealth or hesitated to resign the pleasures of life; none of them put off the evil day in the hope, natural to poverty, that a man, though poor, may one day become rich. They resigned to hope their unknown chance of happiness; but in the face of death they resolved to rely upon themselves alone. And when the moment came they were minded to resist and suffer, rather than to fly and save their lives; they ran away from the word of dishonor, but on the battlefield their feet stood fast, and in an instant, at the height of their fortune, they passed away from the scene not of their fear but of their glory.

Such was the end of these men; they were worthy of Athens, and the living need not desire to have a more heroic spirit, although they may pray for a less fatal issue. The value of such a spirit is not to be expressed in words. Any one can discourse to you forever about the advantages of a brave defense which you know already. But instead of listening to him I would have you day by day fix your eyes upon the greatness of Athens, until you become filled with the love of her; and when you are impressed by the spectacle of her glory, reflect that this empire has been acquired by men who knew their duty and had the courage to do it, who in the hour of conflict had the fear of dishonor always present to them, and who, if ever they failed in an enterprise, would not allow their virtues to be lost to their country, but freely gave their lives to her as the fairest offering which they could present at her feast.

The sacrifice which they collectively made was individually repaid to them; for they received again each one for himself a praise which grows not old, and the noblest of all sepulchres —I speak not of that in which their remains are laid but of that in which their glory sur-

vives, and is proclaimed always and on every
fitting occasion both in word and deed. For
the whole earth is the sepulchre of famous men:
not only are they commemorated by columns
and inscriptions in their own country, but in
foreign lands there dwells also an unwritten
memorial of them, graven not on stone but in
the hearts of men.

(From the funeral speech in honor of the Athenians
who fell in the first year of the Peloponnesian War.)

Thucydides, Book ii
Trans. Benjamin Jowett

THE GIFT AND THE GIVER

Service to Humanity

THE REDEMPTIVE TASK OF EVERYONE

STANTON COIT

English writer and lecturer, 1857 – 1944

Be assured that if thou failest, none other—
not nature, nor man, nor angel, nor Creator—
will render the service or bestow the love due
from thee. According to thine opportunity, thou
must be the strength of the weak, the refuge of
the sorrowful. Thou must have compassion on
those within thy reach who are worn with toil;
thou must defend and cherish the young, bless
and support the aged; welcome strangers who
come thy way; comfort those who are distressed in mind, body, or estate; extend thy
mercy to the oppressed, and especially to those
who suffer injustice or are persecuted for
righteousness' sake. By strength of character
thou art to help in saving the vicious. And
by the sweet mystery of love it will be thy

privilege to soothe into peace the spirit of the
dying.   All this thou must be and do.   Thy defi-
ciencies and imperfections offer no ground for
exemption, for they will themselves be overcome
and dissolved in the redemptive work that waits
for thee.

Social Worship
Ed. Stanton Coit

KING ARTHUR'S ORDER OF CHIVALRY

Alfred Tennyson
English poet, 1809–1892

I was first of all the kings who drew
The knighthood-errant of this realm and all
The realms together under me, their Head,
In that fair Order of my Table Round,
A glorious company, the flower of men,
To serve as model for the mighty world,
And be the fair beginning of a time.
I made them lay their hands in mine and swear
To reverence the King as if he were
Their conscience, and their conscience as their
    King,
To break the heathen and uphold the Christ.

To ride abroad redressing human wrongs,
To speak no slander, no, nor listen to it,
To honor his own word as if his God's,
To lead sweet lives in purest chastity,
To love one maiden only, cleave to her,
And worship her by years of noble deeds
Until they won her; for indeed I knew
Of no more subtle master under heaven
Than is the maiden passion for a maid,
Not only to keep down the base in man,
But teach high thought, and amiable words
And courtliness, and the desire of fame,
And love of truth, and all that makes a man.

Idylls of the King

THE BURNING BUSH *
Hebrew; this passage, eighth century B. C.

Moses was keeping the flock of Jethro his
father in law, and he led the flock to the back
of the wilderness, and came to the mountain
of God. And the angel of the Lord appeared
unto him in a flame of fire out of the midst of
a bush: and he looked, and, behold, the bush
burned with fire, and the bush was not consumed.

And Moses said, "I will turn aside now, and see this great sight, why the bush is not burnt." And when the Lord saw that he turned aside to see, God called unto him out of the midst of the bush, and said, "Moses, Moses."

And he said, "Here am I."

And he said, "Draw not nigh hither: put off thy shoes from off thy feet, for the place whereon thou standest is holy ground. I am the God of Abraham, the God of Isaac, and the God of Jacob."

And Moses hid his face; for he was afraid to look upon God. And the Lord said, "I have surely seen the affliction of my people which are in Egypt, and have heard their cry by reason of their taskmasters; for I know their sorrows; and I am come down to deliver them out of the hand of the Egyptians, and to bring them up out of that land unto a good land and a large, unto a land flowing with milk and honey. Come now therefore and I will send thee unto Pharaoh, that thou mayest bring forth my people out of Egypt."

And Moses said unto God, "Who am I, that I should go unto Pharaoh, and that I should bring forth the children of Israel out of Egypt?"

And he said, "Certainly I will be with thee;

and this shall be a token unto thee, that I have sent thee: when thou hast brought forth the people out of Egypt, ye shall serve God upon this mountain."

And Moses said unto God, "Behold, when I come unto the children of Israel, and shall say unto them, The God of your fathers hath sent me unto you; and they shall say to me, What is his name? what shall I say unto them?"

And God said unto Moses, "Thus shalt thou say unto the children of Israel, I AM hath sent me unto you."

From *The Book of the Exodus*
Old Testament

UNTO THE LEAST
Christian, first century

The son of man shall come, and all the angels with him, and before him shall be gathered all the nations: and he shall separate them one from another, as the shepherd separateth the sheep from the goats: and he shall set the sheep on his right hand, but the goats on the left.

Then shall the king say unto them on his right hand, "Come, ye blessed of my Father, inherit the kingdom prepared for you from the foundation of the world: for I was an hungered, and ye gave me meat: I was thirsty, and ye gave me drink: I was a stranger, and ye took me in; naked, and ye clothed me: I was sick, and ye visited me: I was in prison, and ye came unto me."

Then shall the righteous answer him saying, "Lord, when saw we thee an hungered and fed thee? or athirst, and gave thee drink? and when saw we thee a stranger, and took thee in? and naked, and clothed thee? And when saw we thee sick, or in prison, and came unto thee?"

And the king shall answer and say unto them, "Verily I say unto you, inasmuch as ye did it unto one of these my brethren, even these least, ye did it unto me."

Then shall he say also unto them on the left hand, "I was an hungered, and ye gave me no meat: I was thirsty, and ye gave me no drink: I was a stranger, and ye took me not in; naked, and ye clothed me not; sick, and in prison, and ye visited me not."

Then shall they also answer, saying, "Lord, when saw we thee an hungered, or athirst, or a stranger, or naked, or sick, or in prison, and did not minister unto thee?"

Then shall he answer them, saying, "Verily I say unto you, inasmuch as ye did it not unto one of these least, ye did it not unto me."

From *The Gospel According to Matthew*
New Testament

THE REGENERATION OF MEN [*]
William Booth
English: founder of the Salvation Army; 1829–1912

"Let things alone," the "laws of supply and demand," and all the rest of the excuses by which those who stand on firm ground salve their consciences when they leave their brother to sink, how do they look when we apply them to the actual loss of life at sea? Does "Let things alone" man the lifeboat? Will the inexorable laws of political economy save the shipwrecked sailor from the boiling surf? No desire to make it pay created the National Lifeboat Institution; no law of supply and demand actuates the volunteers who risk their lives to bring the shipwrecked to shore. What we have to do is to apply the same principle to society. We want a Social Lifeboat Institution, a Social Lifeboat Brigade, to snatch from the abyss those who if left to themselves will perish as miserably as the crew of a ship that founders in mid-ocean. The moment that we take in hand this work we shall be compelled to turn our attention seriously to the question whether prevention is not better than cure. It is easier and cheaper, and in every way better, to prevent the loss of home than to have to re-create that home.

The renovation of our social system is a work so vast that no one of us, nor all of us put together, can define all the measures that will have to be taken before we attain even the cab horse ideal of existence for our children and our children's children. All that we can do is attack, in a serious, practical spirit, the worst and most pressing evils, knowing that if we do our duty, we obey the voice of God. He is the Captain of our Salvation. If we but follow where he leads we shall not want for marching orders, nor need we imagine that he will narrow the field of operations.

I am laboring under no delusions as to the possibility of inaugurating the millennium by any social specific. In the struggle of life, the weakest will go to the wall, and there are so many weak. The fittest, in tooth and claw, will survive. All that we can do is to soften the lot of the unfit and make their suffering less horrible than it is at present. No outside propping will make some men stand erect. All material help from without is useful only in so far as it develops moral strength within. And some men seem to have lost even the very faculty of self-help. There is an immense lack of common sense and of vital energy on the part of multitudes. Insoluble the problem is, I am absolutely convinced, unless it is possible to bring new moral life into the soul of these people. This should be the first object of every social reformer, whose work will only last if it is built on the solid foundation of a new birth,—to cry, "You must be born again."

To get a man soundly saved it is not enough to put on him a pair of new breeches, to give him regular work, or even to give him a university education. These things are all outside a man; and if the inside remains unchanged you have wasted your labor. You must in some way or other graft upon the man's nature a new nature, which has in it the element of the divine. To change the nature of the individual, to get at the heart, to save his soul, is the only real, lasting method of doing him any good. In many modern schemes of social regeneration it is forgotten that "it takes a soul to move a body, e'en to a cleaner sty," and at the risk of being misunderstood and misrepresented, I must assert in the most unqualified way that it is primarily and mainly for the sake of saving the soul that I seek the salvation of the body.

But what is the use of preaching the Gospel to men whose whole attention is concentrated upon a mad, desperate struggle to keep themselves alive? You might as well give a tract to a shipwrecked sailor who is battling with the surf which has drowned his comrades and threatens to drown him. He will not listen to you. Nay, he cannot hear you. The first thing to do is to get him at least a footing on firm ground, and to give him room to live. Then you may have a chance. At present you have none. And you will have all the better opportunity to find a way to his heart if he comes to know that it was you who pulled him out.

In Darkest England and the Way Out.

WILLIAM BOOTH[*]
Harold Begbie
English writer, 1871-1929

Civilization can only stand if it is built upon a rock, and the only rock which can withstand the storms of the ages is the rock of the moral law. Man can no more leave God out of his philosophies than he can live without his heart or see without his eyes.

William Booth was one of the last century's greatest prophets of this truth, and certainly its boldest, most courageous, and most effective protagonist. He knew, with but little help from his reason, that the Infinite is not to be examined by the brain of any finite creature; and he knew, with only his moral nature to help him, that the Infinite may be clasped and held by the upstretching hands of love and faith. He has left to the world the memory of a life which deliberately sought the pit, and in the pit worked miracles upon the souls of men by the force of a childlike confidence in God, and by the power of a love which, even if it be judged inferior to the love of the mystic, was nevertheless an infinitely more real and honest love than any carefully measured affection which had hitherto satisfied philanthropy.

Men, indeed, the makers of a civilization founded on combat, have not yet thought what it is to love; and for this reason more than all other reasons religion has failed to transform human existence. No word so common as love, no term so debased, no ideal so woefully unrealized— The love which is sublimely unconscious of self, which is forever at rest, which is unshaken by events and unchanged by time, which seeks only the welfare of another, which lives its life in the life of another, which gives and gives again, never asking, never thinking to ask, for return, which is patient, which is tolerant, which is satisfied—this ministering and adoring love, at once human and divine, at once domestic and religious, this love which "bears it out even to the edge of doom," which seeketh not its own, which is the very centre and principle of the Divine Will, this love, we may say, has hardly yet become even an ideal of the human race.

"The Christian ideal," it is said, "has not been tried and found wanting; it has been found difficult, and left untried." Really to love another person is difficult even for the best of the human race; but how difficult, how almost impossible, when that other person is infamous, degraded, and repulsive. Nevertheless, to read the Gospel in church, to pray for love, and to preach about love, making not one single effort of love in our dealings with the abandoned or the lost, is not this manifestly to live our lives entirely outside the kingdom of heaven? Christianity is, surely, this intense, unselfish, and ministering love or it is no whit different from the ancient religions of terror and superstition.

It is when we reflect upon this absence of love from the world, carefully considering in our minds the difference which exists between social kindness and self-sacrificing love that we are able to see at least something of the greatness of the life of William Booth. His supreme contribution to the religious experience of mankind lies in his proof that by the power of love the worst of men can be changed into the best of men; but his highest and most enduring greatness is the genuine passion of love which urged him into the hells of human existence to work those miracles of conversion. He groaned over the degradation of men, he agonized over the debasement of women, he wept over the sufferings of children. Never has any man whose whole nature so recoiled from the sight of pain, and whose sensitive spirit so shrank from even a recital of grief, waded so far into the sea of agony. He suffered in helping the suffering. He was tortured in rescuing the tortured. If he failed to avert Armageddon, more than any man in the latter part of the nineteenth century he helped to create the social conscience, not by political formula or by any merely philanthropic invention, but by the force and energy of his boundless love.

Life of William Booth—The Founder of
the Salvation Army

THE HEALING TOUCH *
Helen Keller

American: she became deaf, dumb, and blind in infancy, learned to read and write by touch, to converse by signs, and to speak, and received the degree of A.B. from Radcliffe College; 1880—

Those are red-letter days in our lives when we meet people who thrill us like a fine poem, people whose handshake is brimful of unspoken sympathy, and whose sweet, rich natures impart to our eager, impatient spirits a wonderful restfulness which in its essence is divine.

The perplexities, irritations, and worries that have absorbed us pass like unpleasant dreams, and we wake to see with new eyes and hear with new ears the beauty and harmony of God's real world. The solemn nothings that fill our everyday life blossom suddenly into bright possibilities. In a word, while such friends are near us we feel that all is well. Perhaps we never saw them before, and they may never cross our life's path again; but the influence of their calm, mellow natures is a libation poured upon our discontent, and we feel its healing touch.

The hands of those I meet are dumbly eloquent to me. There are those whose hands have sunbeams in them, so that their grasp warms my heart.

I count it one of the sweetest privileges of my life to have known and conversed with many men of genius. Only those who knew Bishop Brooks can appreciate the joy his friendship was to those who possessed it. As a child I loved to sit on his knee and clasp his great hand with one of mine, while Miss Sullivan spelled into the other his beautiful words about God and the spiritual world. I heard him with a child's wonder and delight. My spirit could not reach up to his, but he gave me a real

sense of joy in life, and I never left him without carrying away a fine thought that grew in
beauty and depth of meaning as I grew. Once,
when I was puzzled to know why there were
so many religions, he said: "There is one universal religion, Helen—the religion of love.
Love your Heavenly Father with your whole
heart and soul, love every child of God as much
as ever you can, and remember that the possibilities of good are greater than the possibilities of evil." His life was a happy il-
lustration of this great truth. In his noble
soul love and widest knowledge were blended
with faith that had become insight. He saw
　　God in all that liberates and lifts,
　In all that humbles, sweetens, and consoles.

The Story of My Life

THE RELIEF OF THE POOR [*]
JANE ADDAMS
American: head resident of Hull House, Chicago;
writer on social reforms, 1860–1935

A very little familiarity with the poor districts of any city is sufficient to show how
primitive and genuine are the neighborly re-

lations. There is the greatest willingness to lend or borrow anything, and all the residents of the given tenement know the most intimate family affairs of all the others. The fact that the economic conditions of all alike is on a most precarious level makes the ready outflow of sympathy and material assistance the most natural thing in the world. There are numberless instances of self-sacrifice quite unknown in the circles where greater economic advantages make that kind of intimate knowledge of one's neighbors impossible. An Irish family in which the man has lost his place and the woman is struggling to eke out the scanty savings by day's work will take in the widow and her five children who have been turned into the street, without a moment's reflection upon the physical discomforts involved. The most maligned landlady who lives in the house with her tenants is usually ready to lend a scuttle full of coal to one of them who may be out of work, or to share her supper. A woman for whom the writer had long tried in vain to find work failed to appear at the appointed time when employment was secured at last. Upon investigation it transpired that a neighbor further down the street was taken ill, that the children ran for the family friend, who went of course, saying simply when reasons for her non-appearance were demanded, "It broke me heart to leave the place, but what could I do?"

The evolutionists tell us that the instinct to pity, the impulse to aid his fellows, served man at a very early period, as a rude rule of right and wrong. There is no doubt that this rude rule still holds among many people with whom charitable agencies are brought into contact, and that their ideas of right and wrong are quite honestly outraged by the methods of these agencies. When they see the delay and caution with which relief is given, it does not appear to them a conscientious scruple, but as the cold and calculating action of a selfish man.

The poor man who has fallen into distress, when he first asks aid, instinctively expects tenderness, consideration, and forgiveness. If it is the first time, it has taken him long to make up his mind to take the step. He comes somewhat bruised and battered, and instead of being met with warmth of heart and sympathy, he is at once chilled by an investigation and an intimation that he ought to work. He does not recognize the disciplinary aspect of the situation.

But in our charitable efforts we think much more of what a man ought to be than of what he is or of what he may become; and we ruthlessly force our conventions and standards upon him with a sternness which we would consider stupid indeed did an educator use it in forcing his mature intellectual convictions upon an undeveloped mind.

The Hebrew prophet made three requirements from those who would join the great forward-moving procession led by Jehovah. "To love mercy" and at the same time "to do justly" is the difficult task; to fulfil the first requirement alone is to fall into the error of indiscriminate giving with all its disastrous results; to fulfil the second solely is to obtain the stern policy of withholding, and it results in such a dreary lack of sympathy and understanding that the establishment of justice is impossible. It may be that the combination of the two can never be attained save as we fulfil still the third requirement—"to walk humbly with God," which may mean to walk for many dreary miles beside the lowliest of his creatures, not even in that peace of mind which the company of the humble is popularly supposed to afford, but rather with the pangs and throes to which the poor human understanding is subjected whenever it attempts to comprehend the meaning of life.

Democracy and Social Ethics

IF I WERE IN THEIR PLACE *

JOHN WOOLMAN
American preacher, 1720–1772

Whatsoever ye would that men should do to you, do ye even so to them. Now where such live in fulness on the labor of others, who have never had experience of hard labor themselves, there is often a danger of their not having a right feeling of the laborer's condition, and therefore of being disqualified to judge candidly in their case, not knowing what they themselves would desire were they to labor hard from one year to another to raise the necessaries of life and to pay large rents besides. It is good for those who live in fulness to labor for tenderness of heart, to improve every opportunity of being acquainted with the hardships and fatigues of those who labor for their living, and think seriously with themselves,—Am I influenced with true charity in fixing all my demands? Have I no desire to support myself in expensive customs, because my acquaintances live in those customs? Were I to labor as they do, toward supporting them and their children in a station like mine, in such sort as they and their children labor for us, could I not, on such a change, before I entered into agreements of rent or interest, name some costly articles now used by me or in my family which have no real use in them, the expense whereof might be lessened? And should I not, in such case, strongly desire the disuse of those needless expenses that, less answering their way of life, the terms might be easier to me?

To see our fellow-creatures under difficulties to which we are in no degree accessory tends to awaken tenderness in the minds of all reasonable people; but if we consider the condition of those who are depressed in answering our demand, who labor out of our sight and are often toiling for us while we pass our time in fulness; if we consider that much less than we demand would supply us with all things really needful, what heart will not relent, or what reasonable man can refrain from mitigating that grief which he himself is the cause of?

He who hath been a stranger amongst unkind people, or under their government who were hard-hearted, knows how it feels; but a person who hath never felt the weight of misapplied power comes not to this knowledge but by an inward tenderness, in which the heart is prepared to sympathize with others.

The Journal and Essays

THE LEADEN-EYED

VACHEL LINDSAY
American poet, 1879–1931

Let not young souls be smothered out before
They do quaint deeds and fully flaunt their
    pride.
It is the world's one crime its babes grow dull,
Its poor are ox-like, limp, and leaden-eyed.
Not that they starve, but starve so dreamlessly,
Not that they sow, but that they seldom reap,
Not that they serve, but have no gods to serve;
Not that they die, but that they die like
    sheep.

From The Congo

THE FLOWER FACTORY

FLORENCE WILKINSON EVANS
Contemporary American writer

Lizabetta, Marianina, Fiametta, Teresina,

They are winding stems of roses, one by one, one by one,

Little children who have never learned to play;

Teresina softly crying that her fingers ache today;

Tiny Fiametta nodding, when the twilight slips in, gray.

High above the clattering street, ambulance and fire-gong beat,

They sit, curling crimson petals, one by one, one by one.

Lizabetta, Marianina, Fiametta, Teresina,

They have never seen a rose-bush nor a dew-drop in the sun.

They will dream of the vendetta—Teresina, Fiametta—

Of a Black Hand and a Face behind a grating;

They will dream of cotton petals, endless, crimson, suffocating,

Never of a wild rose thicket or the singing of a cricket;

But the ambulance will bellow through the
    wanness of their dreams,
And their tired lids will flutter with the street's
    hysteric screams.

Lizabetta, Marianina, Fiametta, Teresina,
They are winding stems of roses, one by one,
    one by one.
Let them have a long, long play-time, Lord of
    Toil, when toil is done;
Fill their baby hands with roses, joyous roses
    of the sun.

A Ride Home

TWO FACTORS IN THE INDUSTRIAL
REVOLUTION

WALTER RAUSCHENBUSCH
American: teacher of religion, 1861–1918

The ideal of a fraternal organization of society will remain powerless if it is supported
by idealists only; it needs the firm support
of a solid class whose economic future is staked
on the success of that ideal; and the industrial working class is consciously or uncon-

sciously committed to the struggle for the realization of that principle. It follows that those who desire the victory of that ideal from a religious point of view will have to enter into a working alliance with this class. Just as the Protestant principle of religious liberty and the democratic principle of political liberty rose to victory by an alliance with the middle class which was then rising to power, so the new Christian principle of brotherly association must ally itself with the working class if both are to conquer. Each depends on the other. The idealistic movement alone would be a soul without a body; the economic class movement alone would be a body without a soul. It needs the high elation and faith that come through religion. Nothing else will call forth that self-sacrificing devotion and life-long fidelity which will be needed in so gigantic a struggle as lies before the working class.

Christianity and the Social Crisis

A PRISON CELL

CATHERINE BRESHKOVSKY

Russian: "The Little Grandmother of the Russian Revolution"; for thirty-two years in prison or in exile in Siberia; 1844–1934

This is just the cell in the fortress of St. Peter and St. Paul. Everything is stone, asphalt, and iron; it is very dark in the cells on the first floor, for the wall which surrounds the buildings is high enough to keep out the light of the sun, and you never see the sky and stars. An old creature, like me, can support all the privations of air, light, motion, etc. But the young suffer seriously, and the silence and the mysterious running of all the ways of life there exert a distressing influence on the spirit and imagination. It is like a tomb. No human sounds, but very many sounds coming from outside, and from underground, the origin of which you cannot explain. Nobody answers your questions except the chief, very seldom seen, and you can torture yourself with visions and horrible pictures till you go mad. Many, many young lives have perished in this awful place, the best souls and best characters.

The Little Grandmother of the Russian Revolution
Ed. Alice Stone Blackwell

THE CURE OF THE CRIMINAL

WILFRED T. GRENFELL
English: Christian physician and teacher to
the fishermen of Labrador, 1865–1940

While working eight years in the purlieus
of Whitechapel, I learned beyond all question,
first, that often all the punishments invented
by the law and all the provisions made for the
protection of life and property failed in many
cases; and further, I saw, as I have seen since
that time, that the very men whom the punishments only made worse were perfectly capable
of reformation. Intelligent sympathy and practical love cure individuals who have been pronounced incurable—the very methods the Master advocated and calls for still.

The Adventure of Life

NEITHER DO I CONDEMN THEE
Christian, first century

Jesus went unto the mount of Olives. And
early in the morning he came again into the

temple, and all the people came unto him; and he sat down, and taught them.

And the scribes and the Pharisees bring a woman taken in adultery; and having set her in the midst, they say unto him, "Master, this woman hath been taken in adultery, in the very act. Now in the law Moses commanded us to stone such: what then sayest thou of her?" And this they said, tempting him, that they might have whereof to accuse him.

But Jesus stooped down, and with his finger wrote on the ground. But when they continued asking him, he lifted up himself, and said unto them, "He that is without sin among you, let him first cast a stone at her." And again he stooped down, and with his finger wrote on the ground. And they, when they heard it, went out one by one, beginning from the eldest, even unto the last; and Jesus was left alone, and the woman, where she was, in the midst.

And Jesus lifted up himself, and said unto her, "Woman, where are they? did no man condemn thee?"

And she said, "No man, Lord."

And Jesus said, "Neither do I condemn thee: go thy way; from henceforth sin no more."

From an addition to *The Gospel According to John*
New Testament

BEING HUMAN
William Makepeace Thackeray
English novelist and essayist, 1811-1863

Does a stream rush out of a mountain free and pure, to roll through fair pastures, to feed and throw out bright tributaries, and to end in a village gutter? Lives that have noble commencements have often no better endings; it is not without a kind of awe and reverence that an observer should speculate upon such careers as he traces the course of them. I have seen too much of success in life to take off my hat and huzzah to it as it passes in its gilt coach, and would do my little part with my neighbors on foot that they should not gape with too much wonder, nor applaud too loudly.

Is it the Lord Mayor going in state to mince-pies and the Mansion House? Is it poor Jack of Newgate's procession, with the sheriff and javelin-men, conducting him on his last journey to Tyburn? I look into my heart and think I am as good as my Lord Mayor, and know that I am as bad as Tyburn Jack. Give me a chain and red gown and a pudding before me, and I could play the part of alderman very well, and sentence Jack after dinner. Starve me, keep

me from books and honest people, educate me
to love dice, gin, and pleasure—and put me on
Hounslow Heath, with a purse before me, and
I will take it.

From the *Introduction*

Henry Esmond

THE GOOD BISHOP [*]
VICTOR HUGO
French novelist, 1802–1885

A tragic event occurred at D. A man was
condemned to death for murder. He was a
wretched fellow, not exactly educated, not exactly ignorant, who had been a mountebank at
fairs, and a writer for the public. The town
took a great interest in the trial. On the eve
of the day fixed for the execution of the condemned man, the chaplain of the prison fell
ill. A priest was needed to attend the criminal
in his last moments. They sent for the curé.
It seems that he refused to come, saying, "That
is no affair of mine. I have nothing to do
with that unpleasant task, and with that mountebank: I, too, am ill: and besides it is not my
place." This reply was reported to the Bishop,
who said, "Monsieur le Curé is right: it is not
his place, it is mine."

He went instantly to the prison, descended to the cell of the "mountebank," called him by name, took him by the hand, and spoke to him. He passed the entire day with him, forgetful of food and sleep, praying to God for the soul of the condemned man, and praying the condemned man for his own. He told him the best truths, which are also the most simple. He was father, brother, friend; he was bishop only to bless. He taught him everything, encouraged and consoled him. The man was on the point of dying in despair. He was not sufficiently ignorant to be absolutely indifferent. His condemnation, which had been a profound shock, had in a manner broken through, here and there, that wall which separates us from the mystery of things, and which we call life. He gazed incessantly beyond this world through these fatal breaches, and beheld only darkness. The Bishop made him see light.

On the following day, when they came to fetch the unhappy wretch, the Bishop was still there. He followed him, and exhibited himself to the eyes of the crowd in his purple camail and with his episcopal cross upon his neck, side by side with the criminal bound with cords.

He mounted the tumbril with him, he mounted the scaffold with him. The sufferer, who had been so gloomy and cast down on the preceding day, was radiant. He felt that his soul was reconciled, and he hoped in God. The Bishop embraced him and said to him: "God raises from the dead him whom man slays; he whom his brothers have rejected finds his Father once more. Pray, believe, enter into life: the Father is there." When he descended from the scaffold, there was something in his look which made the people draw aside to let him pass. On his return to the humble dwelling which he designated with a smile as his palace, he said to his sister, "I have just officiated pontifically."

Moreover, he was the same towards people of the world and towards the lower classes. He condemned nothing in haste and without taking circumstances into account. He said, "Examine the road over which the fault has passed."

Les Misérables, Vol. i
Trans. Isabel F. Hapgood

THE SERVANT OF GOD [*]

Hebrew; this passage, sixth or fifth century B. C.

Behold, my servant shall prosper, he shall
be exalted and lifted up, and shall be very high.
Like as many were astonished at thee, (his
visage was so marred from that of man, and
his form from that of the sons of men,) so shall
he startle many nations; kings shall shut their
mouths at him: for that which had not been
told them shall they see, and that which they
had not heard shall they understand.

Who hath believed that which we have heard?
And to whom hath the arm of the Lord been
     revealed?

For he grew up before him as a tender plant,
And as a root out of a dry ground:
     He hath no form nor comeliness, that we
          should look upon him;
     Nor beauty that we should desire him.

He was despised, and rejected of men;
A man of sorrows, and acquainted with grief:
     And as one from whom men hide their face
          he was despised,
     And we esteemed him not.

Surely he hath borne our griefs,
And carried our sorrows:
    Yet we did esteem him stricken,
    Smitten of God, and afflicted.

But he was wounded for our transgressions,
He was bruised for our iniquities:
    The chastisement of our peace was upon
        him;
    And with his stripes we are healed.

All we like sheep have gone astray;
We have turned every one to his own way;
    And the Lord hath laid on him
    The iniquity of us all.

He was oppressed,
Yet he humbled himself,
    And opened not his mouth,
And as a lamb that is led to the slaughter,
And as a sheep that before her shearers is
        dumb;
    Yea, he opened not his mouth.

And they made his grave with the wicked,
And with the rich in his death;
    He shall see his seed, he shall prolong his
        days,

And the pleasure of the Lord shall prosper
    in his hand:
He shall see and be satisfied with the travail
    of his soul.

> From *The Book of Isaiah*
> *Old Testament*

HE SAVED OTHERS *
Christian, first century

If any man would come after me, let him
deny himself, and take up his cross daily, and
follow me. For whosoever would save his life
shall lose it; but whosoever shall lose his life
for my sake, the same shall save it.

Whosoever would become great among you
shall be your minister; and whosoever would become first among you, shall be the servant of
all. For verily the Son of man came not to
be ministered unto, but to minister, and to give
his life a ransom for many.

As they were eating, Jesus took bread, and
blessed, and brake it; and he gave it to the
disciples, and said, "Take, eat: this is my body."

And he took a cup, and gave thanks, and gave to them, saying, "Drink ye all of it; for this is my blood of the covenant, which is shed for many."

Then cometh Jesus with them unto a place called Gethsemane, and saith unto his disciples, "Sit ye here while I go yonder and pray." And he took with him Peter and the two sons of Zebedee, and began to be sorrowful and sore troubled. Then saith he unto them, "My soul is exceeding sorrowful, even unto death: abide ye here, and watch with me." And he went forward a little, and fell on his face, and prayed, saying, "O my Father, if it be possible, let this cup pass away from me: nevertheless, not as I will, but as thou wilt."

And he cometh unto the disciples and findeth them sleeping, and saith unto Peter, "What, could ye not watch with me one hour? Watch and pray, that ye enter not into temptation: the spirit indeed is willing, but the flesh is weak."

Again a second time he went away and prayed, saying, "O my Father, if this cannot pass away, except I drink it, thy will be done."

Pilate called together the chief priests and the rulers and the people, and said unto them,

"Ye brought unto me this man, as one that perverteth the people: and behold, I, having examined him before you, found no fault in this man touching those things whereof ye accuse him: no, nor yet Herod: for he sent him back unto us; and behold, nothing worthy of death hath been done by him. I will therefore chastise him, and release him."

But they cried out all together, saying, "Away with this man, and release unto us Barabbas" (one who for a certain insurrection made in the city, and for murder, was cast into prison).

And Pilate spake unto them again, desiring to release Jesus; but they shouted saying, "Crucify, crucify him."

And he said unto them the third time, "Why, what evil hath this man done? I have found no cause of death in him: I will therefore chastise him and release him." But they were instant with loud voices asking that he might be crucified. And their voices prevailed.

Jesus said, "Father, forgive them; for they know not what they do."

It was the third hour, and they crucified him. And the superscription of his accusation was written over, THE KING OF THE JEWS. And with him they crucify two robbers; one on his right hand, and one on his left. And they that passed by railed on him, wagging their heads, and saying, "Ha! thou that destroyest the temple, and buildest it in three days, save thyself, and come down from the cross." In like manner also the chief priests mocking him among themselves with the scribes said, "He saved others; himself he cannot save."

From the Gospels
New Testament

IN FLANDERS FIELDS

John McCrae
Canadian physician, 1872–1918

In Flanders fields the poppies blow
Between the crosses, row on row,
  That mark our place; and in the sky
  The larks still bravely singing, fly
Scarce heard amid the guns below.

We are the Dead. Short days ago
We lived, felt dawn, saw sunset glow,
  Loved and were loved; and now we lie
    In Flanders fields.

Take up our quarrel with the foe:
To you from failing hands we throw
The torch; be yours to hold it high.
If ye break faith with us who die
We shall not sleep, though poppies grow
In Flanders fields.

In Flanders Fields and Other Poems

THE DEAD

RUPERT BROOKE

English poet, 1887–1915

Blow out, you bugles, over the rich Dead!
There's none of these so lonely and poor of
old
But, dying, has made us rarer gifts than gold.
These laid the world away; poured out the red
Sweet wine of youth; gave up the years to be
Of work and joy, and that unhoped serene
That men call age; and those who would have
been,
Their sons, they gave, their immortality.

Blow, bugles, blow! They brought us, for our
dearth,

Holiness, lacked so long, and love and pain.
Honor has come back, as a king, to earth
And paid his subjects with a royal wage;
And nobleness walks in our ways again:
And we have come into our heritage.

LEADERS AND FRIENDS OF MANKIND

MATTHEW ARNOLD

English essayist and poet, 1822–1888

Servants of God! or sons
Shall I not call you? because
Not as servants ye knew
Your Father's innermost mind,
His, who unwillingly sees
One of his little ones lost—
Yours is the praise if mankind
Hath not as yet in its march
Fainted, and fallen, and died!

See! in the rocks of the world
Marches the host of mankind,
A feeble, wavering line.
Where are they tending? A God
Marshalled them, gave them their goal.

Ah, but the way is so long!
Years they have been in the waste!
Sore thirst plagues them, the rocks,
Rising all round, overawe;
Factions divide them, their host
Threatens to break, to dissolve.—
Ah, keep, keep them combined!
Else, of the myriads who fill
That army, not one shall arrive;
Sole they shall stray: on the rocks
Batter forever in vain,
Die one by one in the waste.

Then, in such hour of need
Of your fainting, dispirited race,
Ye, like angels, appear,
Radiant with ardor divine,
Beacons of hope, ye appear!
Languor is not in your heart,
Weakness is not in your word,
Weariness not on your brow.
Ye alight in our van! at your voice,
Panic, despair, flee away.
Ye move through the ranks, recall
The stragglers, refresh the outworn,
Praise, re-inspire the brave.
Order, courage, return;
Eyes rekindling, and prayers

Follow your steps as you go.
Ye fill up the gaps in our files,
Strengthen the wavering line,
Stablish, continue our march
On, to the bound of the waste,
On, to the City of God.

From *Rugby Chapel*

True Wealth

THE CITY'S CROWN
William Dudley Foulke
American writer, 1848-1935

What makes a city great? Huge piles of stone
Heaped heavenward? Vast multitudes who
    dwell
Within wide circling walls? Palace and throne
  And riches past the count of man to tell,
And wide domain? Nay, these the empty
    husk!
  True glory dwells where glorious deeds are
    done,
Where great men rise whose names athwart the
    dusk
  Of misty centuries gleam like the sun!
In Athens, Sparta, Florence, 'twas the soul
  That was the city's bright immortal part;
The splendor of the spirit was their goal;
  Their jewel, the unconquerable heart!
So may the city that I love be great
Till every stone shall be articulate.

Lyrics of War and Peace

IDEALS OF THE ATHENIAN DEMOCRACY*

PERICLES

Athenian statesman and patron of art, 490–429 B.C.

Our form of government does not enter into rivalry with the institutions of others. We do not copy our neighbors, but are an example to them. It is true that we are called a democracy, for the administration is in the hands of the many and not of the few. But while the law secures equal justice to all alike in their private disputes, the claim of excellence is also recognized; and when a citizen is in any way distinguished, he is preferred to the public service, not as a matter of privilege, but as the reward of merit. Neither is poverty a bar, but a man may benefit his country whatever be the obscurity of his condition. There is no exclusiveness in our public life, and in our private intercourse we are not suspicious of one another, nor angry with our neighbor if he does what he likes; we do not put on sour looks at him which, though harmless, are not pleasant. While we are thus unconstrained in our private intercourse, a spirit of reverence pervades our public acts; we are prevented from doing wrong by respect for authority and for the laws, having an especial regard for those which are ordained for the protection of the injured as well as to those unwritten laws which bring upon the transgressor of them the reprobation of the general sentiment.

And we have not forgotten to provide for our weary spirits many relaxations from toil; we have regular games and sacrifices throughout the year; at home the style of our life is refined; and the delight which we daily feel in all these things helps to banish melancholy. Because of the greatness of our city the fruits of the whole earth flow in upon us; so that we enjoy the goods of other countries as freely as of our own.

We are lovers of the beautiful, yet simple in our tastes, and we cultivate the mind without loss of manliness. Wealth we employ, not for talk and ostentation, but when there is a real use for it. To avow poverty with us is no disgrace; the true disgrace is in doing nothing to avoid it. An Athenian citizen does not neglect the state because he takes care of his own household; and even those of us who are engaged in business have a very fair idea of politics. We alone regard a man who takes no interest in public affairs not as a harmless, but as a useless, character; and if few of us are originators, we are all sound judges, of a policy. The great impediment to action is, in our opinion, not discussion, but the want of that knowledge which is gained by discussion preparatory to action. For we have a peculiar power of thinking before we act and of acting too, whereas other men are courageous from ignorance but hesitate upon reflection. And they are surely to be esteemed the bravest spirits who, having the clearest sense both of the pains and pleasures of life, do not on that account shrink from danger.

Thucydides, Book ii
Trans. Benjamin Jowett

WHERE WEALTH ACCUMULATES
Oliver Goldsmith
Irish poet, dramatist, and novelist, 1728–1774

Ill fares the land, to hastening ills a prey,
Where wealth accumulates and men decay:
Princes and lords may flourish or may fade;
A breath can make them, as a breath has made;
But a bold peasantry, their country's pride,
When once destroyed can never be supplied.

From *The Deserted Village*

THE GOLDEN CALF [*]
Hebrew; this passage, seventh century B.C. or earlier

It is written that Moses went apart from the people to commune with God upon Mount Sinai.

And when the people saw that Moses delayed to come down from the mount, the people gathered themselves together unto Aaron, and said unto him, "Up, make us gods, which shall go before us; for as for this Moses, the man that brought us up out of the land of Egypt, we know not what is become of him."

And Aaron said unto them, "Break off the golden rings, which are in the ears of your wives, of your sons, and of your daughters, and bring them to me."

And all the people brake off the golden rings which were in their ears, and brought them unto Aaron. And he received it at their hand, and fashioned it with a graving tool, and made it a molten calf.

And they said, "These be thy gods, O Israel, which brought thee up out of the land of Egypt."

And when Aaron saw this, he built an altar

before it; and Aaron made proclamation, and said, "To-morrow shall be a feast."

And they rose up early on the morrow, and offered burnt offerings, and brought peace offerings; and the people sat down to eat, and to drink, and rose up to play.

And the Lord spake unto Moses, "Go, get thee down: for thy people, which thou broughtest up out of the land of Egypt, have corrupted themselves: they have turned aside quickly out of the way which I commanded them: they have made them a molten calf, and have worshiped it, and have sacrificed unto it, and said, "These be thy gods, O Israel."

And Moses turned and went down from the mount, and Joshua was with him with the two tables of testimony in his hand; tables that were written on both their sides.

And when Joshua heard the noise of the people as they shouted, he said unto Moses, "There is a noise of war in the camp."

And Moses said, "It is not the voice of them that shout for mastery, neither is it the voice of them that cry for being overcome; but the noise of them that sing do I hear."

And it came to pass, as soon as he came nigh unto camp, that he saw the calf and the dancing:

and Moses' anger waxed hot, and he cast the tables out of his hands, and brake them beneath the mount. And Moses returned unto the Lord and said, "Oh, this people have sinned a great sin and made them gods of gold!"

From *The Book of the Exodus*
Old Testament

LEST WE FORGET*

Hebrew; this passage, late seventh century B. C.

Hear, O Israel: the Lord our God is one Lord: and thou shalt love the Lord thy God with all thine heart, and with all thy soul, and with all thy might. And these words, which I command thee this day, shall be upon thine heart: and thou shalt teach them diligently to thy children, and shalt talk of them when thou sittest in thine house, and when thou walkest by the way, and when thou liest down, and when thou risest up. And thou shalt bind them for a sign upon thine hand, and they shall be for frontlets between thine eyes. And thou shalt write them upon the door posts of thine house, and upon thy gates.

For the Lord thy God bringeth thee into a good land, a land of brooks, of water, of fountains and depths, springing forth in valleys and hills; a land of wheat and barley, and vines and fig trees and pomegranates; a land of oil olives and honey; a land wherein thou shalt eat bread without scarceness, thou shalt not lack anything in it; a land whose stones are iron, and out of whose hills thou mayest dig brass. And thou shalt eat and be full, and thou shalt bless the Lord thy God for the good land which he hath given thee.

Beware lest thou forget the Lord thy God. in not keeping his commandments and his judgments, and his statutes, which I command thee this day: lest when thou hast eaten and art full and hast built goodly houses, and hast dwelt therein; and when thy herds and thy flocks multiply, and thy silver and thy gold is multiplied, and all that thou hast is multiplied; then thy heart be lifted up and thou forget the Lord thy God, and thou say in thine heart, My power and the might of mine hand has gotten me this wealth. But thou shalt remember the Lord thy God for it is he that giveth thee power to get wealth; that he may establish his covenant which he sware unto thy fathers, as at this day.

And it shall be, if thou shalt forget the Lord thy God, and walk after other gods, and serve them, and worship them, I testify against you this day that ye shall surely perish. As the nations which the Lord maketh to perish before you, so shall ye perish; because ye would not harken unto the voice of the Lord your God.

From *The Book of Deuteronomy*
Old Testament

RECESSIONAL
RUDYARD KIPLING
British author, 1865–1936

God of our fathers, known of old,
　　Lord of our far-flung battle-line,
Beneath whose awful Hand we hold
　　Dominion over palm and pine—
Lord God of Hosts, be with us yet,
Lest we forget—lest we forget!

The tumult and the shouting dies;
　　The captains and the kings depart:
Still stands thine ancient sacrifice,
　　An humble and a contrite heart.
Lord God of Hosts, be with us yet,
Lest we forget—lest we forget!

Far-called, our navies melt away;
　　On dune and headland sinks the fire:
Lo, all our pomp of yesterday
　　Is one with Nineveh and Tyre!
Judge of the Nations, spare us yet,
Lest we forget—lest we forget!

If, drunk with sight of power, we loose
　　Wild tongues that have not thee in awe,
Such boastings as the Gentiles use,
　　Or lesser breeds without the Law—
Lord God of Hosts, be with us yet,
Lest we forget—lest we forget!

For heathen heart that puts her trust
　　In reeking tube and iron shard,
All valiant dust that builds on dust,
　　And guarding, calls not thee to guard,
For frantic boast and foolish word—
Thy mercy on thy people, Lord!

The Five Nations

THE GREAT CITY *
WALT WHITMAN
American poet, 1819–1892

What do you think endures?
Do you think a great city endures?

Or a teeming manufacturing state? or a prepared
  constitution? or the best built steamships?

Away! these are not to be cherished for themselves;

They fill their hour, the dancers dance, the
  musicians play for them,

The show passes.

A great city is that which has the greatest
  men and women,

If it be a few ragged huts, it is still the greatest
  city in the whole world.

The place where a great city stands is not the
  place of stretched wharves, docks, manu-
  factures, deposits of produce merely,

Nor the place of the tallest and costliest buildings or shops selling goods from the rest
  of the earth,

Nor the place where money is plentiest, nor the
  place of the most numerous population.

Where the city stands with the brawniest breed
  of orators and bârds,

Where the city stands that is beloved by these,
  and loves them in return and understands
  them,

Where no monuments exist to heroes but in the
  common words and deeds,

Where thrift is in its place, and prudence is in
    its place,

Where the slave ceases, and the master of the
    slaves ceases,

Where the populace rise at once against the
    never-ending audacity of elected persons,

Where outside authority enters always after
    the precedence of inside authority,

Where the citizen is always the head and ideal,

Where children are taught to be laws to them-
    selves, and to depend on themselves,

Where equanimity is illustrated in affairs,

Where speculations on the soul are encouraged,

Where women walk in public processions in the
    streets the same as the men,

Where they enter the public assembly and take
    places the same as the men;

Where the city of the faithfulest friends stands,

Where the city of the cleanliness of the sexes
    stands,

Where the city of the healthiest fathers stands,

Where the city of the best-bodied mothers
    stands—

      There the Great City stands!
        From *Song of the Broad-Axe*

The Church

THE CHURCH
Edwin Ford Piper
American writer, 1871–1939

The blinding July sun at ten o'clock
Glares on the white walls of the little church;—
The shingles silver-gray, the shutters green,
Sunflowers man-high in bloom against the
    wall,—
And glares on dingy wagons trailed by dust,
Slow-jolting to the platform at the door.
Women alight and enter, while the men
Tie sweating teams to the much-gnawed hitch-
    ing-posts.
How drowsily the horses stamp at flies!
The landscape wavers in the shimmering heat.

Come in from the strong sunlight. The pine
    pews
Are filled with settlers. Men with grizzled
    beards,
And faces weathered rough by sun and wind—

Wind that would' wear down granite—listless
    stand,
Awkwardly easing muscles now relaxed
Longer than is their use. The women move
Graceful and gracious, whether pale or tanned,
Thin, nervous, or in rosy health. Their eyes
Are bright, and bearing cheerful. Least at ease
Are growing girls and boys. Welcomes go
    round,
And gossips buzz until the organ wails
The slow, sad measures of the opening hymn.

Beside the open window, dreamily,
A sunflower pokes its stiff and oily head
Droned over by a hairy bumble-bee.
An awkward boy sits gazing; does not hear
Or text or sermon; only sees the flower
Nod in the breeze, and finds the pew grow
    hard,
While muscles twitch and ache for liberty.

A little church; the settlers come for miles.
Some few, unhearing, sit in selfish dreams,—
For life is vilely mingled, sweetly mixed,
Scanty or bounteous in vital force;
But here the most are really worshipers,
Seeking in fellowship a sympathy
With God. Their simple faces plainly show

What feelings stir the heart; for hard looks
    melt,
And thin, worn wretchedness in garb grotesque
Is eased of ugliness while it feeds
On love and hope. This meager hour may lift
Some groveling face to see the blessed sky,
Master a soul and yield it back to life
Tempered against the evil days to be.

A little thing, this church? Remove its roots,
Ossa upon Pelion would not fill the pit.

               Barbed Wire and Wayfarers

HE PRAYETH BEST

SAMUEL TAYLOR COLERIDGE
English poet, 1772–1834

O sweeter than the marriage-feast,
    'Tis sweeter far to me,
To walk together to the kirk
    With a goodly company;

To walk together to the kirk
    And all together pray,
While each to his great Father bends,
Old men, and babes, and loving friends,
    And youths and maidens gay.

Farewell, farewell! but this I tell
To thee thou Wedding-Guest:
He prayeth well, who loveth well
Both man and bird and beast;

He prayeth best who loveth best
All things both great and small:
For the dear God who loveth us,
He made and loveth all.

From *The Rime of the Ancient Mariner*

THE COMING CHURCH *

THEODORE PARKER
American preacher and reformer, 1810–1860

The church that is to lead this century will
not be a church creeping on all fours, mewling
and whining, its face turned down, its eyes
turned back. It must be full of the brave,
manly spirit of the day, keeping also the good
of times past. There is a terrific energy in
this age, for man was never so much developed,
so much the master of himself before. Great
truths, moral and political, have come to light.
They fly quickly. The iron prophet of types
publishes his visions, of weal or woe, to the
near and far. This marvelous age has in-

vented steam, and the magnetic telegraph, apt symbols of itself, before which the miracles of fable are an idle tale. It demands, as never before, freedom for itself, usefulness in its institutions, truth in its teachings, and beauty in its deeds. Let a church have that freedom, that usefulness, truth, and beauty, and the energy of this age will be on its side. But the church which did for the fifth century, or the fifteenth, will not do for this. It must have our ideas, the smell of our ground, and have grown out of the religion in our soul. The freedom of America must be there before this energy will come; the wisdom of the nineteenth century, before its science will be on the churches' side.

A church that believes only in past inspiration will appeal to old books as the standard of truth and source of light, will be antiquarian in its habits, will call its children by the old names and war on the new age, not understanding the man-child born to rule the world. A church that believes in inspiration now will appeal to God; try things by reason and conscience; aim to surpass the old heroes; baptize its children with a new spirit, and, using the present age, will lead public opinion, not follow it.

Let us have a church that dares imitate the

heroism of Jesus; seek inspiration as he sought it; judge the past as he; act on the present like him; pray as he prayed; work as he wrought; live as he lived. Let our doctrines and our forms fit the soul, as the limbs fit the body,—growing out of it, growing with it. Let us have a church for the whole man: truth for the mind, good works for the hands, love for the heart; and for the soul, that aspiring after perfection, that unfaltering faith in God, which, like lightning in the clouds, shines brightest when elsewhere it is most dark.

The True Idea of a Christian Church
Autobiography, Poems, and Prayers

THE BOND OF THE UNIVERSAL CHURCH *

WILLIAM ELLERY CHANNING
American preacher and religious reformer, 1780–1842

All Christians and myself form one body, one church, just as far as a common love and piety possess our hearts. Nothing is more real than this spiritual union.

There is one grand, all-comprehending church; and if I am a Christian, I belong to it, and no man can shut me out of it. You may exclude me from your Roman church, your Episcopal church, and your Calvinistic church, on account of supposed defects in my creed or my sect, and I am content to be excluded. But I will not be severed from the great body of Christ. Who shall sunder me from such men as Fénelon, and Pascal, and Borromeo, from Archbishop Leighton, Jeremy Taylor, and John Howard? Who can rupture the spiritual bond between these men and myself? Do I not hold them dear? Does not their spirit, flowing out through their writings and lives, penetrate my soul? Are they not a portion of my being? Am I not a different man from what I should have been, had not these and other like spirits acted on mine? And is it in the power of synod, or conclave, or of all the ecclesiastical combinations on earth, to part me from them? I am bound to them by thought and affection; and can these be suppressed by the bull of a pope or the excommunication of a council? The soul breaks scornfully these barriers, these webs of spiders, and joins itself to the great and good; and if it possess their spirit, will the great and good, living or dead, cast it off because it has not enrolled itself in this or another sect?

A pure mind is free of the universe. It belongs to the church, the family of the pure, in all worlds. Virtue is no local thing. It is not honorable because born in this community or that, but for its own independent, everlasting beauty. This is the bond of the universal church. No man can be excommunicated from it but by himself, by the death of goodness in his own breast.

In all churches individuals are better than their creed; and, amidst gross error and the inculcation of a narrow spirit, noble virtues spring up, and eminent Christians are formed. It is one sign of the tendency of human nature to goodness that it grows good under a thousand bad influences. To repeat these names does the heart good. They breathe a fragrance through the common air. They lift up the whole race to which they belonged. With the churches of which they were pillars or chief ornaments I have many sympathies; nor do I condemn the union of ourselves to these or any other churches whose doctrines we approve, provided that we do it without severing ourselves in the least from the universal church. On this point we cannot be too earnest. We must shun the spirit of sectarianism as from hell. We must shudder at the thought of shutting up

God in any denomination. We must think no man the better for belonging to our communion, no man the worse for belonging to another. We must look with undiminished joy on goodness, though it shine forth from the most. adverse sect.

The angels and pure spirits who visit our earth come not to join a sect, but to do good to all. May this universal charity descend on us and possess our hearts; may our narrowness, exclusiveness, and bigotry melt away under this mild, celestial fire.

The Church

OUTWITTED

Edwin Markham

American writer, 1852–1940

He drew a circle that shut me out—
Heretic, rebel, a thing to flout.
But Love and I had the wit to win:
We drew a circle that took him in!

The Shoes of Happiness and Other Poems

UNITY, NOT UNIFORMITY, IN RELIGION

Wilfred T. Grenfell

English: Christian physician and teacher to
the fishermen of Labrador, 1865–1940

To suppose that all men's intellectual capacities are identical is absurd, and yet with this premise in a world of utterly imperfect knowledge we play at the solution of religious unity, as if, under the circumstances, it could ever be uniformity, either in thought or in method of expression. There must ever be endless permutations and combinations when it comes to intellectual apprehensions. So long as we cling to any humanly devised definitions which we insist upon as articles of faith necessary to salvation, we shall inevitably insure discord for all time. Together with these initial differences, and with imperfect data, we must take into consideration the changes which new environments and new experiences make in the same individual. Thus for my own part I was once absolutely intolerant of all forms and ceremonies in public worship. Now I expect to value ever more and more beauty and orderliness in the expression of it.

The Adventure of Life

THE CHURCH UNIVERSAL
Samuel Longfellow
American clergyman, 1819–1892

One holy Church of God appears
Through every age and race,
Unwasted by the lapse of years,
Unchanged by changing place.

From oldest time, on farthest shores,
Beneath the pine or palm,
One Unseen Presence she adores,
With silence or with psalm.

Her priests are all God's faithful sons,
To serve the world raised up;
The pure in heart her baptized ones;
Love, her communion-cup.

The truth is her prophetic gift,
The soul her sacred page;
And feet on mercy's errands swift
Do make her pilgrimage.

O living Church, thine errand speed;
Fulfil thy task sublime;
With bread of life earth's hunger feed;
Redeem the evil time!

Hymns of the Spirit

A CHURCH COVENANT
CHARLES GORDON AMES
American preacher, 1828–1912

In the freedom of the truth and in the spirit of Jesus Christ we unite for the worship of God and the service of man.

A Spiritual Autobiography

The State

THE WISDOM OF BENEVOLENCE IN GOVERNMENT *

CONVERSATION WITH KING SEUEN OF TS'E

MENCIUS
Chinese philosopher, 372?–289 B. C.

You collect your equipments of war, endanger your soldiers and officers, and excite the resentment of the other princes. Do these things cause you pleasure in your mind?

The king replied, No. How should I derive pleasure from· these things? My object in them is to seek for what I greatly desire.

Now if your Majesty will institute a government whose actions shall all be benevolent, this will cause all the officers in the empire to wish to stand in your Majesty's court, and the farmers all to wish to plough in your Majesty's fields, and the merchants, both traveling and stationary, all to wish to store their goods in your Majesty's market places, and traveling strangers all to wish to make their tours on your Majesty's roads, and all, throughout the empire, who feel aggrieved by their rulers to wish to come and complain to your Majesty. And when they are so bent, who will be able to keep them back?

The king said, I am stupid. Teach me clearly: I will try to carry your instructions into effect.

Mencius replied, They only are men of education who, without a certain livelihood, are able to maintain a fixed heart. As to the people, if they have not a certain livelihood, it follows that they will not have a fixed heart. And if they have not a fixed heart, there is nothing which they will not do in the way of self-abandonment, of moral deflection, of depravity, and of wild license. When they thus have been involved in crime, to follow them up and punish them,—this is to entrap the people. How can such a thing as entrapping the people be done under the rule of a benevolent man?

When one by force subdues men, they do not submit to him in heart. They submit, because their strength is not adequate to resist. When one subdues men by virtue, in their hearts' core they are pleased, and sincerely submit, as was the case with the seventy disciples in their submission to Confucius.

Trans. James Legge

WHEN POWER AND WISDOM UNITE
PLATO
Greek philosopher: disciple of
Socrates and teacher of Aristotle, 427–347 B. C.

Until philosophers are kings, or the kings
and princes of this world have the spirit and
power of philosophy, and political greatness and
wisdom meet in one, and those commoner natures who pursue either to the exclusion of the
other are compelled to stand aside, cities will
never have rest from their evils—no, nor the human race, as I believe—and then only will this
our State have a possibility of life and behold the
light of day.

The Republic, Book v
Trans. Benjamin Jowett

THE IDEAL STATE *
ARISTOTLE
Greek philosopher and scientist, 384–322 B. C.

It is evident that (the ideal state) is not a
mere community or place; nor is it established
that men may be safe from injury and maintain
an interchange of good offices.   All these things,

indeed, must take place where there is a state, and yet they may all exist and there be no state. A state then may be defined to be a society of people joining together by their families and children to live happily, enjoying a life of thorough independence.

Education and good morals will be found to be almost the whole that goes to make a good man; and the same things will make a good statesman and good king. A state, consisting of a multitude of human beings, ought to be brought to unity and community by education; and who is about to introduce education and expects thereby to make the state excellent will act absurdly if he thinks to fashion it by any other means than by manners, philosophy, and laws. There is no free state where the laws do not rule supreme; for the law ought to be above all. A government in a constant state of turmoil is weak. The only stable state is that where everyone possesses an equality in the eye of the law, according to his merit, and enjoys his own, unmolested.

The Metaphysics
Trans. John H. M'Mahon

WHEN MERCY SEASONS JUSTICE *
WILLIAM SHAKESPEARE
English dramatic poet, 1564–1616

The quality of mercy is not strained.
It droppeth as the gentle rain from heaven
Upon the place beneath: it is twice blest;
It blesseth him that gives, and him that takes:
'Tis mightiest in the mightiest: it becomes
The throned monarch better than his crown;
His sceptre shows the force of temporal power,
The attribute to awe and majesty,
Wherein doth sit the dread and fear of kings;
But mercy is above this sceptred sway;
It is enthroned in the hearts of kings,
It is an attribute to God himself;
And earthly power doth then show likest God's
When mercy seasons justice. Therefore . . .
Though justice be thy plea, consider this,
That in the course of justice none of us
Should see salvation: we do pray for mercy,
And that same prayer doth teach us all to
      render
The deeds of mercy.

The Merchant of Venice

A PETITION *

George Fox
English: founder of the Society
of Friends (Quakers); 1624–1691

Presented to the King, the 21st day of the 11th month, 1660

Our principle is, and our practices have always been, to seek peace and ensue it; to follow after righteousness and the knowledge of God; seeking the good and welfare, and doing that which tends to the peace, of all. All bloody principles and practices, we, as to our own particulars, do utterly deny, with all outward wars, strife, and fighting with outward weapons for any end, or under any pretence whatsoever: this is our testimony to the whole world.

Secondly, we earnestly desire and wait, that (by the word of God's power, and its effectual operation in the hearts of men) the kingdoms of this world may become the kingdoms of the Lord and of his Christ; that he may rule and reign in men by his spirit and truth; that thereby all people, out of all different judgments and professions, may be brought into love and unity with God and with one another; and that all may come to witness the prophet's words fulfilled who said, "Nation shall not lift up sword against nation, neither shall they learn war any more."

For we have not, as some others, gone about cunningly with devised fables, nor have we ever denied in practice what we have proposed in principle, but in sincerity and truth and by the word of God have we labored to be made manifest with all men that both we and our ways might be witnessed in the hearts of all. And whereas all manner of evil hath been falsely spoken of us, we hereby speak the plain truth of our hearts. For although we have always suffered, and do now more abundantly suffer, yet we know it is for righteousness' sake.

For this we can say to all the world: we have wronged no man, we have used no force nor violence against any man, we have been found in no plots, nor guilty of sedition. When we have been wronged, we have not sought to revenge ourselves, we have not made resistance against authority; but wherein we could not obey for conscience' sake, we have suffered the most of any people in the nation. We have been counted as sheep for the slaughter, persecuted, and despised, beaten, stoned, wounded, stocked, whipped, imprisoned, cast into dungeons, shut up from our friends, denied needful sustenance for many days together, with other the like cruelties. And the cause of all these our sufferings is not for any evil, but for things relating to the worship of our God, and in obedience to his requirings. For which cause we shall freely give up our bodies a sacrifice rather than disobey the Lord; knowing as the Lord hath kept us innocent he will plead our cause when there is none in the earth to plead it. So we, in obedience to his truth, seek the good and peace of all men.

And whereas men come against us with clubs, staves, drawn swords, pistols cocked, and beat, cut, and abuse us; yet we never resisted them. It is not an honor to manhood or nobility to run upon harmless people, who lift not an hand against them, with arms and weapons.

Our meetings were stopped and broken up in the days of Oliver under pretence of plotting against him; in the days of the Committee of Safety we were looked upon as plotters to bring in King Charles; and now our peaceable meetings are termed seditious.

Though we have suffered all along because we would not take up carnal weapons to fight against any and are thus made a prey upon and cannot avenge ourselves—These things are left upon your hearts to consider; for we know, as Christ said, "He that takes the sword shall perish with the sword."

This is given forth from the people called Quakers, to satisfy the King, his council, and all that have any jealousy concerning us, that all occasion of suspicion may be taken away, and our innocency cleared.

(Added in the reprinting.)

Courteous reader,

This was our testimony above twenty years ago, and since then we have not been found acting contrary to it, nor ever shall; for the truth that is our guide is unchangeable.

Journal

THE SOCIAL CONTRACT *
JEAN JACQUES ROUSSEAU
French political and social philosopher: "Father of the French Revolution," 1712–1778

Since no man has any natural authority over his fellowmen and since force is not the source of right, conventions remain as the basis of all lawful authority among men.

There is in the State no fundamental law which cannot be revoked, not even (a) social compact; for if all citizens assembled in order to break the compact by a solemn agreement, no one can doubt that it could be quite legitimately broken.

The Social Contract

LAW AND LIBERTY
Voltaire
Eminent French critic and writer, 1694–1778

Liberty embraces all:—That the agriculturist should not be vexed by a tyrant's minion; that no citizen should be imprisoned without immediate trial before his natural judges, who shall decide between him and his prosecutor; that no one shall take from a man his meadow or his vineyard, under pretext of the public good, without ample recompense; that they shall seek the people's good, instead of wishing to rule over them in fattening on their substance; that the law, and not caprice, shall reign.

The human race is ready to endorse all that.

Concerning Fundamental Laws

BEFORE RISING AGAINST ONE'S GOVERNMENT

CATHERINE BRESHKOVSKY

Russian: "The Little Grandmother of the Russian Revolution"; for thirty-two years in prison or in exile in Siberia; 1844–1934

It is a poor patriot who will not thoroughly try his government before he rises against it.

The Little Grandmother of the Russian Revolution
Ed. Alice Stone Blackwell

FREEDOM IN SOCIETY *

ROBERT HALL

English preacher, 1764–1831

Social order would be inevitably dissolved if any man declined a practical acquiescence in every political regulation which he did not personally approve. The duty of submission is, in this light, founded on principles which hold under every government, and are plain and obvious. But the principle which attaches a people to their allegiance, collectively considered, must exactly coincide with the title to authority; as must be evident from the very meaning of the term authority, which, as distinguished from force, signifies a right to demand obedience. Authority and obedience are correlative terms, and consequently in all respects correspond, and are commensurate with each other.

The most capital advantage an enlightened people can enjoy is the liberty of discussing every subject which can fall within the compass of the human mind; while this remains, freedom will flourish; but should it be lost or impaired, its principle will neither be well understood nor long retained. To render the magistrate a judge of truth and engage his authority in the suppression of opinions shows an inattention to the nature and design of political society.

The law hath amply provided against overt acts of sedition and disorder, and to suppress mere opinions by any other method than reasoning and argument is the height of tyranny. Freedom of thought, being intimately connected with the happiness and dignity of man in every stage of his being, is of so much more importance than the preservation of any constitution that to infringe upon the former under pretence of supporting the latter is to sacrifice the means to the end.

Freedom of the Press

THE RIGHT AND LIMITATION OF FREE SPEECH [*]
From the Virginia Statute of Religious Liberty, 1785

To suffer the civil magistrate to intrude his powers into the field of opinion and to restrain the profession or propagation of principles on supposition of their ill tendency is a dangerous fallacy which at once destroys all religious liberty, because he, being of course judge of that tendency, will make his opinions the rule of judgment and approve or condemn the sentiments of others only as they shall square with or differ from his own; it is time enough for the rightful purposes of civil government for its officers to interfere when principles break out into overt acts against peace and good order.

THE RIGHT OF FREE DISCUSSION
WILLIAM ELLERY CHANNING
American preacher and religious reformer, 1780–1842

Freedom of opinion, of speech, and of the press is our most valuable privilege, the very soul of republican institutions, the safeguard of all other rights.

We may learn its value if we reflect that there is nothing which tyrants so much dread. They anxiously fetter the press; they scatter spies through society, that the murmurs, anguish, and indignation of their oppressed subjects may be smothered in their own breasts; that no generous sentiment may be nourished by sympathy and mutual confidence. Nothing awakes and improves men so much as free communication of thoughts and feelings. Nothing can give to public sentiment that correctness which is essential to the prosperity of a commonwealth but the free circulation of truth from the lips and pens of the wise and good.

If such men abandon the right of free discussion; if awed by threats, they suppress their convictions; if rulers succeed in silencing every voice but that which approves them; if nothing reaches the people but what would lend support to men in power,—farewell to liberty. The form of a free government may remain; but the life, the soul, the substance is fled.

Duties of the Citizen in Times
of Trial or Danger.

OPINION IN THE MAKING *
John Stuart Mill
English philosopher and economist, 1806–1873

If all mankind, minus one, were of one opinion, and only one person were of the contrary opinion, mankind would be no more justified in silencing that one person than he, if he had the power, would be justified in silencing mankind. Wrong opinions and practices gradually yield to fact and argument; but facts and arguments, to produce any effect on the mind, must be brought before it. Very few facts are able to tell their own story without comments to bring out their meaning. The whole strength and value, then, of human judgment, depending on the one property that it can be set right when it is wrong, reliance can be placed on it only when the means of setting it right are kept constantly at hand. Not the violent conflict between parts of the truth, but the quiet suppression of half of it, is the formidable evil; there is always hope when people are forced to listen to both sides; it is when they attend only to one that errors harden into prejudices, and truth itself ceases to have the effect of truth, by being exaggerated into falsehood.

We have now recognized the necessity to the mental well-being of mankind (on which all their other well-being depends) of freedom of opinion, and freedom of the expression of opinion, on four distinct grounds; which we will now briefly recapitulate.

First, if any opinion is compelled to silence, that opinion may, for aught we can certainly know, be true. To deny this is to assume our own infallibility.

Secondly, though the silenced opinion be an error, it may, and very commonly does, contain a portion of truth; and since the general or prevailing opinion on any subject is rarely or never the whole truth, it is only by the collision of adverse opinions that the remainder of the truth has any chance of being supplied.

Thirdly, even if the received opinion be not only true, but the whole truth, unless it is suffered to be, and actually is, vigorously and earnestly contested, it will by most of those who receive it be held in the manner of a prejudice, with little comprehension or feeling of its rational grounds. And not only this, but fourthly, the meaning of the doctrine itself will be in danger of being lost, or enfeebled, and deprived of its vital effect on the character and conduct: the dogma becoming a mere formal profession, inefficacious for good, but cumbering the ground, and preventing the growth of any real and heartfelt conviction from reason or personal experience.

On Liberty

THE HIGHER LOYALTY
Theodore Parker
American preacher and reformer, 1810–1860

I think lightly of what is called treason against a government. That may be your duty today, or mine. Certainly it was our fathers' duty not long ago; now, it is our boast and their title to honor. But treason against the people, against mankind, against God is a great sin, not lightly to be spoken of.

From *War*
Sins and Safeguards of Society

LIBERTY FOR ALL
William Lloyd Garrison
American anti-slavery leader, 1805–1879

They tell me, Liberty, that in thy name
I may not plead for all the human race;

That some are born to bondage and disgrace,
Some to a heritage of woe and shame,
And some to power supreme and glorious fame.
With my whole soul I spurn the doctrine base;
And, as an equal brotherhood, embrace
All people, and, for all, fair freedom claim.
Know this, O man! whate'er thy earthly fate,
God never made a tyrant nor a slave;
Woe then to those who dare to desecrate
His glorious image—for to all he gave
Eternal rights, which none may violate,
And by a mighty hand the oppressed he yet
    shall save.

Sonnets and Other Poems

THE TITLE TO WEALTH *
Blaise Pascal
French geometrician and philosopher, 1623–1662

You hold, you say, your wealth from your
ancestors. Do you imagine too that it may
have been by some natural way that this wealth
has passed from your ancestors to you? This
is not true. This order is founded only upon
the mere will of legislators, who may have had
good reasons, but none of which was drawn

from a natural right that you had over these things. Thus the whole title by which you possess your property is not a title of nature but of a human institution.

Opuscules

THIS LAND IS MINE

Jean Jacques Rousseau
French political and social philosopher; "Father of the French Revolution;" 1712–1778

The first man who, having enclosed a piece of ground, bethought himself of saying, *This is mine,* and found people simple enough to believe him, was the real founder of civil society. From how many crimes, wars, and murders, from how many horrors and misfortunes might not any one have saved mankind by pulling up the stakes, or filling up the ditch, and crying to his fellows, "Beware of listening to this impostor; you are undone if you once forget that the fruits of the earth belong to us all, and the earth itself to nobody!"

Discourse on the Origin of Inequality

THE PRESENT CRISIS *

James Russell Lowell
American poet and essayist, 1819–1891

When a deed is done for freedom, through the
broad earth's aching breast
Runs a thrill of joy prophetic, trembling on
from east to west,
And the slave where'er he cowers feels the
soul within him climb
To the awful verge of manhood, as the energy
sublime
Of a century bursts full-blossomed on the
thorny stem of time.

For mankind are one in spirit, and an instinct
bears along
Round the earth's electric circle the swift flash
of right or wrong;
Whether conscious or unconscious, yet humanity's vast frame
Through its ocean-sundered fibres feels the gush
of joy or shame:
In the gain or loss of one race all the rest have
equal claim.

Once to every man and nation comes the moment to decide,

In the strife of truth with falsehood, for the
    good or evil side;
Some great cause, God's new Messiah, offering
    each the bloom or blight,
Parts the goats upon the left hand and the
    sheep upon the right,
And the choice goes by forever 'twixt that dark-
    ness and that light.

Careless seems the great Avenger; history's
    pages but record
One death-grapple in the darkness 'twixt old
    systems and the Word;
Truth forever on the scaffold, wrong forever on
    the throne,—
Yet that scaffold sways the future, and, behind
    the dim unknown,
Standeth God within the shadow, keeping watch
    above his own.

Then to side with truth is noble when we share
    her wretched crust,
Ere her cause bring fame and profit and 'tis
    prosperous to be just;
Then it is the brave man chooses, while the
    coward stands aside,
Doubting in his abject spirit till his Lord is
    crucified,

And the multitude make virtue of the faith they
    had denied.

'Tis as easy to be heroes as to sit the idle
    slaves
Of a legendary virtue carved upon our fathers'
    graves;
Worshipers of light ancestral make the present
    light a crime.
Was the Mayflower launched by cowards, steered
    by men behind their time?
Turn those tracks toward past or future that
    make Plymouth Rock sublime?

They were men of present valor, stalwart old
    iconoclasts,
Unconvinced by axe or gibbet that all virtue was
    the past's;
But we make their truth our falsehood, thinking
    that hath made us free,
Hoarding it in mouldy parchments while our
    tender spirits flee
The rude grasp of that great impulse which
    drove them across the sea.

New occasions teach new duties; time makes
    ancient good uncouth;
They must upward still, and onward, who would
    keep abreast of truth;

Lo, before us gleam her camp-fires! we ourselves must Pilgrims be,
Launch our Mayflower, and steer boldly through
  the desperate winter sea,
Nor attempt the future's portal with the past's
  blood-rusted key.

FROM THE MAGNA CHARTA *
Granted in 1215

John, by the grace of God, King of England,
to the archbishops, bishops, abbots, earls, barons, justiciars, foresters, sheriffs, reeves, servants, and all bailiffs, and to his faithful people,
greetings:

We have granted to God, and by this our
present charter confirmed for us and our heirs
forever, that the English Church shall be free,
and shall hold its rights entire and its liberties
uninjured.

We have granted, moreover, to all free men of
our kingdom, for us and our heirs forever, all
the liberties written below to be had and holden
by themselves and their heirs from us and our
heirs.

The city of London shall have all its ancient

liberties and free customs, as well by land as by water. Moreover, we will and grant that all other cities and boroughs and villages and ports shall have all their liberties and free customs.

A free man shall not be fined for a small offense, except in proportion to the gravity of the offense; and for a great offense he shall be fined in proportion to the magnitude of the offense, saving his freehold; and a merchant in the same way, saving his merchandise; and the villein shall be fined in the same way, saving his wainage, if he shall be at our mercy; and none of the above fines shall be imposed except by the oaths of honest men of the neighborhood.

No constable or other bailiff of ours shall take any one's grain or other chattels without immediately paying for them in money, unless he is able to obtain a postponement at the good will of the seller.

No sheriff or bailiff of ours, or any one else, shall take horses or wagons of any free man, for carrying purposes, except on the permission of that free man.

Neither we nor our bailiffs will take the wood of another man for castles, or for anything else which we are doing, except by the permission of him to whom the wood belongs.

No free man shall be taken, or imprisoned,

or dispossessed, or outlawed, or banished, or in any way injured; nor will we go upon him, nor send upon him, except by the legal judgment of his peers, or by the law of the land.

To no one will we sell, to no one will we deny or delay, right or justice.

If anyone shall have been dispossessed or removed by us, without legal judgment of his peers, from his lands, castles, franchises, or his right, we will restore them to him immediately; and if contention arises about this, then it shall be done according to the judgment of the twenty-five barons, of whom mention is made below concerning the security of peace.

Since, moreover, for the sake of God, and for the improvement of our kingdom, and for the better quieting of the hostility sprung up lately between us and our barons, we have made all these concessions; wishing them to enjoy these in a complete and firm stability forever, we make and concede to them the security described below; that is to say, that they shall elect twenty-five barons of the kingdom, whomsoever they will, who ought with all their power to observe, hold, and cause to be observed, the peace and liberties which we have conceded to them, and by this our present charter confirmed to them.

It has been sworn, moreover, as well on our part as on the part of the barons, that all these things spoken of above shall be observed in good faith, and without any evil intent.

Given by our hand in the meadow which is called Runnymede, between Windsor and Staines, on the fifteenth day of June, in the seventeenth year of our reign.

American Idealism

THE MAYFLOWER COMPACT
William Bradford
One of the Pilgrim Fathers, second governor of
the Plymouth Colony; 1590–1657

In ye name of God, Amen. We whose names
are underwritten, the loyall subjects of our
dread soveraigne Lord, King James, by ye grace
of God, of Great Britaine, Franc, and Ireland
king, defender of ye faith, &c., haveing undertaken, for ye glory of God, and advancemente
of ye Christian faith, and honor of our king and
countrie, a voyage to plant ye first colonie in
the Northerne parts of Virginia, doe by these
presents solemnly & mutualy in ye presence of
God, and one of another, covenant & combine
our selves togeather into a civill body politick,
for our better ordering & preservation & fur-
therance of ye ends aforesaid; and by vertue
hearof to enacte, constitute, and frame such just
& equall lawes, ordinances, acts, constitutions,

& offices, from time to time, as shall be thought most meete & convenient for ye generall good of ye Colonie, unto which we promise all due submission and obedience. In witnes wherof we have hereunder subscribed our names at Cap-Codd ye 11. of November, in ye year of ye raigne of our soveraigne lord, King James, of England, France, & Ireland ye eighteenth, and of Scotland ye fiftie-fourth. Ano. Dom. 1620.

History of Plymouth Plantation

(The forms *ye* and *yt* mean, and are pronounced, *the* and *that* respectively. Ed.)

THE PILGRIMS' PROSPECTS *
WILLIAM BRADFORD
One of the Pilgrim Fathers, second governor of
the Plymouth Colony; 1590–1657

But hear I cannot but stay and make a pause, and stand half amased at this poore peoples presente condition; and so I thinke will ye reader too, when he well considers ye same. Being thus passed ye vast ocean, and a sea of troubles before in their preparation (as may be remembered by yt which wente before), they had now no freinds to wellcome them, nor inns to entertaine or refresh their weatherbeaten bodys, no houses or much less townes to repaire too, to seeke for succoure. It is recorded in scripture (Act. x 28) as a mercie to ye apostle & his shipwraked company, yt the barbarians shewed them no smale kindnes in refreshing them, but these savage barbarians, when they mette with them (as after will appeare) were readier to fill their sids full of arrows then otherwise. And for ye season it was winter, and they yt know ye winters of yt cuntrie know them to be sharp & violent, & subjecte to cruell & feirce stormes, deangerous to travill to known places, much more to serch an unknown coast. Besids, what could they see but a hidious & desolate wildernes, full of wild beasts & wild men? and what multituds ther might be of them they knew not. Nether could they, as it were, goe up to ye tope of Pisgah to vew from this wildernes a more goodly cuntrie to feed their hops; for which way soever they turnd their eys (save upward to ye heavens) they could have litle solace or content in respecte of any outward objects. For summer being done, all things stand upon them with a wetherbeaten face; and ye whole countrie, full of woods & thickets, represented a wild & savage heiw. If they looked behind them, ther was ye mighty ocean which they had passed, and was now as a maine barr & goulfe to seperate them from all ye civill parts of the world. What could now sustaine them but ye spirite of God & his grace? May not & ought not the children of these faithers rightly say: *Our faithers were Englishmen which came over this great ocean, and were ready to perish in this willdernes; but they cried unto ye Lord, and he heard their voyce, and looked on their adversitie, &c. Let them therfore praise ye Lord, because he is good, & his mercies endure for ever. Yea, let them which have been redeemed of ye Lord, shew how he hath delivered them from ye hand of ye oppressour. When they wandered in the deserte willdernes out of ye way, and found no citie to dwell in, both hungrie, & thirstie, their sowle was overwhelmed in them. Let them confess before ye Lord his loving kindnes, and his wonderfull works before ye sons of men.*

History of Plymouth Plantation

(The forms *ye* and *yt* mean, and are pronounced, *the* and *that* respectively. Ed.)

THE PILGRIMS' FIRST WINTER
William Bradford
One of the Pilgrim Fathers, second governor of
the Plymouth Colony; 1590–1657

In these hard & difficulte beginings they
found some discontents & murmurings arise
amongst some, & mutinous speeches & carriags
in other; but they were soone quelled & overcome by ye wisdome, patience, and just & equall
carrage of things by ye Gov'r and better part,
wch clave faithfully togeather in ye maine.
But yt which was most sadd & lamentable
was, yt in 2. or 3. moneths time halfe of their
company dyed, espetialy in Jan: & February,
being ye depth of winter, and wanting houses &
other comforts; being infected with ye scurvie
& other diseases, which this long vioage & their
inacomodate condition had brought upon them;
so as ther dyed some times 2. or 3. of a
day, in the aforesaid time; that of 100. & odd
persons, scarce 50. remained. And of these in
ye time of most distres, ther was but 6. or 7.
sound persons, who, to their great comendations
be it spoken, spared no pains, night nor day,
but with abundance of toyle and hazard of their
owne health, fetched them woode, made them
fires, drest them meat, made their beads, washed

their lothsome cloaths, cloathed & unclothed them; in a word, did all ye homly & necessarie offices for them wch dainty & quesie stomacks cannot endure to hear named; and all this willingly & cherfully, without any grudging in ye least, shewing herein their true love unto their freinds & bretheren. A rare example & worthy to be remembered. Tow of these 7. were Mr. William Brewster, ther reverend Elder, & Myles Standish, ther Captein & military comander, unto whom my selfe, & many others, were much beholden in our low & sicke condition. And yet the Lord so upheld these persons as in this generall calamity they were not at all infected either with sicknes, or lamnes. And what I have said of these, I may say of many others who dyed in this generall vissitation, & others yet living, yt whilst they had health, yea, or any strength continuing, they were not wanting to any that had need of them. And I doute not but ther recompence is with ye Lord.

History of Plymouth Plantation

(The forms *ye* and *yt* mean, and are pronounced, *the* and *that* respectively. Ed.)

THANKSGIVING, 1623

William Bradford

One of the Pilgrim Fathers, second governor of the Plymouth Colony; 1590–1657

I may not here omite how, notwithstand all their great paines & industrie, and ye great hops of a large cropp, the Lord seemed to blast, & take away the same, & to threaten further & more sore famine unto them, by a great drought which continued from ye 3. weeke in May, till about the midle of July, without any raine, and with great heat (for ye most parte), insomuch as ye corne begane to wither away, though it was set with fishe, the moysture wherof helped it much. Yet at length it begane to languish sore, and some of ye drier grounds were partched like withered hay, part wherof was never recovered. Upon which they sett a parte a solemne day of humilliation, to seek ye Lord by humble & fervente prayer, in this great distrese. And he was pleased to give them a gracious & speedy answer, both to their owne, & the Indeans admiration, that lived amongest them. For all ye morning, and greatest part of ye day, it was clear weather & very hotte, and not a cloud or any signe of raine to be seen, yet toward evening it begane to overcast, and shortly after to raine, with shuch sweete and gentle showers, as gave them cause of rejoyceing, & blesing God. It came, without either wind, or thunder, or any violence, and by degreese in yt abundance, as yt ye earth was thorowly wete and soked therwith. Which did so apparantly revive & quicken ye decayed corne & other fruits, as was wonderfull to see, and made ye Indeans astonished to behold; and afterwards the Lord sent them shuch seasonable showers, with enterchange of faire warme weather, as, through his blessing, caused a fruitfull & liberall harvest, to their no small comforte and rejoycing. For which mercie (in time conveniente) they also sett aparte a day of thanksgiveing.

History of Plymouth Plantation

(The forms *ye* and *yt* mean, and are pronounced *the* and *that* respectively. Ed.)

A TRIBUTE TO THE PILGRIMS
JOHN MASEFIELD
English author, 1875—

A generation fond of pleasure, disinclined towards serious thought, and shrinking from hard ship, even if it may be swiftly reached, will find it difficult to imagine the temper, courage, and manliness of the emigrants who made the first Christian settlement of New England. For a man to give up all things and fare forth into savagery in order to escape from the responsibilities of life, in order, that is, to serve the devil, "whose feet are bound by civilization," is common. Giving up all things in order to serve God is a sternness for which prosperity has unfitted us.

Some regard the settling of New Plymouth as the sowing of the seed from which the crop of Modern America has grown. For all the Mayflower's sailing there is, perhaps, little existing in modern England or America "according to the Primitive Patern in the Word of God." It would be healthful could either country see herself through the eyes of those pioneers, or see the pioneers as they were. The pilgrims leave no impression of personality on the mind. They were not "remarkable." Not one of them had compelling personal genius, or marked talent for the work in hand. They were plain men of moderate abilities, who, giving up all things, went to live in the wilds, at unknown

cost to themselves, in order to preserve to their
children a life in the soul.

From the *Introduction*
Chronicles of the Pilgrims

THE CITIZEN'S VOTE *
Massachusetts, about 1634

I doe promise to give my voice for the elect-
ing of such psone and psones unto voide places
as I shall thinke to be the wisest, godliest, &
ablest for the discharg, men of wisedome &
courage—feareinge God & hateing covetousness.

(From the freeman's oath, which appears in the
handwriting of Thomas Dudley, second governor of
Massachusetts Colony.)

Historical Manuscripts and Reprints

THE PUBLIC SCHOOL
A law enacted in Massachusetts in 1647

It being one chiefe project of that ould de-
luder, Sathan, to keepe men from the knowledge
of the Scriptures, as in former times by keeping

them in an unknowne tongue, so in these latter
times by perswading from the use of tongues
that so at least the true sence and meaning of
the originall might be clouded by false glosses
of saint seeming deceivers, that learning may
not be buried in the grave of our fathers in the
church and comonwealth, the Lord assisting our
endeavors:—

It is therefore ordered, that every township
in this jurisdiction, after the Lord hath increased them to the number of fifty household-
ers, shall then forthwith appoint one within their
towne to teach all such children as shall resort
to him to write and reade, whose wages shall be
paid either by the parents or masters of such
children, or by the inhabitants in generall, by
way of supply, as the maior part of those that
order the prudentials of the towne shall appoint; provided, those that send their children
be not oppressed by paying much more than
they can have them taught for in other townes;
and it is further ordered, that where any towne
shall increase to the number of one hundred
families or househoulders they shall set up a
gramer schoole, the master thereof being able to
instruct youth so farr as they may be fited for
the university; provided, that if any towne neglect the performance hereof above one yeare,

that every such towne shall pay 5s. to the next
schoole till they shall performe this order.

Records of Massachusetts, Vol. ii

FROM THE CHARTER OF RHODE ISLAND *
Granted by Charles II, 1663

They [1] in their humble address have freely
declared that it is much on their hearts (if they
may be permitted) to hold forth a lively experiment, that a most flourishing civil State may
stand and best be maintained, and that among
our English subjects, with a full liberty in religious concernments. Now, know ye, that we,
being willing to encourage the hopeful under-
taking of our said loyal subjects, and to secure
them in the free exercise and enjoyment of all
their civil and religious rights appertaining to
them; and to preserve unto them that liberty,
in the true Christian faith and worship of God
which they have sought with so much travail,
and with peaceable minds; and because some of
the people and inhabitants of the same colony

---

[1] The petitioners to King Charles II, including
Roger Williams.

cannot, in their private opinions, conform to the public exercise of religion, according to the liturgy, forms, and ceremonies of the Church of England, or take or subscribe the oaths and articles made and established in that behalf; and for that the same, by reason of the remote distances of those places, will (as we hope) be no breach of the unity and uniformity established in this nation: Have therefore thought fit, and do hereby publish, grant, ordain and declare that our royal will and pleasure is that no person within the said colony, at any time hereafter, shall be in any wise molested, punished, disquieted, or called in question, for any differences in opinion in matters of religion, and do not actually disturb the civil peace of our said colony; but that all and every person and persons may, from time to time, and at all times hereafter, freely and fully have and enjoy his and their own judgments and consciences, in matters of religious concernments, throughout the tract of land hereafter mentioned, they behaving themselves peaceably and quietly.

Witness ourself at Westminster, the eighth day of July, in the fifteenth year of our reign.

By the King: HOWARD

Documents Illustrative of American History
Ed. Howard Preston

LIBERTY AND THE COMMON WEAL*
ROGER WILLIAMS
English colonist and preacher; founder of
the State of Rhode Island, 1604–1684

There goes many a ship to sea with many
hundred souls in one ship, whose weal and woe
is common, and it is a picture of a commonwealth, or an human combination of society.
It hath fallen out sometimes that both Papists
and Protestants, Jews and Turks, may be em-
barked into one ship. Upon which supposal, I
affirm that all the liberty of conscience that ever
I pleaded for turns upon these two hinges: that
none of the Papists, Protestants, Jews, or Turks
be forced to come to the ship's prayers or worship; nor compelled from their own particular
prayer or worship, if they practise any. I further add that I never denied that, notwithstanding this liberty, the commander of this
ship ought to command that justice, peace, and
sobriety be kept and practised, both among the
seamen and all the passengers. If any of the
seamen refuse to perform their service, or passengers to pay their freight; if any refuse to
help in person or purse toward the common
charges or defense; if any refuse to obey the
common laws and orders of the ship concerning

their common peace or preservation; if any shall mutiny and rise up against their commanders and officers; if any should preach or write that there ought to be no commanders nor officers because all are equal in Christ, therefore no masters nor officers, no laws nor orders, no corrections nor punishments: in such cases, whatever is pretended, the commander or commanders may judge, resist, compel, and punish such transgressors, according to their deserts and merits.

(Roger Williams, after becoming a Puritan, left England for America in 1631. He was called to the church in Salem, Massachusetts, as teaching Elder, and later became minister of that church.

He held marked views of religious toleration and non-conformity, which offended many of the church members. He also preached against the holding of the land by the Massachusetts colonists under patent from the King, believing that the King could not dispose of the land of the Indians without their consent. Again, he insisted that the magistrate should not "deal in matters of conscience and religion."

In these ways, incurring the displeasure of the government, in 1635 he was banished.

Although he considered himself thus treated unjustly, he never appeared to harbor revenge, but instead, when learning through his intimate mingling with the Indians that they plotted to massacre the

inhabitants of the settlement from which he had been
banished, he gave the information that saved their
lives. He "employed himself continually in acts of
kindness to his persecutors, affording relief to the distressed, offering an asylum to the persecuted." Ed.)

Rhode Island Historical Society
Collections, Vol. i

THE BROTHER INDIAN *
Roger Williams
English colonist and preacher, founder of
the State of Rhode Island, 1604–1684

There is a savour of civility and courtesie
even amongst these wild Americans, both
amongst themselves and towards strangers.

More particular:

1. The courteous Pagan shall condemne
      Uncourteous Englishmen,
   Who live like Foxes, Beares, and Wolves,
      Or Lyon in his Den.

2. Let none sing blessings of their soules
      For that they courteous are:
   The wild Barbarians with no more
      Then nature goe so farre:

3. If natures Sons both wild and tame,
    Humane and courteous be:
  How ill becomes it Sonnes of God
    To Want Humanity!

Sweet rest is not confind to soft Beds, for, not only God gives his beloved sleep on hard lodgings; but also Nature and custome gives sound sleep to these Americans on the earth, on a boord or mat. Yet how is Europe bound to God for better lodging, &c.

  More particular:
1. God gives them sleep on ground, on straw,
    on sedgie mats or boord:
  When English softest beds of downe
    sometimes no sleep affoord.

2. I have knowne them leave their house and
    mat,
    to lodge a friend or stranger,
  When Jews and Christians oft have sent
    Christ Jesus to the manger.

3. 'Fore day they invocate their Gods,
    Though many false and new:
  O how should that God worshipt be,
    Who is but one and true?

Nature knowes no difference between Europe
and Americans in blood, birth, bodies, &c.   God
having of one blood made all mankind.   Acts
17.

More particular:
Boast not, proud English, of thy birth and
    blood:
Thy Brother Indian is by birth as good.
Of one blood God made Him, and Thee, and
    All—
As wise, as faire, as strong, as personall.
By nature, wrath's his portion, thine, no more
Till Grace his soule and thine in Christ restore.
Make sure thy second birth, else thou shalt see
Heaven ope to Indians wild, but shut to thee.

Rhode Island Historical Society
Collections, Vol. i

WISDOM OF THE NORTH AMERICAN
INDIAN

Canonicus (a sachem of the Narragansetts)
to Roger Williams: I have never suffered any
wrong to be done the English, since they
landed, nor ever will.

Garangula, or Grangula (an orator of the Onondagas, 1684): We are born free. We depend neither on Yonondio (France) nor on Corlaer (England).

Honayawus, or Farmer's Brother (famous chief of the Senecas): The Great Spirit spoke to the whirlwind and it was still. (Said in 1798 of the war of the Revolution and its close.)

Metakoosega (a chief of the western Ojibwa): Am I a dog, that I should lie? (Said in 1826 when Gov. Cass suggested that he should bind himself by an oath.)

Miantunnumoh (a sachem of the Narragansetts): When your people come to me, they are permitted to use their own fashions, and I expect the same liberty when I come to you. (Said to Governor Dudley in 1640.)

Moanahonga (an Iowa Indian): I am ashamed to look upon the sun. I have insulted the Great Spirit by selling the bones of my fathers. It is right that I should mourn. (He wore a blackened face to the day of his death.)

I'll go with you. A brave man dies but once. Cowards are always dying. (Said when surrendering to the whites.)

Tecumseh (the famous Shawnee chief): These lands are ours. No one has a right to remove us, because we were the first owners.

The Great Spirit above has appointed this place for us, on which to light our fires, and here we will remain. As to boundaries, the Great Spirit knows no boundaries, nor will his red children acknowledge any. (Said in 1810 to the messenger of the President of the United States.)

My father? The sun is my father, and the earth is my mother; and on her bosom I will repose. (Said, indignantly, at Vincennes, in 1810, when told, "Your father requests you to take a chair." Tecumseh, in Indian fashion, sat on the ground.)

Sell a country! Why not sell the air, the clouds and the great sea, as well as the earth? Did not the Great Spirit make them all for the use of his children?

Collected by Alexander Francis Chamberlain
Proceedings of the American
Antiquarian Society

FROM THE DECLARATION OF INDEPENDENCE *

The Representatives of the United States of America in General Congress assembled, July 4th, 1776

When, in the course of human events, it becomes necessary for one people to dissolve the political bands which have connected them with another, and to assume, among the powers of the earth, the separate and equal station to which the laws of nature and of nature's God entitle them, a decent respect to the opinions of mankind requires that they should declare the causes which impel them to the separation.

We hold these truths to be self-evident: that all men are created equal; that they are endowed by their Creator with certain inalienable rights; that among these are life, liberty, and the pursuit of happiness; that, to secure these rights, governments are instituted among men, deriving their just powers from the consent of the governed; that whenever any form of government becomes destructive of these ends, it is the right of the people to alter or to abolish it, and to institute a new government, laying its foundation on such principles and organizing its powers in such form as to them shall seem most likely to effect their safety and happiness. Prudence, indeed, will dictate that governments long established should not be changed for light and transient causes; and, accordingly, all experience hath shown that mankind are more disposed to suffer, while evils are sufferable, than to right themselves by abolishing the forms to which they are accustomed. But, when a long train of abuses and usurpations, pursuing invariably the same object, evinces a design to reduce them under absolute despotism, it is their right, it is their duty, to throw off such government, and to provide new guards for their future security.

We, therefore, the representatives of the United States of America, in General Congress assembled, appealing to the Supreme Judge of the world for the rectitude of our intentions, do, in the name, and by the authority, of the good people of these colonies, solemnly publish and declare that these united colonies are, and of right ought to be, free and independent States; that, as free and independent states, they have full power to levy war, conclude peace, contract alliances, establish commerce, and to do all other acts and things which independent states may of right do. And, for the support of this declaration, with a firm reliance on the protection of Divine Providence, we mutually pledge to each other our lives, our fortunes, and our sacred honor.

Prepared by Thomas Jefferson
Signed by John Hancock and fifty-six others

PREAMBLE TO THE CONSTITUTION
OF THE UNITED STATES
Philadelphia Convention, September 17, 1787

We, the people of the United States, in order to form a more perfect Union, establish justice, insure domestic tranquillity, provide for the common defence, promote the general welfare, and secure the blessings of liberty to ourselves and our posterity, do ordain and establish this Constitution for the United States of America.

CIVIL LIBERTIES
First amendment to the Constitution of the United States, 1791

Congress shall make no law respecting an establishment of religion, or prohibiting the free exercise thereof; or abridging the freedom of speech or of the press; or the right of the people peaceably to assemble, and to petition the government for a redress of grievances.

THE GETTYSBURG ADDRESS

ABRAHAM LINCOLN

President of the United States during the Civil War; preserver of the Union, and emancipator of the slaves; 1809–1865

Fourscore and seven years ago, our fathers brought forth upon this continent a new nation, conceived in liberty, and dedicated to the proposition that all men are created equal.

Now we are engaged in a great civil war, testing whether that nation, or any nation so conceived and so dedicated, can long endure. We are met on a great battlefield of that war. We have come to dedicate a portion of that field as a final resting-place for those who here gave their lives that that nation might live. It is altogether fitting and proper that we should do this.

But in a larger sense we cannot dedicate, we cannot consecrate, we cannot hallow this ground. The brave men, living and dead, who struggled here have consecrated it far above our power to add or detract. The world will little note nor long remember what we say here, but it can never forget what they did here. It is for us, the living, rather to be dedicated here to the unfinished work which they who fought here have thus far so nobly advanced. It is rather for us to be here dedicated to the great task remaining before us, that from these honored dead we take increased devotion to that cause for which they gave the last full measure of devotion; that we here highly resolve that these dead shall not have died in vain; that this nation, under God, shall have a new birth of freedom; and that government of the people, by the people, for the people shall not perish from the earth.

FROM THE SECOND INAUGURAL ADDRESS *

ABRAHAM LINCOLN

President of the United States during the Civil War; preserver of the Union, and emancipator of the slaves; 1809–1865

Four years ago, all thoughts were anxiously directed to an impending civil war. All dreaded it—all sought to avert it. Both parties deprecated war; but one of them would make war rather than let the nation survive; and the other would accept war rather than let it perish. And the war came.

With malice toward none, with charity for all, with firmness in the right, as God gives us to see the right, let us strive on to finish the work we are in, to bind up the nation's wounds, to care for him who shall have borne the battle, and for his widow, and his orphans—to do all which may achieve and cherish a just and lasting peace among ourselves and with all nations.

PIONEERS! O PIONEERS!*

WALT WHITMAN

American poet, 1819–1892

O you youths, Western youths,
So impatient, full of action, full of manly pride
and friendship,
Plain I see you, Western youths, see you tramp-
ing with the foremost,
Pioneers! O pioneers!

Have the elder races halted?
Do they droop and end their lesson, wearied
over there beyond the seas?
We take up the task eternal, and the burden and
the lesson,
Pioneers! O pioneers!

O to die advancing on!
Are there some of us to droop and die? has the
hour come?
Then upon the march we fittest die; soon and
sure the gap is filled,
Pioneers! O pioneers!

Life's involved and varied pageants,
All the forms and shows, all the workmen at
their work,
All the seamen and the landsmen, all the mas-
ters with their slaves,
Pioneers! O pioneers!

All the hapless silent lovers,
All the prisoners in the prisons, all the right-
eous and the wicked,
All the joyous, all the sorrowing, all the living,
all the dying,
Pioneers! O pioneers!

I too with my soul and body,
We, a curious trio, picking, wandering on our
way,
Through these shores amid the shadows, with
the apparitions pressing,
Pioneers! O pioneers!

Not for delectations sweet
Not the cushion and the slipper, not the peace-
ful and the studious,
Not the riches safe and palling, not for us the
tame enjoyment,
Pioneers! O pioneers!

Do the feasters gluttonous feast?
Do the corpulent sleepers sleep? have they
lock'd and bolted doors?
Still be ours the diet hard, and the blanket on
the ground,
Pioneers! O pioneers!

Has the night descended?
Was the road of late so toilsome? did we stop
discouraged, nodding on our way?
Yet a passing hour I yield you in your tracks to
pause oblivious,
Pioneers! O pioneers!

Till with sound of trumpet,
Far, far off the daybreak call—hark! how loud
and clear I hear it wind—
Swift! to the head of the army!—swift! spring
to your places,
Pioneers! O pioneers!

THE FOUNDATIONS OF THE REPUBLIC *

EDWARD EVERETT HALE
American preacher and writer, 1822–1909

The success of the American Republic is due to the empire of the moral forces. In our new century the moral forces are to control the physical forces of America. We have created these giants which we call power stations or engines or dynamos, and they are to serve us. They will serve us; they will have to obey God and man. God and man are the moral forces.

When the French Republic was well established, Guizot said to (James Russell) Lowell, "How long do you think the American Republic will endure?" That was naturally the question for a man who had seen his own handiwork go to pieces. And Lowell answered, "So long as the ideas of its founders continue to be dominant."

The remark conveys to the world the true idea as to what the foundations of a commonwealth are. It is not on this or that bit of paper, or this or that parchment, that we build. It is not by calling a king a president that you make a republic. It is not by calling an Assembly a Congress that you make a republic. The republic is the government of the people, for the people, by the people. If the ideas on which you build it are the eternal ideas, it will stand. If you forget them; if, as Paul says, you build on gold or silver or precious stones, or wood or hay or stubble, they last no longer than the gold lasts, or the stubble. If your republic is really founded on faith, hope, and love—these are the eternities—it will endure.

But this was not the first foundation. As Lowell said, we have to go back to the traditions of their race.

The first instance occurs to every one. It is the tradition of equality which existed in the practice of the eight northern states, and which existed in the theories of the five southern states. Second, and akin to this, is the instinct for "together." To the students of social order who talk of the breach between capital and labor I have to commend this tradition of the fathers, the tradition of together.

Given the idea of equality, given the gospel idea of together, and, almost of course, you have another of the great ideas of the fathers, which I will name next, the idea of local government—home government, we call it now—the two are one and the same.

Equality, brotherhood, home government,

which is local government, these were conditions of government quite as much matters of course among the fathers as the English language in whose words they were written. And with this, all along, first, second, and last, the undercurrent of them all, was the religious character or disposition or training of the fathers. Of nine-tenths of them the American history was the history of emigration for religion's sake. And of the other tenth, the custom, what you might call the common law, was bred in their habits of worship and of ecclesiastical administration. In practice, every church was an independent organization. Here comes in that reverent acknowledgment of the will of God, and of the presence of God, which in the minds of the fathers is wrought in with all they enact or do. Law is to them the voice of infinite justice, it is not a temporary arrangement made by a few neighbors with each other. It is something eternal.

For your life and mine, today, and tomorrow, if we wish to maintain a republic, we must keep in mind our own part in living up to the ideas of the fathers. This is not because they were the ideas of the fathers, but because they are infinite ideas. They represent the eternities, which are but three. They represent faith,

hope, and love. If you please to put it so, they
rest on absolute religion, the religion in which
all men are of one blood, every man is a son of
God, every man bears his brother's burdens.
He who is first of all is the bond-servant of all.

Our special duties, then, are given to us in
the words *equality of rights, together, local
government.* And all along, he who is greatest
is to be your servant. And we are to remember that these words imply duties. Remember
as well that there is no duty unless there is a
present recognition of the present God.

The Foundations of the Republic

THE RIGHT OF THE PEOPLE TO RULE *

THEODORE ROOSEVELT
President of the United States; 1858–1919

Friends, our task as Americans is to strive
for social and industrial justice, achieved
through the genuine rule of the people; this is
our end, our purpose. The methods for achiev-
ing the end are merely expedients, to be finally
accepted or rejected according as actual experience shows that they work well or ill. But

in our hearts we must have this lofty purpose, and we must strive for it in all earnestness and sincerity, or our work will come to nothing.

In order to succeed, we need leaders of inspired idealisms, leaders to whom are granted great visions, who dream greatly and strive to make their dreams come true; who can kindle the people with the fire from their own burning souls.

In the long fight for righteousness, the watchword for us all is, "Spend and be spent."

We here in America hold in our hands the hope of the world, the fate of the coming years; and shame and disgrace will be ours if in our eyes the light of high resolve is dimmed, if we trail in the dust the golden hopes of men. If on this new continent we merely build another country of great but unjustly divided material prosperity, we shall have done nothing; and we shall do as little if we merely set the greed of envy against the greed of arrogance, and thereby destroy the material well-being of all of us. To turn this government either into government by a plutocracy or into government by a mob would be to repeat on a larger scale the lamentable failures of the world that is dead.

We stand against all tyranny, by the few or

by the many. We stand for the rule of the many in the interest of all of us, for the rule of the many in a spirit of courage, of common sense, of high purpose; above all, in a spirit of kindly justice toward every man and woman. We not merely admit, but insist, that there must be self-control on the part of the people, that they must keenly perceive their own duties as well as the rights of others; but we also insist that the people can do nothing unless they not merely have, but exercise to the full, their own rights.

The worth of our great experiment depends upon its being in good faith an experiment—the first that has ever been tried—in true democracy on the scale of a continent, on a scale as vast as that of the mightiest empires of the old world. Surely this is a noble ideal, an ideal for which it is worth while to strive, an ideal for which at need it is worth while to sacrifice much; for our ideal is the rule of all the people in a spirit of friendliest brotherhood toward each and every one of the people.

The American Spirit

DEMOCRACY

JANE ADDAMS

American: head resident of Hull House, Chicago; writer on social reforms, 1860–1935

The doctrine of Democracy, like any other of the living faiths of men, is so essentially mystical that it continually demands new formulation. To fail to recognize it in a new form, to call it hard names, to refuse to receive it, may mean to reject that which our fathers cherished and handed on as an inheritance not only to be preserved but also to be developed.

The Spirit of Youth

THE SHIP OF STATE

HENRY WADSWORTH LONGFELLOW

American poet, 1807–1882

Thou, too, sail on, O Ship of State!
Sail on, o UNION, strong and great!
Humanity with all its fears,
With all the hopes of future years,
Is hanging breathless on thy fate.
We know what Master laid thy keel,
What workmen wrought thy ribs of steel,

Who made each mast, and sail, and rope,
What anvils rang, what hammers beat,
In what a forge and what a heat
Were shaped the anchors of thy hope.
Fear not each sudden sound and shock,
'Tis of the wave and not the rock;
'Tis but the flapping of the sail,
And not a rent made by the gale.
In spite of rock and tempest's roar,
In spite of false lights on the shore,
Sail on, nor fear to breast the sea.
Our hearts, our hopes, are all with thee,
Our hearts, our hopes, our prayers, our tears,
Our faith triumphant o'er our fears,
Are all with thee,—are all with thee!

From *The Building of the Ship*

THE VOYAGE OF DEMOCRACY
WALT WHITMAN
American poet, 1819–1892

Sail, sail thy best, ship of Democracy,
Of value is thy freight: 'Tis not the present
    only;
The past is also stored in thee.
Thou holdest not the venture of thyself alone,
    not of the Western continent alone;

Earth's résumé entire floats on thy keel, O ship,
    is steadied by thy spars;
With thee Time voyages in trust; the antece-
    dent nations sink or swim with thee,
With all their ancient struggles, martyrs, heroes,
    epics, wars, thou bearest the other conti-
    nents:
Theirs, theirs as much as thine, the destination-
    port triumphant;
Steer then with good strong hand and wary eye,
    O helmsman, thou carriest great compan-
    ions!

        From *Thou Mother with Thy Equal Brood*

I AM AN AMERICAN

ELIAS LIEBERMAN
American poet; born in Russia, 1883—

I am an American.
My father belongs to the Sons of the Revolu-
    tion;
My mother, to the Colonial Dames.
One of my ancestors pitched tea overboard in
    Boston Harbor;
Another stood his ground with Warren;

Another hungered with Washington at Valley
    Forge.
My forefathers were America in the making:
They spoke in her council halls;
They died on her battle-fields;
They commanded her ships;
They cleared her forests.
Dawns reddened and paled.
Staunch hearts of mine beat fast at each new
   • star
In the nation's flag.
Keen eyes of mine foresaw her greater glory:
The sweep of her seas,
The plenty of her plains,
The man-hives in her billion-wired cities:
Every drop of blood in me holds a heritage of
    patriotism.
I am proud of my past.
I am an American.

I am an American.
My father was an atom of dust,
My mother, a straw in the wind,
To His Serene Majesty.
One of my ancestors died in the mines of
    Siberia;
Another was crippled for life by twenty blows
    of the knout;

Another was killed defending his home during
    the massacres.

The history of my ancestors is a trail of blood
To the palace gate of the Great White Czar.
But then the dream came—
The dream of America.

In the light of the Liberty torch
The atom of dust became a man,
And the straw in the wind became a woman,
For the first time.

"See," said my father, pointing to the flag that
    fluttered near,
"That flag of stars and stripes is yours;
It is the emblem of the promised land.
It means, my son, the hope of humanity.
Live for it—die for it!"

Under the open sky of my new country I swore
    to do so;
And every drop of blood in me will keep that
    vow.

I am proud of my future.
I am an American.

Paved Streets

THE POSITION OF WOMEN [*]

JAMES BRYCE
British historian and statesman; ambassador to
the United States; 1838–1922

It has been well said that the position which
women hold in a country is, if not a complete
test, yet one of the best tests of the progress it
has made in civilization. When one compares
nomad man with settled man, heathen man with
Christian man, the ancient world with the
modern, the eastern world with the western,
it is plain that in every case the advance in
public order, in material comfort, in wealth, in
decency and refinement of manners among the
whole population of a country—for in these
matters one must not look merely at the upper
class—has been accompanied by a greater respect for women, by a greater freedom accorded
to them, by a fuller participation on their part
in the best work of the world. Americans are
fond of pointing, and can with perfect justice
point, to the position their women hold as an
evidence of the high level their civilization has
reached.

If women have on the whole gained, it is clear
that the nation gains through them. As mothers they mould the character of their children,

while the function of forming the habits of society and determining its moral tone rests greatly in their hands. But there is reason to think that the influence of the American system tells directly for good upon men as well as upon the whole community. The respect for women which every American man either feels, or is obliged by public sentiment to profess, has a wholesome effect on his conduct and character, and serves to check the cynicism which some other peculiarities of the country foster. No country seems to owe more to its women than America does, nor to owe to them so much of what is best in social institutions and in the beliefs that govern conduct.

The American Commonwealth, Vol. ii
1910 edition

THE PRINCIPLES OF A LIBERATED MANKIND *

WOODROW WILSON

President of the United States during the World War; 1856–1924

We are a composite and cosmopolitan people. We are of the blood of all nations that are at war. We wished nothing for ourselves that we were not ready to demand for all mankind—fair dealing, justice, the freedom to live and be at ease against organized wrong.

There are many things still to do at home, to clarify our own politics and give new vitality to the industrial processes of our own life, and we shall do them as time and opportunity serve; but we realize that the greatest things that remain to be done must be done with the whole world for stage and in coöperation with the wide and universal forces of mankind. We are provincials no longer. The tragical events of the thirty months of vital turmoil through which we have just passed have made us citizens of the world. There can be no turning back. Our own fortunes as a nation are involved, whether we would have it so or not.

And yet we are not the less Americans on that account. We shall be the more American if we but remain true to the principles in which we have been bred. They are not the principles of a province or of a single continent. We have known and boasted all along that they were the principles of a liberated mankind. These, therefore, are the things we shall stand for, whether in war or in peace:—

That all nations are equally interested in the peace of the world and in the political stability of free peoples, and equally responsible for their maintenance;

That the essential principle of peace is the actual equality of nations in all matters of right or privilege;

That peace cannot securely or justly rest upon an armed balance of power;

That governments derive all their just powers from the consent of the governed and that no other powers should be supported by the common thought, purpose, or power of the family of nations;

That the seas should be equally free and safe for the use of all peoples, under rules set up by common agreement and consent, and that, so far as practicable, they should be accessible to all upon equal terms;

That national armaments should be limited to the necessities of national order and domestic safety;

That the community of interest and of power upon which peace must henceforth depend imposes upon each nation the duty of seeing to it that all influences proceeding from its own citizens meant to encourage or assist revolution in other states should be sternly and effectually suppressed and prevented.

The shadows that now lie dark upon our

path will soon be dispelled and we shall walk
with the light all about us if we be but true to
ourselves,—to ourselves as we have wished to
be known in the counsels of the world and in
the thought of all those who love liberty and
justice and the right exalted.

From *The Second Inaugural Address*

AN EPISTLE TO THE AMERICANS *
EDWIN D. MEAD
American publicist, 1849–1937

Faith is the substance of things hoped for,
the evidence of things not seen. For by it the
fathers obtained a good report. Columbus
sailed through unknown seas for many days, mid
perils of wind and perils of water, mid perils
from faint hearts, mid perils from false brethren, and revealed a new world, and died knowing not what he had seen. By faith Puritan-
ism, beginning even as a grain of mustard seed,
brought forth Eliot and Hampden and Crom-
well and Milton and Vane and planted New
England. By faith the Pilgrim Fathers, when
they were called to go out into a place which
they should after receive for an inheritance,

obeyed; and they went out, not knowing whither they went. By faith they sojourned in the land of promise, as in a strange country, with Winthrop and Cotton and Roger Williams, heirs with them of the same promise.

By faith Samuel Adams refused to admit of bondage, and was not afraid of the king's commandment. By faith Washington drew his sword, and Jefferson saw that which was invisible. By faith independence was declared by a nation that was not yet a nation. By faith the farmers stood at Bunker Hill, by faith they endured at Valley Forge, by faith they conquered at Yorktown.

And what shall I more say? For the time would fail me to speak of Lafayette and the faith that worked mightily for us in other lands; of Franklin and Madison and Hamilton, who by faith brought us out of confusion into order; of Lincoln, also, and the noble army of those who redeemed the land from slavery; of Garrison, who worked mightily with the newspaper, of Phillips on the platform, and Parker in the pulpit, and Whittier with the song, and Sumner in the senate, and John Brown on the scaffold; of America in the council of nations, of faithful soldiers coming up from lowly homes and lying down in unknown graves; of faithful women giving up brothers and sons and husbands. And some had trial of bonds and imprisonment, being destitute, afflicted, tormented. These all, having obtained a good report through faith, labored for our welfare and to safeguard democracy throughout the world; and posterity has entered into the fruits of their labor.

Wherefore, seeing we are compassed about with so great a cloud of witnesses, and that with so great a price freedom has been purchased, let us lay aside every weight of selfishness and sloth, and the sins of partisanship and pride, which so easily beset us, let us walk worthy of our great inheritance, let us be creditors of the future even as we are debtors to the past; and let us know that the spirit of history is the God of nations, whose other name is Justice.

Lessons of History

HYMN TO AMERICA *
WALT WHITMAN
American poet, 1819-1892

Thou Mother with thy equal brood,
Thou varied chain of different States, yet one
    identity only,

A special song before I go I'd sing o'er all the
  rest,
For thee, the future.

The conceits of the poets of other lands I'd
  bring thee not,
Nor the compliments that have served their turn
  so long,
Nor rhyme, nor the classics, nor perfume of
  foreign court or indoor library;
But an odor I'd bring as from forests of pine
  in Maine, or breath of an Illinois prairie,
With open airs of Virginia or Georgia or Ten-
  nessee, or from Texas uplands, or Florida's
  glades,
Or the Saguenay's black stream, or the wide
  blue spread of Huron,
With presentment of Yellowstone's scenes, or
  Yosemite,
And murmuring under, pervading all, I'd bring
  the rustling sea-sound,
That endlessly sounds from the two Great Seas
  of the world.

And for thy subtler sense, subtler refrains,
  dread Mother,
Thou! mounting higher, diving deeper than we
  knew, thou transcendental Union!

Thought of man justified, blended with God,
Through thy idea, lo, the immortal reality!
Through thy reality, lo, the immortal idea!

Brain of the New World, what a task is thine,
To formulate the Modern!
By vision, hand, conception, on the background
    of the mighty past, the dead,
To limn with absolute faith the mighty living
    present!
Thou but the apples, long, long, long a-growing,
The fruit of all the Old ripening to-day in thee.

Thee in thy future,
Thee in thy larger, saner brood of female, male
    —thee in thy athletes, moral, spiritual:
    South, North, West, East,
Thee in thy moral wealth and civilization (until
    which thy proudest material civilization
    must remain in vain)
Thee in thy all-supplying, all-enclosing worship
    —thee in no single bible, saviour, merely,
Thy saviours countless, latent within thyself,
    equal to any, divine as any,
Thee in thy pinnacles, intellect, thought, thy
    topmost rational joys, thy love and godlike
    aspiration,
These! these in thee (certain to come) today I
    prophesy.

(Lo, where arise three peerless stars
To be thy natal stars, my country, Ensemble,
    Evolution, Freedom,
Set in the sky of law!)

The storm shall dash thy face, the murk of
    war and worse than war shall cover thee all
    over,
(Wert capable of war, its tug and trials? Be
    capable of peace, its trials,
For the tug and mortal strain of nations come
    at last in prosperous peace, not war;)
In many a smiling mask death shall approach,
    beguiling thee,
But thou shalt face thy fortunes, thy diseases,
    and surmount them all,
Thou globe of globes! thou wonder nebulous!
Thou mental, moral orb—thou New, indeed
    new, Spiritual World!
The present holds thee not—for such vast
    growth as thine,
For such unparalleled flight as thine, such brood
    as thine,
The future only holds thee, and can hold thee.

From *Thou Mother with Thy Equal Brood*

AMERICA THE BEAUTIFUL
KATHARINE LEE BATES
American writer and teacher, 1859–1929

O beautiful for spacious skies,
  For amber waves of grain,
For purple mountain majesties
  Above the fruited plain!
    America! America!
God shed his grace on thee,
And crown thy good with brotherhood
  From sea to shining sea!

O beautiful for pilgrim feet,
  Whose stern, impassioned stress,
A thoroughfare for freedom beat
  Across the wilderness!
    America! America!
God mend thine every flaw,
Confirm thy soul in self-control,
  Thy liberty in law!

O beautiful for heroes proved
  In liberating strife,
Who more than self their country loved
  And mercy more than life!
    America! America!
May God thy gold refine,

Till all success be nobleness,
   And every gain divine!

O beautiful for patriot dream
   That sees beyond the years
Thine alabaster cities gleam
   Undimmed by human tears!
      America! America!
   God shed his grace on thee,
And crown thy good with brotherhood
   From sea to shining sea!

America the Beautiful and Other Poems

The Coming Day

SWORDS AND PLOWSHARES
Hebrew; this passage, after 500 B. C.

And it shall come to pass in the latter days
that the mountain of the Lord's house shall be
established at the head of the mountains, and
shall be exalted above the hills; and all nations
shall flow unto it. And many peoples shall go
and say, Come ye, and let us go up to the mountain of the Lord, to the house of the God of
Jacob; and he will teach us of his ways, and we
will walk in his paths: for out of Zion shall go
forth the law, and the word of the Lord from
Jerusalem. And he shall judge between the
nations, and shall reprove many peoples: and
they shall beat their swords into plowshares,
and their spears into pruninghooks: nation shall
not lift up sword against nation, neither shall
they learn war any more.

From *The Book of Isaiah*
Old Testament

THE NEW YEAR

ALFRED TENNYSON
English poet, 1809–1892

Ring out, wild bells, to the wild sky,
  The flying cloud, the frosty light:
  The year is dying in the night;
Ring out, wild bells, and let him die.

Ring out the old, ring in the new,
  Ring, happy bells, across the snow:
  The year is going, let him go;
Ring out the false, ring in the true.

Ring out the grief that saps the mind,
  For those that here we see no more;
  Ring out the feud of rich and poor,
Ring in redress to all mankind.

Ring out a slowly dying cause,
  And ancient forms of party strife;
  Ring in the nobler modes of life,
With sweeter manners, purer laws.

Ring out the want, the care, the sin,
  The faithless coldness of the times;
  Ring out, ring out my mournful rhymes,
But ring the fuller minstrel in.

Ring out false pride in place and blood,
　The civic slander and the spite;
　　Ring in the love of truth and right,
Ring in the common love of good.

Ring out old shapes of foul disease;
　Ring out the narrowing lust of gold;
　　Ring out the thousand wars of old,
Ring in the thousand years of peace.

Ring in the valiant man and free,
　The larger heart, the kindlier hand;
　　Ring out the darkness of the land,
Ring in the Christ that is to be.

In Memoriam

THE LAW OF WAR AND THE LAW
OF PEACE

Louis Pasteur

French: founder of the science
of bacteriology, 1822–1895

Two contrary laws seem to be wrestling with
each other nowadays: the one, a law of blood
and of death, ever imagining new means of destruction and forcing nations to be constantly

ready for the battle field—the other, a law of peace, work, and health, ever evolving new means of delivering man from the scourges which beset him.

The one seeks violent conquests; the other, the relief of humanity. The latter places one human life above any victory; while the former would sacrifice hundreds of thousands of lives to the ambition of one. The law of which we are the instruments seeks, even in the midst of carnage, to cure the sanguinary ills of the law of war; the treatment inspired by our antiseptic methods may preserve thousands of soldiers. Which of those two laws will ultimately prevail, God alone knows. But we may assert that French science will have tried, by obeying the law of humanity, to extend the frontiers of life.

The Life of Pasteur
René Vallery-Radot
Trans. Mrs. R. L. Devonshire

WAR *

Gilbert Murray
English classical scholar, 1866—

Among all the evil aspects in which war has revealed itself to our generation there is none more horrible or more widely felt than its enslavement of whole nations to the will of the few.

Whatever view a man may take of the origin of the World War, it remains clear that millions of poor men in divers regions of the world have been dragged suddenly, and without any previous action of their own, into a quarrel which they neither made, nor desired, nor understood; and in the course of that quarrel have been subjected again and again to the very extremity of possible human suffering, while those at whose will they fight for the most part contemplate the battles from a distance or else sit at home in glory. To say this is not necessarily to blame the belligerent governments, but even if no one was to blame at all, it would make no difference. The fact is unchanged that, under the present conditions of state organization and national sovereignty, the life and liberty and property and happiness of the common man throughout the world are at the absolute mercy of a few persons whom he has never seen, involved in complicated quarrels that he has never heard of.

No artisan, no peasant, no remote wood-cutter or shepherd in the whole of Europe, however law-abiding and God-fearing, can be sure that he will not suddenly by due process of law be haled away to a punishment more cruel than that normally reserved for the worst criminals. He must lose not only his happiness but his innocence also. He must do things which his whole soul abominates. He must give himself up to the work of killing other men like himself and previously as innocent as himself. And all of it owing to no fault and no will of his own!

True, when he is called upon to come and fight for his country, the matter is generally put to him in such a light that the average man responds with instinctive loyalty. He joins the colors willingly, and he fights bravely. But this trustful innocence of the victims does not diminish the moral hideousness of the whole transaction.

To educate a man for the army; to accustom him to the thought that war, when it comes, will bring him a chance to use all his powers, to serve his country, to rise in his profession, and to leap perhaps from obscurity to the most dazzling form of glory that humanity knows: to do all this and then expect him not to desire war is surely to demand too much of human nature. Of course a conscientious soldier will often work conscientiously to avoid war. But

one has only to talk intimately in time of peace
to a few young officers to realize how their spirits naturally leap up at the prospect of putting
in practice the art to which they have devoted
their lives.

It is no doubt quite the reverse with the average unprofessional army, whether volunteer or
conscript.

*The League of Nations and the
Democratic Idea*

WOULD YOU END WAR?

JAMES OPPENHEIM
American writer, 1882–1932

Would you end war?
Create great peace—
The peace that demands all of a man,
His love, his life, his veriest self;
Plunge him in the smelting fires of a work that
    becomes his child;
Coerce him to be himself at all hazards, with the
    toil and the mating that belong to him;
Compel him to serve—
Give him a hard peace: a peace of discipline
    and justice—

Kindle him with vision, invite him to joy and
    adventure;
Set him at work, not to create things
But to create men,
Yes, himself.

Go search your heart, America—
Turn from the machine to man,
Build, while there is yet time, a creative peace—
While there is yet time!
For if you reject great peace.
As surely as vile living brings disease,
So surely shall your selfishness bring war.

From *1914—and After*
War and Laughter

THE UNITED STATES OF EUROPE *
Victor Hugo
French novelist and poet, 1802–1885

If four centuries ago, at the period when war
was made by one district against the other, between cities, and between provinces, some one
had dared to predict to Lorraine, to Picardy, to
Normandy, to Brittany, to Auvergne, to Provence, to Dauphiny, to Burgundy,—"A day shall

come when you will no longer make wars,—a
day shall come when you will no longer arm
men one against the other:—you will still have
many disputes to settle, interests to contend for,
difficulties to resolve; but do you know what
you will substitute instead of armed men, instead of cavalry and infantry, of cannon, of
falconets, lances, pikes and swords?—you will
select, instead of all this destructive array, a
small box of wood, which you will term a ballot-
box, and from which shall issue—what?—an
assembly—an assembly in which you shall all
live—an assembly which shall be, as it were, the
soul of all—a supreme and popular council,
which shall decide, judge, resolve everything—
which shall make the sword fall from every
hand, and excite the love of justice in every
heart—which shall say to each, 'Here termi-
nates your right, there commences your duty:
lay down your arms! Live in peace!' And in
that day you will all have one common thought,
common interests, a common destiny; you will
embrace each other, and recognize each other as
children of the same blood, and of the same
race; that day you will no longer be hostile
tribes,—you will be a people; you will no longer
be Burgundy, Normandy, Brittany, or Provence,
—you will be France! You will no longer

make appeals to war—you will do so to civilization."

If some one had uttered these words, all men of a serious and positive character, all prudent and cautious men, all the great politicians of the period, would have cried out, "What a dreamer! what a fantastic dream! How little this pretended prophet is acquainted with the human heart! What ridiculous folly! what an absurd chimera!" Yet, time has gone on and on, and we find that this dream, this folly, this absurdity, has been realized! And the man who would have dared to utter so sublime a prophecy would have been pronounced a madman for having dared to pry into the designs of the Deity.

We who are assembled here say to France, to England, to Prussia, to Austria, to Spain, to Italy, to Russia—we say to them, "A day will come when from your hands also the arms you have grasped will fall. A day will come when war will appear as absurd and be as impossible between Paris and London, between St. Petersburg and Berlin, between Vienna and Turin, as it would be now between Rouen and Amiens, between Boston and Philadelphia. A day will come when you, France—you, Russia—you,

Italy—you, England—you, Germany—all of you, nations of the Continent, will, without losing your distinctive qualities and your glorious individuality, be blended into a superior unity, and constitute a European fraternity, just as Normandy, Brittany, Burgundy have been blended into France. A day will come when the only battle-field will be the market open to commerce and the mind opening to new ideas. A day will come when bullets and bombshells will be replaced by votes, by the universal suffrage of nations, by the venerable arbitration of a great Sovereign Senate, which will be to Europe what the Parliament is to England, what the Diet is to Germany, what the Legislative Assembly is to France. A day will come when a cannon will be exhibited in public museums, just as an instrument of torture is now, and people will be astonished how such a thing could have been. A day will come when these two immense groups, the United States of America and the United States of Europe, shall be seen placed in presence of each other, extending the hand of friendship across the ocean, exchanging their produce, their commerce, their industry, their arts, their genius, clearing the earth, peopling the deserts, improving creation under the eye of the Creator, and uniting, for the good of all, these two irresistible and infinite powers, the fraternity of men and the power of God."

Nor is it necessary that four hundred years should pass away for that day to come. We live in a rapid period, in the most impetuous current of events and ideas which has ever borne away humanity; and at the period in which we live, a year suffices to do the work of a century.

But, French, English, Germans, Russians, Slavs, Europeans, Americans, what have we to do in order to hasten the advent of that great day? We must love each other! To love each other is, in this immense labor of pacification, the best manner of aiding God!

From *The Presidential Address*
International Peace Congress, 1849

THE TWO ALTARS
GIUSEPPE MAZZINI
Italian patriot, and defender of
republicanism, 1805–1872

When before young Europe's dawn all the **a**ltars of the old world have fallen, two altars shall be raised upon the soil that the divine Word has made fruitful: and the finger of the herald-people shall inscribe upon one, *Fatherland,* and upon the other *Humanity.*

Like sons of the same mother, like brothers who will not be parted, the people shall gather around those two altars and offer sacrifice in peace and love. And the incense of the sacrifice shall ascend to heaven in two columns that shall draw near each other as they mount, until they are confounded in one point, which is God.

And so often as they move asunder whilst they rise, fratricide shall be on earth, and mothers shall weep on earth and angels in heaven.

From *The Faith of Young Europe*
The Duties of Man and Other Essays

PREAMBLE TO THE COVENANT OF THE LEAGUE OF NATIONS
Paris Peace Conference, April 28, 1919

In order to promote international coöperation and to achieve international peace and security, by the acceptance of obligations not to resort to war, by the prescription of open, just, and honorable relations between nations, by the firm establishment of the understandings of international law as to actual rule of conduct among Governments, and by the maintenance of justice and a scrupulous respect for all treaty obligations in the dealings of organized peoples with one another, the high contracting parties agree to this covenant of the League of Nations.

THE VISION OF THE WORLD
Alfred Tennyson
English poet, 1809–1892

I dipt into the future, far as human eye could
    see,
Saw the Vision of the world, and all the wonder
    that would be;

Saw the heavens fill with commerce, argosies of
    magic sails,
Pilots of the purple twilight, dropping down
    with costly bales;

Heard the heavens fill with shouting, and there
    rained a ghastly dew
From the nations' airy navies grappling in the
    central blue;

Far along the world-wide whisper of the south-
    wind rushing warm,
With the standards of the peoples plunging
    thro' the thunder-storm;

Till the war-drum throbb'd no longer, and the
    battle-flags were furl'd
In the Parliament of man, the Federation of the
    world.

There the common sense of most shall hold a
    fretful realm in awe,
And the kindly earth shall slumber, lapped in
    universal law.

From *Locksley Hall*

THE SOURCE OF INTERNATIONAL
GOODWILL *
WILLIAM McDOUGALL
English psychologist, 1871–1938

As soon as man understands that his fellow
man suffers the same pains and joys as himself, longs for the same good, fears the same
evils, throbs with the same emotions and desires, then he shares with him in some degree

these feelings, in virtue of that fundamental law of all social beings, the law of primitive sympathy; then also pity and sympathetic sorrow and tender regard are awakened in his breast; then his fellow man is no longer the object of his cold or hostile glances, as a certain rival and probable enemy, but is seen to be a fellow toiler and sufferer whom he is willing to succor, a fellow creature whose joys and sorrows alike he can but share in some degree.

Only through increase of knowledge of others is each man's knowledge of himself slowly built up and enriched, until it renders him capable of enlightened self-direction. So the development of the group mind, the increase of its self-knowledge, of its power of self-direction, is through increase of knowledge of other human societies.

The self-knowledge of the individual grows chiefly through intercourse with his fellows; his idea of himself develops in fulness and accuracy in the light of his knowledge of other selves, and this knowledge in turn develops in the light of his increasing knowledge of himself. Just so the self-knowledge of nations is now growing rapidly through the intercourse of each nation with others, an intercourse far freer, more multiplex, than ever before in the history of the

world; a result largely of the improved means
of communication which we owe to science and
the spirit of inquiry.

Thus the group spirit, rising above the level
of a narrow patriotism that regards with hostility all its rivals, recognizing that only through
the further development of the collective life of
nations can man rise to higher levels than he
has yet known, becomes the supreme agent of
human progress.

The Group Mind

THE COMING DAY

JOHN ADDINGTON SYMONDS
English critic and poet, 1840-1893

These things shall be,—a loftier race
Than e'er the world hath known shall rise
With flame of freedom in their souls,
And light of knowledge in their eyes.

They shall be gentle, brave, and strong
To spill no drop of blood, but dare
All that may plant man's lordship firm
On earth, and fire, and sea, and air.

Nation with nation, land with land,
Unarmed shall live as comrades free;

In every heart and brain shall throb
The pulse of one fraternity.

New arts shall bloom of loftier mould,
And mightier music thrill the skies,
And every life shall be a song
When all the earth is paradise.

There shall be no more sin, nor shame,
Though pain and passion may not die,
For man shall be at one with God
In bonds of firm necessity.

New and Old

NATIONS AND THE MORAL LAW

Giuseppe Mazzini

Italian patriot, and defender of
republicanism, 1805–1872

The end of politics is the application of the moral law to the civil constitution of a nation in its double activity, domestic and foreign. The end of economics is the application of the same law to the organization of labor in its double aspect, production and distribution. All that makes for that end is good and must be promoted; all that contradicts it or gives it no help must be opposed till it succumb. People and government must proceed united, like thought and action in individuals, towards the accomplishment of that mission. And what is true for one nation is true as between nations. Nations are the individuals of humanity. The internal national organization is the instrument with which the nation accomplishes its mission in the world. Nationalities are sacred, and providentially constituted to represent, within humanity, the division or distribution of labor for the advantage of the peoples, as the division and distribution of labor within the limits of the state should be organized for the greatest benefit of all the citizens. If they do not look to that end they are useless and fall. If they persist in evil, which is egotism, they perish; nor do they rise again unless they make atonement and return to the good.

The Duties of Man and Other Essays

THE CITY OF LIGHT
Felix Adler
American: writer upon ethical subjects, 1851–1933

Have you heard the golden city
Mentioned in the legends old?

Everlasting light shines o'er it,
Wondrous tales of it are told.
Only righteous men and women
Dwell within its gleaming wall;
Wrong is banished from its borders,
Justice reigns supreme o'er all.

We are builders of that city;
All our joys and all our groans
Help to rear its shining ramparts,
All our lives are building-stones.
But the work that we have builded,
Oft with bleeding hands and tears,
And in error and in anguish,
Will not perish with the years.

It will be at last made perfect
In the universal plan;
It will help to crown the labors
Of the toiling hosts of man.
It will last and shine transfigured
In the final reign of right;
It will merge into the splendors
Of the City of the Light.

Ethical Addresses

THE NEW FAITH
William M. Salter
American writer and lecturer, 1853–1931

The conception of evolution—the fruit of geological and biological and historical study—is a modern product. It was unknown to Confucius, unknown to Buddha, unknown to Socrates and Marcus Aurelius and Jesus as truly as to the author of Ecclesiastes. It signifies more than order—mere cause and effect; it signifies progress, the unfolding of effects whose causes were latent and hidden before. The world is not ever the same; if it is, how happens it that there are suns and planets now where ages ago there were none?

The old idea was that the earth, like the "everlasting hills" upon it, had always been. But life is not ever the same; it is ascending. Man is not ever the same; at happy junctures new races have been born. History need not always repeat itself. Dowered with reason and social feeling, man has within him the possibility of indefinite advance. It is in the make of things that the possibilities of progress lie. Why is not, then, a world-state in which all are brothers, a "Kingdom of God," conceivable?

In face of the magnificent story of evolution in the past, who will set limits to its future course? If the diviner order of which Marcus Aurelius and Jesus dreamed would be the cap and crown of things, what hinders us from actually anticipating it?

I see a new faith rising in the hearts of men, and organizing itself in human society. It will have the human interests, the practical sense, the sanity of Confucius, but in the service of the grand ideals of a Marcus Aurelius or a Jesus; it will, with Buddha, loosen the cords that bind men so tightly to the earth, and master all other loves than the love of right and the love of love; and yet it will seek to organize right and love in the daily work of the world, and no service to man shall be so material or so low that it may not also be holy; it will, with Socrates, inspire to all science, but the darling effort of science shall be to find the way to those far and shining heights that shall be anew the object of the aspirations and worship of men—to ascertain the laws and true methods of advance. Under the stress of the new faith, wrought organically out of the present and the past, men will again look beyond themselves, will again be sanctified, will again feel a glow

in the heart, and feel themselves happy in
contributing ever so little to so divine a result.

Social Worship
Ed. Stanton Coit

FORWARD THROUGH THE AGES

FREDERICK LUCIAN HOSMER
American preacher and hymn writer, 1840–1929

Forward through the ages,
In unbroken line,
Move the faithful spirits
At the call divine:
Gifts in differing measure,
Hearts of one accord,
Manifold the service,
One the sure reward.

Wider grows the kingdom,
Reign of love and light;
For it we must labor,
Till our faith is sight.
Prophets have proclaimed it,
Martyrs testified,
Poets sung its glory,
Heroes for it died.

Not alone we conquer,
Not alone we fall;
In each loss or triumph
Lose or triumph all.
Bound by God's far purpose
In one living whole,
Move we on together
To the shining goal!

The Thought of God

HUMAN PROGRESS *
Walt Whitman
American poet, 1819–1892

Allons! after the great Companions, and to belong to them!
They too are on the road—they are the swift
and majestic men—they are the greatest
women;
Journeyers over consecutive seasons, over the
years, the curious years, each emerging
from that which preceded it;
Journeyers gaily with their own youth, journeyers with their bearded and well-grained
manhood,
Journeyers with their womanhood, ample, un-
surpassed, content,

Journeyers with their own sublime old age of manhood or womanhood,
Old age, calm, expanded, broad with the haughty breadth of the universe.

Allons! to that which is endless as it was beginningless,
To see nothing anywhere but what you may reach it and pass it,
To look up or down no road but it stretches and waits for you, however long but it stretches and waits for you,
To know the universe itself as a road, as many roads, as roads for traveling souls.

All parts away for the progress of souls!
All religion, all solid things, arts, governments—all that was or is apparent upon this globe or any globe falls into niches and corners before the procession of souls along the grand roads of the universe.
Of the progress of the souls of men and women along the grand roads of the universe, all other progress is the needed emblem and sustenance.

Forever alive, forever forward,
Stately, solemn, sad, withdrawn, baffled, mad, turbulent, feeble, dissatisfied,

Desperate, proud, fond, sick, accepted by men,
   rejected by men,
They go! they go! I know that they go, but I
   know not where they go;
But I know that they go toward the best—
   toward something great.

> From *Song of the Open Road*

ACKNOWLEDGMENTS
AND
INDEXES

638   ACKNOWLEDGMENTS

ACKNOWLEDGMENTS

The editor wishes to acknowledge his indebtedness to the following authors, publishers, and owners of copyright material who have granted permission to include in this anthology material which they control:—

Adler, Felix, for the poem "The City of Light."

American Unitarian Association, for the selections from "The Works of William Ellery Channing."

Appleton, D. & Co., New York, for the selections from "History of the United States" by George Bancroft and "Life and Letters of Thomas Huxley" by Leonard Huxley.

Barrus, Clara, literary executrix of John Burroughs, for the selection from "Accepting the Universe" (copyright, Houghton, Mifflin Co.).

Bates, Katharine Lee, for the hymn "America the Beautiful."

Bobbs-Merrill Co., for the selection from "Fathers and Mothers" by George H. Betts. Copyright 1915. Used by special permission of the publishers.

Carruth, Mrs. Katharine M., for the poem "Each in His Own Tongue" by Dr. William A. Carruth (copyright, G. P. Putnam's Sons).

Century Co., The, for the poem "Would You End War?" by James Oppenheim; and for the selections from "Lincoln the Lawyer" by Frederick Trevor Hill and for "The American Boy" by Theodore Roosevelt.

Coit, Stanton S., for the selections from "Social Worship."

Cornhill Publishing Co., for the poem "And What Shall You Say?" from "The Band of Gideon" by Joseph S. Cotter, Jr.

Crowell Co., Thomas Y., for the selection from Victor Hugo's "Les Misérables," translated by Isabel F. Hapgood; and for the poem "America the Beautiful" by Katharine Lee Bates.

Curtis Bridgham, for the selection from "The Indian's Book" by Natalie Curtis, Paul Burlin (Harper & Brothers).

Dodd, Mead & Co., for the poems "The Dead" by Rupert Brooke, "The Debt" by Paul Laurence Dunbar; and for the selection from "Scott's Last Expedition."

Donohue & Co., M. A., for the selection from "Natural Law in the Spiritual World" by Henry Drummond.

Doran Co., George H., for the selections from the "Outlines of a Philosophy of Religion" by Auguste Sabatier.

Doubleday, Page & Co., for the poem "If" by Rudyard Kipling; for miscellaneous poems from "Leaves of Grass" by Walt Whitman; and for the selection from the preface to "The Nigger of the Narcissus" by Joseph Conrad.

Eliot, Estate of Charles W., for the selection from "The Durable Satisfactions of Life."

Ellis Co., George H., for the selection from "Messages of Faith, Hope, and Love" by James Freeman Clarke.

Evans, Florence W., for the poem "The Flower Factory."

Everybody's Magazine for the selection from "The Undying Story of Captain Scott," (also published as "Scott's Last Expedition" by Dodd, Mead & Co.).

Funk & Wagnalls Co., for the sonnet from "Poems" by Richard Realf. Copyright, 1898.

Gannett. Mrs. Mary T. L., for poems by Dr. William Channing Gannett.

Garland, Hamlin, for the selection from "A Pioneer Mother."

Grenfell, Wilfred T., for the selections from "The Adventure of Life," and "Labrador Days."

Harper & Brothers for poems by Algernon Charles Swinburne and for the selection from "Henry Esmond" by William Makepeace Thackeray.

Heinemann, Ltd., William, for the selections from "Mutual Aid" by Peter Alexeivich Kropotkin and "Dream Tales and Prose Poems" by Ivan Sergievich Turgenev.

Holt, Henry & Co., for the selection from "Principles of Psychology" by William James.

Hosmer, F. L., for hymns.

Houghton, Mifflin Co., for the selections from the works of Ralph Waldo Emerson, Henry Wadsworth Longfellow, James Russell Lowell, Oliver Wendell Holmes and John Greenleaf Whittier; and for the selections from "The Wisdom of Goethe" (a translation by John Stuart Blackie), "Science and Immortality" by William Osler, the translation of Virgil's "Aenid" by Theodore Chickering Williams, "Accepting the Universe" by John Burroughs, and "Everyday Religion" by James Freeman Clarke.

Johnston, Charles, for the selections from his translation of "Bhagavad-Gita."

Kennerley, Mitchell, for the poem "The Jew to Jesus" by Florence Kiper Frank.

Kipling, Rudyard, for the poem "If" from "Rewards and Fairies." (All rights reserved *including* that of translation into foreign languages *including* the Scandinavian).

Little, Brown & Co., for the selections from "The Little Grandmother of the Russian Revolution" by Alice Stone Blackwell, Ed.

Loeb Classical Library for the selections from Hippocrates' "The Oath" and "Precepts for Physicians", and the selection from "Hesiod, The Poems and Fragments Done into English Prose" by A. W. Mair.

Longmans, Green & Co., for the selections from "The Will to Believe" and "Is Life Worth Living?" by William James.

Lothrop, Lee & Shepard Co., for the selections from "Reminiscences of Froebel" by Baroness von Bülow.

MacMillan Co., for the selections from "The American Commonwealth" Vol. II, by James Bryce, "The Spirit of Youth" and "Democracy and Social Ethics" by Jane Addams, "The Life of William Booth" by Harold Begbie, "Abt Vogler" by Robert Browning, "The Psychology of Power" by J. Arthur Hadfield, "Poems" by W. E. Henley, "The Congo" by Vachel Lindsay, "Christianity and the Social Crisis" by Walter Rauschenbusch, "The Crescent Moon" by Rabindranath Tagore, "Barbed Wire and Wayfarers" by Edwin Ford Piper and "Dream Tales and Prose Poems" by Ivan S. Turgenev.

McBride & Co., Robert F., for the selection from "Psychology & Morals," by J. Arthur Hadfield. Published 1923. Reprinted by permission of the publishers.

Markham, Edwin, for the poems "Outwitted" and "Inbrothered."

Murray, John, for the poem "The Coming Day" by John Addington Symonds.

Orr, Hugh Robert, for the poem "They Softly Walk."

Oxford University Press for the selections from "Sacred Books of the East."

Oxford University Press and the Jowett Trustees for the selections from Jowett's translation of Thucydides.

Piper, Edwin Ford, for the poem "The Church."

Pott & Co., James, for the selection from "Foundations of the Republic" by Edward Everett Hale.

Princeton University Press, for the selections from "Heredity and Environment in the Development of Man" by Edwin Grant Conklin.

Putnam's Sons, G. P., of New York and London, for the poem "In Flanders Fields" by John McCrae; and for the selections from "The Group Mind" by William McDougall and "The Outline of Science" by J. Arthur Thomson.

Rankin, Henry B., for the selection from "Personal Recollections of Abraham Lincoln."

Remington Co., Norman, for the selection from "Walter Reed and Yellow Fever" by Howard A. Kelly.

Scribner's Sons, Charles, for the selection from "Poems" by George Santayana, "Development of Religion and Thought in Ancient Egypt" by James Henry Breasted, "Poems and Ballads" by Robert Louis Stevenson and "Note Books of Leonardo da Vinci," trans. Edward McCurdy.

Small, Maynard & Co., for the selection from "Chants Communal" by Horace Traubel.

Stokes Co., Frederick A., for the selections "Music of the Spheres" and "The Torch Bearers" from "Watchers of the Sky" by Alfred Noyes. Copyright, 1922, by Frederick A. Stokes Co.

Stratford Co., for the poem "The Teacher" from "Wings of Oppression" by Leslie Pinckney Hill.

University of Chicago Press, for the selections from "A Translation of the New Testament" by Edgar J. Goodspeed.

World Book Co., Yonkers-on-Hudson, New York, for the selections from Anderson's "Divine Comedy of Dante Alighieri." Copyright, 1921, by World Book Company.

Yale University Press, for the selections from "The Meaning of God in Human Experience" by William Ernest Hocking and "Marcus Aurelius" by Henry Dwight Sedgwick.

Note: Careful effort was made to trace the ownership of all copyright material included in this book and to secure permission to use the desired selections. If any such material has been inadvertently included without the necessary permission, the editor desires hereby to express his regrets for such oversight, and will be glad, upon receiving the proper notification, to make due acknowledgment in future editions.

INDEX OF TITLES

INDEX OF AUTHORS AND SOURCES